CLAIR, René. Cinema yesterday and today, tr. by Stanley Appelbaum.
Dover, 1972. 260p il 74-177483. 3.50 pa. ISBN 0-486-
22775-8
This delightful book contains autobiographical reflections, notes on film
theory, bits of film history and criticism. The arrangement of material
is unusual. Clair combines essays or bits of essays written in the 20s
and 30s with comments made in 1950 and 1970. Much of the material
was first published in Clair's *Reflections on the cinema* (1953). Comments on comments and revisions of revisions show the development of
Clair's thoughts on cinema. Among the high points in the book are his
defense of comedy and his comments on the *auteur* theory growing out
of his discussion of Chaplin in an essay published in 1929. A special
feature of the book is the collection of stills from his major films. An
essential book for film collections.

CINEMA
yesterday and today

by RENÉ CLAIR

Translated by STANLEY APPELBAUM

Edited,
and with an Introduction and Annotations, by
R C DALE

ASSOCIATE PROFESSOR OF FRENCH,
UNIVERSITY OF WASHINGTON, SEATTLE

DOVER PUBLICATIONS, INC., NEW YORK

Cinema Yesterday and Today, first published by
Dover Publications, Inc., in 1972, is a new English
translation, by Stanley Appelbaum, of the complete
text of *Cinéma d'hier, cinéma d'aujourd'hui,* ©
1970 by Editions Gallimard, Paris. A new introduction and notes to the text have been written
specially for the present edition by R C Dale; the
indexes of persons and of films have been revised;
and a selection of illustrations has been added.
The publisher is grateful to Mr. René Clair, the
Museum of Modern Art Film Stills Archive, Mr.
Herman G. Weinberg and Prof. R C Dale for making their photographs available for reproduction.

International Standard Book Number: 0-486-22775-8
Library of Congress Catalog Card Number: 74-177483

Manufactured in the United States of America
Dover Publications, Inc.
180 Varick Street
New York, N. Y. 10014

Introduction to the English Edition

One afternoon not so long ago René Clair and I sat in his study debating the propriety of artistic revision. In conducting research for a book I am writing on his work, I had come across a number of variant versions of his films, including one that had somehow been reduced to an incoherent jumble, no longer resembling the original cut in any way. He told me that he, too, had seen that monstrous recut, and had spoken about it to the direction of the Cinémathèque Française. They had responded with horror to his suggestion that the copy be destroyed, but they accorded his request that it never again be shown. While I had to agree that the recut print was no longer his own work, I also had to defend the archivist's and scholar's duty to preserve all the works of great artists, no matter what their condition, rather than let them perish completely.

"An artist should have the right to destroy his own work if it doesn't satisfy him, or to revise it if he feels that revision has become necessary," he countered. "I've made a few films in my career for the wrong reasons—films that didn't spring from my own heart—that I completely disown. If I were a painter, I could paint them over; if I were a novelist, I could turn over the sheets of paper and write another novel on the other side. Why should a film-maker, more than any other artist, be bound to a once-and-forever version—the first one—of his work? In film-making, one is under terrific financial pressure to finish, and to finish rapidly. One may make a decision on the final day of cutting that one later—two days or twenty years—realizes was wrong. With another picture, I dropped out a whole reel at the première on the advice of my producers. I thought they were right at the time, and I still think they were right, forty years later, even though I made that decision in a few seconds, after the picture had been completed and just as it was about to be premièred. A couple of decades later, I cut some more material out of that film because it no longer seemed appropriate—and I also added a shot that I had long since come to realize was necessary. The Museum of Modern Art in New York wrote me a letter complaining that I was messing up "their" film when they saw the revised version after I had recut it. I've experienced similar reactions when I've tried to restore some of the other films that somehow had become scrambled. It seems that the archivists prefer to keep *their* version intact at any expense—even if it doesn't have much to do with the original—because in their minds it has been sanctified by tradition. I wonder what they would do if I suddenly decided to substitute an alternate ending I once shot for a later film, and eventually abandoned? It rather changes the outcome of the picture. As a matter of fact, I got an infuriated letter from Cocteau after he saw the picture telling me I was crazy not to have used that other ending."

Seeing the irrefutable logic in René Clair's artistic-prerogative argument didn't affect my own bias as a student of his work, to whom *all* of his versions must remain equally interesting simply because they are all the products of his creative imagination. I realized that our discussion had reached an ideological impasse. "The trouble is," I helpfully suggested, "that you've been working in the wrong art all these years. If you were a poet, say Blake for instance, you could revise to your heart's content whenever you feel like it, and all the different versions could be printed together. Then everyone would be happy. Or you might have been an essayist, like Montaigne. I've always admired his attitude toward revision: 'Maybe I'm wrong now and was right at first,' he would say. 'What do I know? So I'll add on my later ideas but never exclude any of my initial ones.' "

"Ah, yes," René Clair replied. "Montaigne was right, as usual. And now that you mention it, I guess I am following Montaigne's method right down the line with the new work I've undertaken, a revision of my old book *Reflections on the Cinema.*" His guess was accurate, for in *Cinema Yesterday and Today* we find his Montaignesque revision of revisions, those 1970 reflections on 1950 reflections on reflections from the previous thirty-odd years that document his sometimes thoughtful, sometimes outrageous, always provocative examinations of self and cinema over that long and important period of time. Fifty years in which the matured form of silent cinema gave way to a squalling infant, sound film, and in which sound film came to develop a maturity of its own. Fifty years of love, devotion, patience, petulance, agony and delight centered on this unruly artistic genius of our century. Fifty years of engaged thought by one of world cinema's most gifted creative artists.

Fifty years ago, in 1921, René Clair was making his entry into cinema—a very casual entry, it might be added. The previous year, as a sort of lark, he had taken a part in a film just to see what it was like, to pick up a little money—and perhaps even to meet some of the lovely girls who were said to be working on the picture. He had no serious intentions about cinema whatsoever. "I went into the studios for three days," he says, "and stayed there all my life." In 1921, he worked as the juvenile lead for several directors, notably Protazanoff and Louis Feuillade, now famous for his early serials *Fantômas* and *Judex*. The following year, growing more and more intrigued by cinema, René Clair worked with director Jacques de Baroncelli, and began to compose screenplays. At the same time, he took over the film section of the magazine *Théâtre et Comœdia Illustrés*, which he continued to edit for two years. In 1923, he directed his first film, *Paris qui dort* (*The Crazy Ray*), and the rest is history: twenty-four feature films, five shorts or contributions to omnibus films, numerous screenplays, and frequent forays into fiction as well as other forms of the dramatic arts.

René Clair's French friends might call his passion for literature a *"violon d'Ingres":* Ingres, the neo-classical painter, was never very happy over the fact that his muse had destined him to become a great painter rather than a violinist. Similarly, René Clair longed for a career as a man of letters, as a poet and novelist. His earliest works were stories and poems, and even after he began work in cinema, he continued to hold out his hopes for a literary life—to the extent that the young man born René Chomette actually took on the pseudonym René Clair for his "temporary" work in cinema so that he could keep his real name untainted for his literary works.

As you read the following pages, you will doubtlessly admire the deep affection René Clair has held over the years for the literary traditions of France and England. It may seem odd that a man with such a strong inclination toward the written word should have been such a staunch enemy of literary traditions whenever they entered into the making of a film. Indeed, we might very easily expect a man of those leanings to sanction the invasion of cinema by literature. But the exact opposite is true. In every instance where any extra-cinematic tradition has threatened the autonomy of film, René Clair throughout his life has rushed in to expose it and to exorcise it with the same candid lucidity we have come to recognize as a hallmark of his films. From the very beginning, René Clair was a *cinéaste,* whether he knew it or not, whether he preferred it or not. He was born with an instinct for cinema, an instinct that manifested itself in his very first writings and has continued to do so throughout the years. Although it would take a well-trained film historian to appreciate fully the originality found in many of these ideas once considered scandalous and now universally accepted, any reader interested in cinema will recognize the consistency with which he has advocated the right and duty of film-makers to keep their art pure and free of contamination from foreign elements of any sort. There is no need to talk here about the other manifestations of his instinct for cinema, the films themselves, which have assured him a permanent place in the pantheon of great original film creators.

And in exercising his *violon d'Ingres,* René Clair also has a talent for words—a talent that has already earned this book a French award for the best work on cinema to appear in 1970–71. We can thank that talent for having placed this work, unique in the history of cinema, before us. That talent has produced a fifty-year record of cinema seen from the inside, seen by a man who lived with it intimately, seen by a man who first loved it with a passion that engendered romantically zealous declarations of immaculate fidelity, then with a more mature love bringing a less truculent and more tolerant understanding that allowed him to acknowledge his youthful follies, and finally by the philosopher who realizes that the love he has nurtured and cherished all his life is indeed strong enough to withstand all the seductions wrought upon it by ill-intentioned or misguided corruptors. In one sense, this work forms an unparalleled commentary on the vicissitudes of cinema; in another, it bears witness to a touching declaration of faith in our century's most vibrant art form.

As we finished talking about his book, René Clair asked me if I would oversee the American translation as its editor, to make sure that the work is totally accessible to American readers, some of whom may not understand all of his many references to French culture. I agreed willingly, and have attempted to do so in the footnotes that follow, which have been given numbers and labeled "ED." to differentiate them from the author's own notes (with asterisks). In my notes, I have confined myself entirely to explanatory remarks, although in the text I have occasionally exercised the editor's prerogative to correct a faulty detail that resulted from a lapse of factual memory on the author's part while describing the action of films seen long ago. These lapses are very rare, and the corrections pass without comment, since the details never alter a point the author is making. In order to avoid loading down the pages with unnecessary annotations, I have commented only on French names or cultural references that must be recognized and understood in order to obtain a full appreciation of the text. The translator has also supplied film titles in English as well as in their original form where applicable, along with their director's name and their date of release, in the title index. Our mutual aim has been, of course, to provide the American reader with the most helpful edition possible of this fascinating work.

It seems unnecessary to say any more, for René Clair himself will tell you as you turn the pages how this remarkable book came to be composed, and then will lead you on a fascinating journey that crisscrosses those eventful years on hundreds of different paths, from hundreds of different angles, to build up an intriguing and informative composite chart of his and cinema's mutual metamorphoses over the fifty engaging years they have spent together.

R C DALE

Contents

In Self-Defense   149

Film sense — Jean-Paul Sartre and Pirandello — Marcel Pagnol enters the scene — On poets and Tristan Corbière — Authors — New men needed

Theater and Cinema   159

Renewal of the theater — For a true Conservatory — What is a good film? — Production and manufacture

Beginning to Take Stock   170

Useless regrets — Cinema, theater and novel — If the theater had not existed — Difference in techniques — The argument goes on — What the public wants — Condition of the film author

Speed and Shape   186

The frenetic past — Change of ratio — A lucky poker hand — A regret

On Hollywood   192

Pioneers and financiers — Robert Florey — Cecil B. DeMille — A hero in the studios — Orson Welles — Preston Sturges — A wartime cinema — A government matter — The idea of pleasure

On International Cinema   203

The screens invaded — Intellectual and commercial value

A Retroactive Revolution   206

The concept of "anti" — Expressing oneself — The quest for genius — Blushing in good company — The official avant-garde — Mayakovsky — Meetings that failed to take place

On the Morals of Our Day   217

In a "house" — Commercial boldness — Against the current

On Comedy   223

What is the best film? — The tragic and the beautiful — Laughter and liberty

List of Illustrations

NOTE: Those portions of the text flanked at the left by a vertical rule are the essays or parts of essays dating from the past which René Clair is anthologizing here. The remainder of the text represents the author's new statements and commentary from the standpoint of 1950 and 1970.

Foreword

In the eyes of the historian, no document is unimportant. That is undoubtedly why in 1950 Georges Sadoul, who was beginning to publish his *Histoire générale du cinéma,* urged me to assemble into one volume various articles I had written in the past.

These articles, which I barely remembered, had been composed between 1922 and 1935, and dealt with the last years of the silent film and the first years of the sound film. Leafing through them, I felt that the questions raised by the cinema in that vital period of its development had not lost all their significance, but I felt also that my feelings in regard to them had changed on many points. And in the course of my reading, finding fault here, giving my approval there, commenting on whatever called for commentary, I struck up a sort of dialogue across the years with the author of these old articles.

This was the form adopted by a book entitled *Réflexion faite,* published in 1951, which gathered together various notes "as aids for a history of film art from 1920 to 1950."[1] The final pages of the book contained the following passage:

Before sending these notes to the printer, I have just reread them. How many topics they include which no longer have more than a historical or at least retrospective interest! In less than thirty years, how many changes in an "art" the development of which depends so closely on technology! We may well ask what will remain in thirty years of what our contemporaries call cinema. And in three hundred years, when Corneille will not have many more readers than the *Chanson de Roland* has today, when the name of Charlie Chaplin will be mentioned only by a few scholars? No doubt our cinema will then appear as the primitive form of a medium of expression which it is difficult for us to imagine; or perhaps the memory of it will be merely one of the strangest traces of a vanished civilization.

Anyone who has browsed through the shelves of used book stores, or has meditated on the fragility of human things in

---

[1] Published in English as *Reflections on the Cinema* (London: W. Kimber, 1953). "Upon Reflection" gives a more accurate idea of the pun contained in the French title.—ED.

some rural attic, knows that chance can save from destruction the least important books as well as the most weighty. By virtue of this egalitarian law, it is not absolutely impossible that a copy of the present book will still exist in five hundred years. Let us suppose that this copy then comes into the hands of an inquisitive man who, bewildered by his find, shows it to some student he knows. The student, who cannot make out the subject of this sorcerer's manual written in an archaic language, will perhaps offer it to one of his professors for examination. This professor, an authority on the history of twentieth and twenty-first-century customs, opens my book. "What," he wonders, "is this unknown author talking about? What was this thing he calls a 'film?' What was this 'cinematic art' which seems to have been so important in the life of the good people of that era?"

Time is a skillful magician. He distracts our attention so cunningly that the trick is performed without our noticing his subterfuges. No need to traverse centuries to ascertain the result; a few seasons are enough. When the prospect of a new edition of *Réflexion faite* arose, I opened this little book and noticed that a number of passages which corresponded to my reflections of not so long ago showed signs of age themselves. Surely the cinema has not evolved so drastically that it is necessary to explain today what it was like twenty years ago. Nevertheless, I considered it not unuseful to take new bearings and to add a third voice to the dialogue outside of time which I had carried on with myself, a voice which would be—forgive me—my own once again.

I wrote in 1950 and I must repeat today in order to avoid any misunderstanding:

This is not a history of the cinema. I would be quite incapable of writing one. The pages gathered together here may not have any other merit than an extremely obvious lack of objectivity hardly befitting a historian.

The reader may also find that I have paid too much attention to one topic or neglected another; in fact, a number of interesting things and more than one memorable name have gone unmentioned in this book. But I had neither an overall plan nor specific references, and it was often chance that furnished the subject of these reflections. Far from wishing to draw up an honor roll, I have merely assembled old notes, sketched various general notions of a profession that is also an art, and recalled to life a few images of its past. If I do not speak much about the present—that is, about contemporary cinema—it is not because I fail to recognize the importance of its accomplishments. But to judge them without the necessary perspective and before time has sifted their contributions, would be to engage in criticism. And I am no more a critic than I am a historian.

One word further: if the three voices which will carry on the dialogue in this book are not always in unison, this will not trouble me very much; I even hope that their discord will be of some interest. What would freedom of expression be if it were not guaranteed by the inalienable right of self-contradiction?

To begin, let us contradict chronology and, before turning back toward a recent past, venture a few steps into a more or less distant future. When people say, as they do in many different places today, that the cinema is experiencing a crisis, the term is incorrect. At the end of a crisis, the thing that was affected by it returns more or less to its former state. Now, in this particular case, that cannot happen. What the cinema is suffering from is its failure to adapt to the possibilities of an era in which everything is changing with inconceivable rapidity. Though it is a modern medium of expression, it has remained paradoxically attached to its past. And aren't we all behind our times like those generals who were preparing for an earlier war?[1] When we talk about "film," we are using a word which will soon be inadequate to define the audiovisual forms of expression that are now being developed.

What forms? Strolling on a beach the other day, I thought

---

[1]When the French military command belatedly recognized in the late thirties that war with Germany was unavoidable, they prepared their defense by constructing the Maginot Line, a series of trenches along their Eastern front. Although the French were convinced that the Second World War would be conducted according to the same trench strategy as the first war had been, the Germans entertained other ideas on the subject, and eventually proved the French generals to be disastrously wrong.—ED.

that if Venus Astarte were to issue from the briny wave today, her divine foot would be sullied by the deposits of fuel oil that wash up on our shores. Why do we still use the unclean oil called petroleum which we have great difficulty extracting from the bowels of the earth, where prudent Nature placed it out of our reach? Isn't it surprising that after so many years the automobile is still faithful to the internal combustion engine of its beginnings? Is it true that no other means has been found of making our cars go? In an era when the astronauts' ships glide through "infinite space," we continue here on earth to manufacture clumsy engines which rattle our brains with their noise, while our lungs, as well as the foliage on our trees, are eaten away by their fumes.

"What," the reader may well ask, "does this have to do with the cinema?"

The automobile is not the only thing that has remained fundamentally unchanged since its earliest days. The physical basis of film-making, which is just as old as the automobile, has not developed any more than cars have. After eighty years, more or less, have passed and fabulous treasures have been expended on these two industries! One, with its gasoline, is still back in the good old days of the Marquis de Dion;[1] the other, with its celluloid, is still in the days of the Lumière Brothers.

"And color, sound, wide screen?"

Trifles! Nothing essential has changed; a transparent ribbon moved along by a sprocket wheel, with a light behind it and a white canvas in front of it: we are still at the point of departure. If you want to talk about new technology, take a look at what television is accomplishing! At the very moment an event takes place, let us say in Japan, the image of it is transmitted via the United States and, relayed by some satellite, joins up again on European screens with the sound, which is routed through Canada or some other path around the earth. In a day when such miracles are taking place, the technology of the cinema seems ridiculously primitive.

"Let's be fair. Progress has been made. The sensitivity of film has been heightened, cameras and sound equipment have been lightened considerably, and . . . ."

---

[1] The Marquis de Dion was a French automotive pioneer.—ED.

This progress has made it possible to shoot films in a different style. But this is not yet the "new cinema," which is talked about more than it is seen. It is from technology that a complete renewal is to be expected. Just as the arrival of sound revolutionized the dramaturgy of the story film, it is the evolution of technology that will give this dramaturgy its new forms.

If the theater has not undergone substantial transformations in two thousand years, it is because its material existence was not dependent on technology. From the Greek theater to the medieval mystery plays and to contemporary drama, whether the stage be Elizabethan, Chinese or Italian, the principle is the same: a platform and a passion, to quote a good phrase. It matters very little whether this platform is made of wood or of marble, whether it does or does not have a revolving stage and elevators. The sun of Athens was as good as all our spotlights, and the acoustics at Epidaurus make loudspeakers unnecessary.

But the cinema is still the "scientific toy" that it was to its inventors, and continues to depend on science body and soul. That is why, after more than a half-century of immobility, it is on the eve of surprising metamorphoses. Look at what happened with radio: in the early days radio receivers had the form of enormous boxes linked to long antennas. Today the voices of the whole world issue from a tiny case, soon from a thimble. Miniaturization still has surprises in store for us. It is not madness to predict that before long film images and sound will be recorded by means of a tiny apparatus and that transmitted images will appear within a frame similar to that of a wristwatch.*

Even now the smallest model television camera transmitting pictures by radio and cable is the size of an ordinary pocket flashlight. And an American Senate committee has made upsetting discoveries in the course of an inquiry into industrial espionage. In particular, it seems that during the exclusive première of a new fashion line, two television cameras were found in the brassiere of one lady guest.

That sounds like science fiction, but the distance between fiction and science is lessening daily. In his book *Automation et humanisme* Georges Elgozy writes:

---

*It seems that the size of the components of all electronic devices has been reduced 100,000 times between 1948 and 1970.

The time intervening between a basic discovery and its industrial applications is growing shorter every year. From a hundred years for photography, it went to fifty years for the telephone, fourteen for the airplane, seven for television, six for the peaceful uses of atomic energy, five for the use of communication satellites.

In the past, monks continued to make manuscript copies even after printing had been invented. By a similar survival of an anachronistic practice, copies of a film are still transported from one city to another even though a single television station could telecast the film, through the air or by cable, to a thousand theaters at the same time. That is what will happen some day, and it can be predicted that after this large-scale telecast, another television channel will present the same picture on home screens for those who prefer to see it without going out. Finally, films will be printed in a smaller format and will be sold, like long-playing records, to film lovers who want to acquire a personal collection. When these varied modes of distribution have come into use, it will be seen that what was called a crisis of the cinema was only one of the phases of its development.

All that would still only be a variant, an extension of what we already know. The kinetic arts are in their infancy, and their future is as little known to us as that of photography was in the reign of Louis XIII. In a short novel published quite some time ago,[1] the present writer conceived the idea of a gigantic film projected onto the sky. We cannot be sure that this fanciful notion will not become a reality some day.

There is already talk of projection without a screen, virtual images that would have an existence only as we look at them. . . . For us benighted people, this seems scarcely more mysterious than the simple process of recording on magnetic tape which shows no visible trace of the sound it conceals. Moreover, aren't we told that the laser makes it possible to obtain an image each fragment of which potentially contains the entire image, and that this image can show not only the front of an object but also what is located *behind* the object and is hidden by it? That it is possible to divide the laser beam in two and form a three-dimensional image by the interference of

---

[1] René Clair's *Adams* (Paris: Grasset, 1926), published in English translation as *Star Turn* (London: Chatto & Windus, 1936).—ED.

the reconverging double beam, that a hologram with the aid of a computer gives rise to a kinoform, and that thanks to this newcomer a mere *idea,* not corresponding to any real figure, can become a concrete form . . . ?

I would be quite lost if I had to explain these wonders; since I would not understand them myself if they were explained to me, I prefer taking the specialists at their word. But I can still dream about them. The past teaches us that what is possible for still pictures becomes possible sooner or later for moving pictures. No doubt this is the path that will lead to three-dimensional films, that old problem which has not yet been solved satisfactorily. It is amusing to imagine forms as immaterial as those stage ghosts whose appearance is created by means of trick mirrors, creatures issuing from the framework of the screen and entering our three-dimensional universe. If these inventions are applied commercially and placed within the reach of all, these forms could gambol about with full freedom in everybody's home, whereas the television figures we see today are still imprisoned in a depthless limbo. A priceless resource for the elegiac poet! In his room his beloved, picked up by a home receiver, could materialize at will like the figures— impalpable, unfortunately—who pass through our dreams.

As for the epic poet, the sky would be his domain. I see this sky peopled by shades as mighty as gods or swarming with the activity of another world—not that antiworld whose existence is suspected by the scientists, but an additional world to which we could relegate a portion of our desires and misery. By means of projections every country would create its own empire there, with its own army, of course. And if a war broke out we would be the spectators of battles in which only spectral blood was shed . . . . Unless the human race never gets to conquer these dream spaces because it is blown to bits by the creations of its genius, the thickness of the earth from surface to center no longer being "sufficiently honorably deep."*

But let us return to our own time. No matter how far-fetched our ramblings may be and how implausible they appear, one thing is certain: the story film will not retain the form in which we know it, and in the face of the upheavals that await us, how laughable the arguments about the ethics and esthetics of

---

*Alfred Jarry, *Gestes et opinions du docteur Faustroll.*

contemporary productions seem! The future of the media of expression, of which our cinema is only a forerunner, defies our reason. If we wish to adapt to an era fertile in marvels, we must not be afraid to call upon Lady Imagination. At times the face of this madwoman in our brain, when seen in the fantastic light of our century, shows some points of resemblance to Minerva's. But surely that goddess of wisdom cannot look without a smile at what we call progress.

By Way of an Epigraph

Between 1920 and 1924, the Compagnie des Ballets Suédois (Swedish ballet company) became the most Parisian of all dance troupes. Its director, Rolf de Maré, surrounded by co-workers whose names testify to his second sight or clairvoyance, had rented the Théâtre des Champs-Elysées, which had been since 1914 a Sleeping Beauty's palace—new, sumptuous and empty.

This theater, the direction of which he had entrusted to Jacques Hébertot, was at the time a delightful beehive of artistic activity. On the main stage, among other memorable attractions, the Ballets Suédois were followed by Diaghilev's Ballets Russes, the Vienna Opera, Stanislavsky's company and that of the Kamerny Theater of Moscow, which put on works as different as Racine's *Phèdre* and Lecocq's *Giroflé-Girofla* in productions that would make the boldest innovators of today turn pale. At the Comédie and the Studio,[1] Jouvet, Pitoëff and Baty were working. And in the corridors, in the midst of the dancers, singers, conductors and actors of every nationality, could be found Claudel, Cocteau, Cendrars, Honegger, Milhaud, Poulenc, Auric, Bonnard, de Chirico, Laprade, Léger, Foujita and others. "Others" of quality. Not far away, the outdoor tables of Chez Francis served as a second lounge of the theater. There Giraudoux would see a bizarrely befeathered old lady pass by every evening at the same hour. Through the grace of poetry, she became the Madwoman of Chaillot.

In November 1924, the final production of the Ballets Suédois was announced as follows:

> RELÂCHE[2]
> Instantaneist ballet in two acts
> and a cinematographic entr'acte
> and *The Dog's Tail,* by Francis
> Picabia. Music by Mr. Erik Satie.
> Sets by Mr. Picabia. Cinemato-
> graphic entr'acte by Mr. René Clair.
> Choreography by Mr. Jean Borlin.

---

[1] The two smaller auditoriums in the Théâtre des Champs-Elysées.—ED.

[2] *"Relâche"* means "relaxation," but in theatrical parlance it means that performances have been temporarily suspended. The phrase could be translated as "closed today," "day off," or "no performance tonight."—ED.

For the benefit of future historians of the performing arts, I must add that it was never known precisely why this ballet was "instantaneist." As for *The Dog's Tail,* no one ever saw hide or hair of it. But Picabia, one of the great inventive minds of that period, was not likely to run short of inventions. When I met him he explained to me that he wanted to have a film projected between the two acts of his ballet, something that had been done during the intermission of café-concert performances before the World War. Since I was the only staff member who worked in cinema, I was the one called upon.

What good luck for a beginner! My unit was quickly formed: I hired a cameraman, two young men who were called assistant directors and had all sorts of chores, and a property man not the easiest of whose duties was to find parking space every evening for a hearse rented from a funeral parlor. Nobody would take the trouble to give shelter for the night to this vehicle, to which a camel was harnessed in the daytime. That is what the scenario called for.

All Picabia knew about this scenario was what he had written on a sheet of stationery bearing the letterhead of the restaurant Maxim's, and I was mightily pleased when I showed him the completed film and heard him laugh at what I had added to it. As for Satie, the old master of young music, he timed every sequence with meticulous care, thus preparing the first musical composition written in perfect synchronization with a film, and this at a time when the cinema was still silent. Extremely conscientious, he was afraid he would not complete his work by the assigned date, and he would send me friendly but urgent appeals couched in an inimitable handwriting:

> And the film? . . . Time goes by *(and doesn't come back again).* Am "jittery" thinking you have forgotten me. Yes . . . Send me quickly the details of your so wonderful work. Thank you much. Truly yours I am.

Time went by and did not come back again, but on the date planned everything was ready. The sumptuous décor Picabia had conceived for his ballet, consisting solely of metal reflectors, was set up on the main stage. The dancers rehearsed for the last time under Jean Borlin's direction. Désormière gave his last-minute instructions to the large orchestra he was conducting.

For our film, a projection booth was set up in the second balcony. And the great night arrived.

Picabia had not failed to provoke the future spectators by writing in the program: "I would rather hear them yell than applaud." For his part, Satie, after declaring that he had composed a piece of "pornographic" music for us "good boys," toned down that declaration by adding that he did not intend "to make a lobster or an egg blush." And the cream of Parisian first-nighters, always attracted by the hope of a scandal, had swooped down upon the Théâtre des Champs-Elysées fully prepared to savor the most insulting surprises.

The surprise was not one that would normally have been expected. The ticket holders—gentlemen in white-tie evening dress, ladies with bare shoulders, furs and diamonds—stepped out of their cars beneath Bourdelle's marble sculpture only to learn that the doors of the theater were locked and that the performance would not take place. There was a lively explosion of shouts, to which were added the comments of the knowledgeable: "We should have suspected it . . . That's what the title meant: *No Performance* . . . This is the apotheosis of Dada . . . That joker Picabia's best stunt . . . ."

The truth, however, was simpler. Jean Borlin—ill or perhaps compelled by excitement to take too powerful a stimulant—was not in shape to appear on the stage. But that explanation satisfied no one, and most of those who returned home in their gala dress fully believed that they had been the victims of an excellent joke. A few days later, they had to admit their mistake when the curtain rose on the first act of *Relâche*.

A brief filmed prologue which I had shot at the request of the authors showed them descending from heaven in slow motion—an unforgettable view of Satie: white wispy beard, pince-nez, derby and umbrella—and firing a cannon shot that announced the beginning of the performance. The first part of the ballet was well received and the audience was still applauding when a screen descended from the flies. The projection of *Entr'acte* began.

From the very first frames, a noise composed of discreet laughter and muttered grumbling rose from the crowd of spectators, and a slight shudder ran up and down the rows of seats. This is the sign of a coming storm, and soon the storm broke. Picabia, who had wished he could hear the audience yell, had every reason to be satisfied. Shouts and whistles mingled with the melodious clowning of Satie, who undoubtedly had the connoisseur's appreciation of the harmonic support the protesters were lending his music. The bearded ballerina and the mortuary camel were received as was fitting, and when the whole audience felt itself swept away on the roller coaster of the amusement park, their howls brought the general disorder and our pleasure to their peak. Imperturbable, Roger Désormière, with furious forelock and set features, seemed to be simultaneously conducting the orchestra and unleashing a burlesque hurricane with his commanding baton. Thus was born, amid sound and fury, this little film, the end of which was greeted with applause as loud as the catcalls and whistles.

Now that *Entr'acte* is shown in film societies and film libraries with all the deference due to an antique, I am tempted to pay my respects to those who once hissed it. Snobbism has done the arts so many favors that it should not be damned indiscriminately. But it is healthy only if it remains the prerogative of a certain class of intelligence. When its effects become the common property of the entire audience, it is to be feared that this phenomenon presages the abandonment of individual judgment, acceptance of any sort of conformity, submission to every dictatorship of tastes and ideas. Nothing is more distressing than a tame, disciplined audience that feels obliged to applaud in cadence even what it finds dull, even what it dislikes. That audience is ready to do the goosestep. The audience of the Ballets Suédois had the courage to get angry. It was a real audience, a living audience . . . .

The critics were kind to us: not only such young revolutionaries as Léon Moussinac and Robert Desnos, but even such pontiffs as Lucien Descaves and Paul Souday, who admitted that they had laughed. But it was the subtle Alexandre Arnoux who bestowed the most flattering praise on us. Seeing *Entr'acte* again at some film society, long after the première at the Champs-Elysées, he wrote: "This film is still young. Even today you feel like hissing it."

Some people have wondered just how much of what is called "sincerity" goes into an enterprise of this nature. That is a pertinent question, but one not easy to answer. I myself am incapable of drawing the line between the provocation, the mystification and the serious side of my own contribution to a

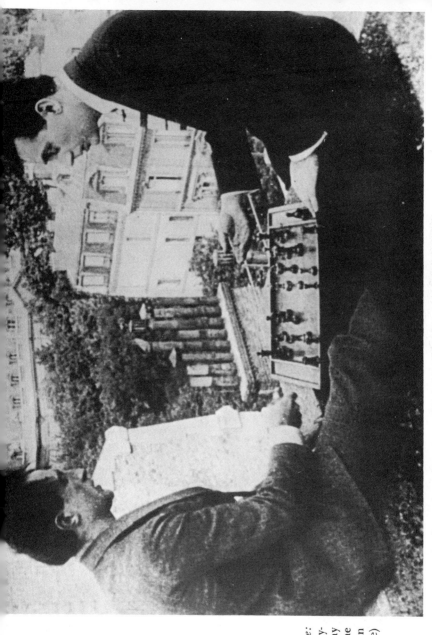

A scene from *Entr'acte*: Marcel Duchamp playing chess with Man Ray on a roof. (The Museum of Modern Art Film Stills Archive)

A scene from *Entr'acte*: The funeral procession arrives at the roller coaster. (The Museum of Modern Art Film Stills Archive)

work which was improvised for showing on a few evenings and which has survived by chance. And my uncertainty on this point leads me to raise the same question in regard to various artistic productions of our time. I hope that one day some future Ph.D. will write a thesis entitled: *On the Role of Conscious or Unconscious Mystification in Contemporary Art.* Believe me, it is not an unimportant subject.

I have wondered at times why the name of Francis Picabia has not been cited more often among the names of those who, for better or worse, have contributed to the creation of our era. I think I know the answer to this question, which other people have asked themselves as well: he never felt like playing the part of the "accursed" creator, and the people of our time (no doubt to obtain forgiveness for the various conformities to which they are attached) have a taste for official "accursedness."[1]

The young people who frequent film societies can see in our old film a funeral scene in which, by Francis Picabia's request, his initials appear on the mortuary escutcheon along with Erik Satie's. Now that he has rejoined Satie in our memory, I recall that elegant challenge which that lover of life seemed to be sending death. And I repeat to myself these lines taken from a manifesto published at the time of *Entr'acte,* these sincere and serious lines in which he seems to define the whole of his artistic production, as well as himself:

> *Entr'acte* does not believe in much—in the pleasure of living, perhaps; it believes in the pleasure of inventing, it respects nothing except the desire to burst out laughing, for laughing, thinking and working have the same value and are indispensable to one another.

"The pleasure of inventing . . . ." Stendhal could not have put it better. Permit me to place this profession of faith at the beginning of these notes, by way of an epigraph.

---

[1]The French word is *"maudit,"* a combination of tormented, damned, accursed, and tortured. Although it usually respectfully designates certain nineteenth-century poets, Clair uses it here pejoratively to connote a pseudo-artistic self-pitying role.—ED.

A Dialogue

If the dialogue resulting from this discussion gives rise to many "I's" and "me's," please do not hold it against me.* Despite the disadvantage of using the first person, the best way of bearing witness is still to say: "I was there. Such a thing happened to me."

Two years before the event that has just been narrated, I had joined the staff of the Théâtre des Champs-Elysées, where Jacques Hébertot was not content merely to manage his three stages. In the basement of the building constructed by the Perret Brothers, he had set up a printing shop, where *Paris-Journal* first saw the light of day. Its first editor-in-chief was Aragon; under the direction of Pierre Scize and Georges Charensol it became the most representative weekly of its era. In its pages appeared an article signed by the novice Marcel Pagnol, as well as *La Confession dédaigneuse* (The scornful confession) by André Breton. In addition, Jacques Hébertot published two monthly magazines, *La Danse* and *Le Théâtre*. I was assigned to write for *Le Théâtre* a cinema supplement called "Films," which was published from December 1922 to December 1924.

If you are willing to believe it possible to wander about in the past in some way other than in memory, permit me to return to that era and to appear as I am today—that is, laden with a good number of superfluous years—on the Champs-Elysées, where the sumptuous chestnut trees had not yet given way to the spindly sycamores of today.

Following the Avenue Montaigne amid the passersby who fail to notice the anachronism of my appearance, I arrive at the blind alley located on the side of the Théâtre des Champs-Elysées. There, in a sort of triangular closet which passes for an office, sits a thin young man busy correcting printer's proofs.

I: René Clair, I presume?

THE YOUNG MAN: Speaking.

Let us now imagine that these two people enter into conversation and that the older of the two asks the younger one what the

_____
*R.C., *Réflexion faite*, 1951.

latter thinks of the cinema in this year 1923. The young man, somber and resolute as one can be only at that age, replies without hesitation:

R. C. 1923: The cinema is too young, too imperfect, to satisfy us if it remains stationary. From the moment it ceases to advance, it seems to move backwards.*

THE OTHER: What do you mean exactly by "cinema?" It is a word that may be taken in different ways in future years.

R. C. 1923: It is time to have done with words. Nothing is being improved because we are not wiping the slate clean. Real cinema cannot be put in words. But just try to get that across to people—you, myself and the rest—who have been twisted by thirty-odd centuries of chatter: poetry, the theater, the novel. . . . They must learn again to see with the eyes of a savage, of a child less interested in the plot of a Punch and Judy show than in the drubbings the puppets give each other with their sticks.

THE OTHER: Certainly. But while waiting for the unlikely fulfillment of that wish, do you have reason to despair?

R. C. 1923: When optimism revives, the cinema appears to be in good health. Everything has been done to stifle it from its infancy. It is growing up all the same, and it will continue to grow; it will become something monstrous, an incomplete giant, to the surprise of those who wanted to keep it in diapers. When I say cinema, I am not speaking of the film industry, which seems to be going from bad to worse, thanks to the impotent hangers-on and con men who make their living by it along with a few loyal and innocent souls. I am speaking of the cinema as a means of expression—or a means of making us appreciate silence. Just think that at the beginning stage plays were filmed with their stage sets and their stage actors and their red make-up which showed up as blackface! Just think that thousands of novels, written works, have been adapted to this art of moving pictures!

---

*This dialogue is not completely imaginary. The words put into the mouth of the young man of 1923 are taken from one of the articles I published at that time in *Le Théâtre*.

Just think that even today, there is the cinema that points a moral, the cinema with a message, and that we are told to expect color cinema and three-dimensional cinema. As if the things that surround us—in fact, our whole existence—were so beautiful that they just had to be reproduced exactly as they are! And the cinema is not dead. We are astonished at all the vitality it has. No doubt Providence wants to console us for our charming modernity— a five-year war, bankruptcies, remote-control destruction, taxes, poverty, influenza epidemics, stock market speculation —and for the still rosier future it holds in store, by making us a gift of this universal toy and then watching us to see that we do not break it.

THE OTHER: Please let's not talk about war and remote-control destruction. I would be afraid of the accuracy of your predictions. . . . Instead, tell me what ought to be done if your cinema is to realize its destiny fully.

R. C. 1923: The whole public should be sent to a school where nothing is taught. School or rather vacuum-cleaning agency. There, my dear millions of friends, your heads would be purged of all those dregs of outmoded literature, all those artistic tranquilizers you absorb from your childhood on, which keep you from observing the world and works of art with an individual eye, which repress your savage's sensitivity to the point where you no longer cry out in ecstasy—except in certain all too prearranged circumstances. Dregs of literature: Michel Zévaco, Stendhal, Mallarmé, the *Jeudi de la jeunesse,* ministerial declarations, etc. All those things which your particular tastes and upbringing have caused to dance before your eyes, prevent them from focusing. Now, what the cinema requires of you is to learn to *see.*

THE OTHER: It seems difficult to carry any further the statement of a mystique of the cinema as you understand it. Your remarks, in accordance with the fashion of that time, are tinged with the note of inspiration, and also with that taste for provocation which makes you challenge the standing of Stendhal and Mallarmé, in order to assert that you are ready for any sacrifice, am I not right?[1]

---

[1]Clair here groups together worthless scribbling with the work of some of his favorite writers, so he is not simply knocking conventional reputations, as his interlocutor suggests.—ED.

R. C. 1923 (who has preferred not to hear this last remark) : If I could give you an oblivion treatment, I would make beautiful savages of you. Before the screen, which would be blank at first, you would marvel at elementary visions: leaf, hand, water, ear; then: tree, body, river, face; then: wind in the leaves, a man walking, a river flowing, simple facial expressions. In the second year you would answer visual riddles. You would be taught the basic rudiments of interim syntax. You would have to figure out the meaning of certain series of images in the way that a child or a foreigner has to guess little by little the significance of the sounds he hears. A few years later—or after a few generations have passed by (I am not a prophet)—people would come to respect visual conventions, which would be as practical as, and not more tedious than, those of speech.

THE OTHER: And after that?

R. C. 1923: After that? We would invent something else. Perhaps conventions of touch or smell.

THE OTHER (who remembers just in time that young men of 1923 are not afraid to add a certain aggressive humor to their most heartfelt assertions) : So by means of the cinema you want to create a new language, a sort of visual Esperanto, to escape from the "old bondage to speech?"[1] Perhaps this hope that drives you will make you smile some day, although it must be admitted it does not lack grandeur. But, to return to the present . . .

R. C. 1923: Starting right now, let us learn to take what pleases us in a film. Everyone knows that the bad taste of most movie-goers, producers and directors requires bad literature and cheap sentimentality. Since the film industry cannot live if it neglects the majority, let us wink an eye from time to time.

THE OTHER: The public makes no demands. Sooner or later you will realize that the public is a child perpetually ready to accept whatever amuses it: sometimes an excellent work of art,

---

[1] The line comes from an essay by Alexandre Arnoux that Clair will discuss at greater length on pp. 128 and 129.—ED.

sometimes a piece of nonsense. At this period in which I am speaking with you, aren't the greatest successes the films of Charlie Chaplin and Douglas Fairbanks?

R. C. 1923: Let's not always ask for masterpieces. Let's be content at times to be swept along by a torrent of images. Thirty seconds of pure cinema in the course of a film that runs an hour are enough to keep our hope alive. When we cease to care about a ridiculous plot and surrender ourselves instead to the charm of a series of images, forgetting the pretext for their appearance on the screen, we can taste a new pleasure. Images: a landscape in motion passes by. A hand appears. The bow of a boat. A woman's smile. Three trees outlined against the sky. Images . . . . Do not tell me what they mean according to the arbitrary rules of your language. It is enough for me to see them, to take pleasure in their harmony and in their contrasts. Let's learn to look at what is in front of us. Words have acquired a highly exaggerated importance. We know almost all the combinations of words by heart. We have eyes, yet we see not.

¶ It is time to interrupt this conversation between two interlocutors who are separated by so many years. The younger one's remarks do not sound very rational today, but if a few exaggerations are eliminated, they reflect a state of mind which was not unusual at that time. That is what the next chapter will show us.

An Opinion Poll

In 1923 writers and artists had just discovered the cinema, and I thought it of interest to ask some of them what type of films they liked most and what type of films they would like to see made.

These questions were asked without any malice, and the replies that were submitted give a rather precise idea of what people then thought about "the seventh art." For example:

LOUIS ARAGON:[*] I like films without stupidity, the ones in which people kill each other and make love. I like films in which the characters are good-looking and have magnificent skin—you know, that can be seen close up. I like Mack Sennett comedies with women in bathing suits, German films with magnificent romantic scenes, the films made by my friend Delluc, in which there are people who desire each other for a whole hour until the people in the audience make their seats rattle. I like films in which there is blood. I like films in which there is no morality, in which vice is not punished, in which there are no fatherland or soldier boys, in which there is no Breton woman at the foot of an outdoor cross, *in which there is no philosophy or poetry. Poetry isn't something you look for, it's something you find.* . . .

PIERRE ALBERT-BIROT: *The work of art begins where imitation ends.* . . . I remember the first film comedies very dimly. It seems to me that they were really creative and, what is more, dynamic, truly born of the new medium of expression put at man's disposal. Moreover, even now *it is in film comedies that that basic quality has best been preserved.* . . .

JEAN COCTEAU: The cinema is in a blind alley. On the first day, since people were dazzled by the invention, *the mistake began. They photographed stage plays.* Gradually these plays became cinematic plays, but never pure cinema. Such progress can only be disastrous. Better and better: *three-dimensionality, color, speech; we will soon have a cinema as dreary as our theater.* At the end of this blind alley, on a wall which young people will have to demolish, I see, as the perfect outcome of a mistake: *A Dog's Life* by Chaplin, for example.

---

[*]Louis Aragon (born 1897), poet and novelist, one of the founders of the Surrealist movement. Pierre Albert-Birot, writer. Jean Cocteau (1889–1963), poet, novelist, and film-maker. Fernand Léger (1881–1955), painter and film experimenter. Pierre Mac Orlan (1882–1970), writer. Léon Pierre-Quint, writer, author of the first essay devoted to Marcel Proust. Philippe Soupault (born 1897), writer, poet, one of the founders of the Surrealist movement. Paul Valéry (1871–1945), writer and poet.

Caligari is the first step toward a more serious error, which consists in photographing eccentric sets in a flat manner instead of producing surprises with the camera.

FERNAND LÉGER: In the future, I hope for this:
A cinematic concept that finds its own methods. *As long as the film is based on fiction or the theater, it will be nothing.*
As long as it uses stage actors, it will be nothing.
It will be everything—that is, the indispensable complement of modern life—when its actors are "mimes" specially trained to be projected as images.
When they learn to shut their mouths and make appropriate gestures.
When film-makers develop the consequences of the close-up, which is the cinematic architecture of the future. A detail of an object transformed into an absolute whole is personified when projected in large dimensions; a portion of a human being is personified when projected in large dimensions. This is the dramatic element of the future.

PIERRE MAC ORLAN: For my tastes, the cinema is an admirable art: in fact, it is the only art that can render our era literally in expressionist and simultaneist form, with all its secret rhythms which music has already grasped, *but which the art of writing cannot render because language imposes a rigid framework that cannot be dislocated.* In this case, the tool exaggerates its personality at the cost of the creation. The cinema allows a faithful translation of the psychology of our time. It might even be said that the cinematic art was discovered instinctively, in order to bestow upon our era its unique medium of expression.

LÉON PIERRE-QUINT: The first automobile was indistinguishable from the horse-drawn cab. *The film is too much like the theater and the newspaper serial, themselves outworn genres.*

PHILIPPE SOUPAULT: (1) Charlie Chaplin's films especially, Swedish films and without any doubt most documentaries.
(2) Films in which *all the resources of the cinema* would be used. It is a truism, but one that should be repeated at every opportunity and inscribed in every studio. Film-makers are making an effort to limit the cinema, *to reduce it to the proportions of the theater. . . .*

PAUL VALÉRY: I think that there is a need to institute an art of pure cinema, or cinema reduced to its own means. *This art should steer clear of those—theater or novel—that deal in speech.*

1950. It can be seen that these replies from the most diverse personalities all agreed more or less: the cinema is an autonomous medium of expression which ought to seek its future only in itself. It should be noted that, a few years before the appearance of the talking picture, no one was sorry that the film was silent and no one wished to see it cured of its muteness. Even a playwright like Sacha Guitry, when asked about the relationships between the theater and the cinema, answered:

> It seems to me that these two arts are not destined to live together long. *Whenever the cinema approaches the dramatic procedures of the theater, I hate it.* But I love it whenever it becomes objective, documentary. . . .

This small group of quotations, in which I have italicized the most significant passages, are a reflection of the opinions generally expressed between 1918 and 1928. These opinions may seem extravagant to those who did not know that era, in which the world of cinematic expression, imperfect as it was, aroused such lively curiosity and awakened such great expectations.

1970. It was while recalling that passion for the silent film, for that art which was to contrast with those "that deal in speech," that the arrival of the talking picture led me to write: "In a few years, young people will no longer understand what the word 'cinema' meant to an entire generation."

If my chief at the time I started in the cinema, Louis Feuillade, could have read that last sentence, he would have smiled. Not only did that master of the film serial, or "film novel," never imagine that the technology of the cinema could ever change; he even thought that films in general, and naturally his own, would be shown to the public indefinitely. "Soon so many films will be available that it will be unnecessary to make any more," he asserted. "The same films will be shown in the theaters all the time. And later on, seeing what we accomplished, people will say: 'Those folks really knew their job!'"

A sturdy craftsman, Louis Feuillade did not worry his head with artistic problems and never took the trouble to write out a detailed scenario. Every Monday he would distribute to his co-workers a single sheet of paper on which he had sketched out the episode to be filmed during the week. Taking his departure from this brief outline, he would invent the situations, incidents and direction as he went along. I would not swear that he even knew what would happen in the final episodes of his serial while the first episodes were already running in theaters. As you see: the absence of a scenario and confidence in improvisation, so highly recommended by the latest crop of theorists, are not as new as they are thought to be.

The young film-makers of the period were not at all interested in the popular vehicles manufactured by the prolific author of *Judex*, whom they spoke of with some disdain. But what can be predicted? Today the esthetic experiments of that era are forgotten or no longer arouse much interest, whereas film societies show *Fantômas* or *The Vampires* to respectful houses. Louis Feuillade was not that wrong: his works still have an audience, and a particularly alert audience! That would really have surprised Louis Delluc and his friends (that is, it would truly have surprised *me*), if some fortune teller had predicted it to them. This adventure, along with so many others—the history of the theater is full of them—forces a quite natural question upon our curiosity: what will people fifty years from now think about the things we esteem most highly today?

A scene from Feuillade's serial *Judex* (1917), with René Cresté in the title role. (The Museum of Modern Art Film Stills Archive)

A scene from Sjöström's *The Outlaw and His Wife* (1917), with Sjöström and Edith Erastoff. "*The Treasure of Arne, The Outlaw and His Wife* and *The Phantom Carriage* marked the apogee of Swedish production" (p. 43). (The Museum of Modern Art Film Stills Archive)

Children of the Age

1962. What fancies were spawned by that cinema of the heroic period! Its muteness seemed like a virtue to us. Its infirmity made its devotees believe that it was going to create an art out of nothing but moving images, painting in motion, dramaturgy without words, which would become a language common to all countries. As naïve as the ambition we cherished may seem today, it must be admitted that it did not lack grandeur. Our art was then young, and it is in the nature of youth to dream of noble revolutions. If anyone should smile at our lost illusions, we could make the same reply to him that a statesman made to an adversary who was criticizing his past: "Sir, I pity the man who was not a revolutionary when he was twenty."[1]

This idea of revolution gripped the liveliest minds during the years that followed the First World War. Revolutionary in art, revolutionary in literature, never did a generation show such joyous ferocity in laying waste the work of its predecessors, who were separated from it by the monstrous four-year war that marked the end of an era.

It is difficult for young people to imagine that anyone was young before they were. "What?" those of today will say. "Don't you think we are laying things waste even better than you did?"

Everyone is entitled to his view of history and his own illusions! But can it be denied that 1914 marked the true end of the nineteenth century and 1918 the start of another age? By that date, the main lines of the contemporary period were already traced: the Soviets were ruling in Russia, the industrial supremacy of the United States was established, the old structure of the Victorian world had turned to dust.

The upheaval that had just taken place within a few years could not fail to have an effect on arts and letters. Traditions and technologies were thrown overboard like the officers of the "Potemkin," the representatives of an old order.[2] The very prin-

---

[1] From Clair's *Discours de réception à l'Académie française*, the speech he delivered upon becoming a member of the French Academy on June 17, 1960. —ED.

[2] Clair refers to the events detailed in Eisenstein's *The Battleship Potemkin*, which centers on a mutiny that eventually contributed to the Russian revolution.—ED.

ciples of artistic activity were called into question. Why paint?
Why write? Historians would be wrong to lend too much importance to the outward show of provocation adopted from time
to time by those demonstrations in which a certain form of humor
did not completely hide a certain form of despair. Let them
remember that among those young people were some who also
wondered "Why live?" and could find no answer to that ultimate
question.

In an era when for some among us fiction and drama seemed
to belong to a worm-eaten age whose rubbish was being hauled
away by the Dada moving men, at a moment when the word
"revolution" seemed to be the key to all artistic problems, the
cinema was seen as the medium of expression that was newest
and the least compromised by its past—in a word, the most revolutionary. The following lines express this feeling, which I was
surely not alone in experiencing:

1925. Will our generation know what to think about any given
question raised by film and about film itself?* I doubt it. Such
an attitude may be judged to be irreconcilable with that knowledge of his art which people pretent to demand of an artist.
Let us claim for the cinema the right to be judged only by its
promises.

For my part, I could easily resign myself to admitting neither
rules nor logic into the world of images today. The wonderful
barbarity of this art charms me. Here at last are virgin territories.
It is not unpleasing to me to be ignorant of the laws of this world
that is coming into being and that is not overwhelmed by any
enslaving law of gravity. When I see these images I experience
a pleasure that is often not the one their maker wished to arouse
in me—a feeling of musical freedom . . . .

Prose sentences could not flout logic for very long without preparing their own death. But why should this series of images, not
connected with any absolute meaning and not bound by the old
cords of thought, concern itself with logic?

You raise your blonde head, and your parting hair unveils your
face. I can give to this glance, to this gesture toward the imagined
door, any meaning that I choose. If words were giving you life,

---

*R.C., "Rythme," in *Les Cahiers du mois,* 1925.

it would be impossible for me to release you from their confining power; you would be their slave. O image, be my mistress!

You are mine, dear optical illusion. Mine this reconstructed universe whose obliging perspectives I orient as I wish.

1950. Amid the exaggeration which all writers of manifestos are prone to (the manifesto tone was then used on all occasions), the above-cited passage reveals the desire to cast light on the "supernatural" nature of the cinema. A reverse supernatural, if I may say so, since it is the spectator who finds himself "in that state of reverie" Gérard de Nerval spoke of as early as the mid-nineteenth century. (See the later chapter "Pure Cinema and Poetry.")

In these remarks about "barbarity" and the nonlogic of the world of images, perhaps there was the secret hope of discovering the laws of a logic that would be proper to it and of establishing a particular order in it, but the essential thing at that period was to keep oneself in a state of "perfect availability"[1] and to do everything possible to preserve for the cinema that characteristic of being a revolutionary novelty, a trait so perfectly suited to a revolutionary age.

Another characteristic of the cinema attracted us then, perhaps without our realizing it: that of being a popular art. It seemed that poetry, music and the traditional visual arts were becoming closed domains to which only an ever-straitening gate gave access. Poetry for men of letters, music for musicians, painting for painters; the public seemed to be left out of games of which only specialists knew the rules, and all art seemed headed for a dead end in which it would lose its reason for existence.

The cinema was made for the masses and could not live without them; certain films affected the most demanding spectators as much as the mass audiences. Of what contemporary literary or artistic work could the same have been said between 1920 and 1930? What revolution in the already known forms of expression was as intoxicating as the discovery and exploration of the one

---

[1]The expression *"disponibilité parfaite"* comes from Gide, who posited it as an ideal state of freedom, one that would allow its possessor to engage in any new activity without constraints imposed by past commitments. Clair was a great admirer of Gide in his twenties, and his novel *Adams* shows a considerable stylistic debt to him.—ED.

that seemed miraculously destined for all men, whatever their social class, language or nation?

1927. If it does not die in its youth, the cinema will be . . . In fact, what will it be? It is not what it was yesterday, it will not be what it is today. It will be what the children of the cinematic age make of it. Our task is limited to preparing the instrument that they will use tomorrow.

Indeed, the best that can be said about a creator of films today is that he has a film sense. The compliment is not often bestowed. This proves that we expect a great deal from the art of the film and, on the other hand, that most of the productions offered to us are still unworthy of that expectation. What painter would be flattered to hear that he has a painting sense? It would seem like faint praise to him. In the art of images, it is precious. This is a measure of the difference between a mature art and an art in formation, whose craftsmen have not yet discovered its elementary laws. The film sense we are striving to acquire will, I believe, come quite naturally to those who follow us. The cinema generation is growing.

We expect a great deal from that generation which, as soon as it opened its eyes onto the world, saw Douglas Fairbanks scoffing at the laws of gravity and Charlie Chaplin scorning fate. These men of tomorrow, because they have not, like all the rest of us, come to the film too late, will not experience our uncertainties, it may be hoped, or that dizziness which sometimes overcomes us when faced with the blank screen "protected by its whiteness."[1] They will consider perfectly rational the following declaration which most respectable people today can appreciate only as a paradox:

> It is from the cinema that our era borrows its color, its picturesqueness, and the moral atmosphere in which it breathes; one lives as a function of the other, and it would be a waste of time to try to determine the consequences of this dizzying marriage. The lens confers an aura of legend upon everything

---

[1] "*Que la blancheur défend.*" This hemistich from Mallarmé's "Brise marine" carries resonances of other Mallarmé poems. The image centers on the immaculate purity of the void, represented by a blank sheet of paper, which resists the artist's attempt to fill it, to create something in, on, of, and from it. Clair appropriately modifies the image from a sheet of paper to a motion-picture screen.—ED.

that comes near it; it transports all that falls into its field of vision out of reality, onto a plane where only appearance, sham and artifice reign. It is impossible for us today to consider an aspect of the world without immediately divesting it of its visible form and then thinking of nothing but the representation of it we have seen in a film, removing it from the material domain it occupies and placing it in the vague realm of dream and abstraction, where all perspectives are confounded and abolished. This transition from the sensory to the spiritual, from the concrete to the imaginary, is accomplished without our knowledge, and to experience it we need only have faith.

These lines by Albert Valentin are taken from his "Introduction à la magie blanche et noire" (Introduction to black and white magic), which, if it had not been published so soon, might have been the preface of that cinematic *Hernani* which the generation of tomorrow will fight over.[1] That indefinable "film sense" was never better expressed than in these pages. In my opinion, nothing is missing there, neither enthusiasm nor lucidity, nor even the melancholy of the believer who cannot make those who are not chosen share his certainty:

> Those who have made music, poetry or painting the object of their worship have no trouble justifying their choice. Enough works have been conceived and carried out with love, ever since men have been expressing their torment with the aid of sounds, words or colors, to remove our doubts about the quality of their labors and the nature of the admiration they arouse. . . . Unfortunately, we cannot say the same about the cinema, and we understand all too well the doubts and hesitations of those whom we would like to bring round to its side! They ask us in

---

[1]Victor Hugo's historical drama *Hernani* became the center of the growing controversy between the conservative neo-classicists and the revolutionary romantics when it was first performed in 1830. Forewarned members of the opposing factions entered the theater fully prepared to engage in physical combat with one another. At the play's very outset, members of the audience gasped in admiration or disgust, depending on their allegiances, as Hugo provocatively inserted a line referring to a hidden staircase. The reference outraged the neo-classicists because hidden staircases were supposed to belong to melodrama, not the tragedy genre they had come to defend, so it defied their sacrosanct persuasion that the various genres must be kept pure. That offense was bad enough, but in the same line Hugo added insult to injury by creating a flagrantly intolerable breakdown in the regularity of alexandrine scansion. Thus the battle was launched in the play's first minute and so it continued relentlessly throughout the evening as Hugo defiantly broke one dramatic code after another with the audience bellowing its appreciation or rejection of his daring.—ED.

vain to take them by the hand and to lead them into some darkened theater where they can applaud the ideal visual drama, the one that will effect their conversion to the cause we serve. Sacrilegious as it may be to confess it, and painful as it is to do, we must admit that to our knowledge the film does not exist yet. . . .

Such faith and such warmth in expressing it gives us a foretaste of the enthusiasm which I expect the children of the cinematic age to have. Later on we shall view the effects of this enthusiasm with surprise, and no doubt will not understand them very well.

A hundred years ago today, the Romantic battle was being waged. At the thought of this, some good people sigh. "We will not again see an era like that," they say, "in which young men ardently defended a newly created art form, in which a few verses constituted a revolution. Young people today only think about automobiles, and not one of them is ready to devote his life to an artistic ideal." I spare you the rest of the refrain. It is customary for every era to misjudge itself and, in its self-ignorance, to turn with regret toward the past.

Open your eyes, good people! Another battle is taking shape next to which the Battle of *Hernani* will some day look like a minor squabble among writers. It is no longer a question of deciding whether "the hidden staircase" is a bold stroke worthy of praise or an enjambment to be censured, whether beggars ought to be given monologues like princes. It is no longer a question of verses. It is no longer a question of literature. Is it still a question of art?

I quote the same author:

> For us, the cinema is the latest of the media of expression given to man. It has a claim to our wholehearted affection, and its youth alone makes up for its lack of great accomplishments so far.

Inspired by thoughts like this, the children of the cinematic age will rise up and fight for the triumph of their art over the stifling encroachment of the other arts, over the reign of money, over the reign of stupidity. This new art which will be their art, although so far it is just a new mystique *which already has its gods, its priests, its faithful and, in addition, its merchants in the Temple.*

1950. In this profession of faith I was echoing the one that
Léon Moussinac had placed at the beginning of his *Naissance du
cinéma* (Birth of the cinema) in 1925:

> In the midst of our great modern uproar, an art is being born,
> is developing, is discovering its own laws one by one, is slowly
> progressing toward its perfection, an art that will be the very
> expression—bold, powerful, original—of the ideal of the new
> era. . . .

I must admit that our optimism was not fully justified, that
"the children of the cinematic age" have not triumphed over
either the reign of money or the reign of stupidity, and that,
although the cinema may be progressing "toward its perfection,"
this progress slows down fairly often. In our ardor, we were
wrong to believe that the destiny of the cinema was determined
once and for all, to forget that the arts progress in irregular fashion
and that, in their history, creative eras are followed by periods of
slumber and imitation. But the most serious error caused by our
enthusiasm was to project into a limitless future the image of the
only cinematic art we knew at the time, failing to imagine the
technological changes which were going to alter its looks permanently.

1970. Léon Moussinac, poet and historian of the theater, had
dedicated to his friend Louis Delluc that *Naissance du cinéma*
the preface of which, in the period after the First World War,
became the manifesto of a new generation of film-makers. Even
today, this prophetic book still surprises readers with the boldness of its remarks, but it is more surprising to those who knew
the era in which it was written. It was the time when a small
group, of whom Moussinac was one of the leaders, was creating
the Ciné-Club de France, ancestor of the film societies that now
exist even in the smallest cities of our nation. It was the time
when *only one* movie theater was to be found on the Champs-
Elysées—also, the time when "independent" critics could be
counted on the fingers of one hand.

As a critic, Moussinac was not content with reviewing the films
he had seen. From his very first articles, he constituted himself a
historian and theorist of the art he saw arising. As a polemicist,

calling down insults and lawsuits upon himself, he fought against all those who claimed that the cinema should be subjected to the laws of business alone. In a letter addressed to one of these people, he wrote: "I strive to remain constantly, remorselessly, in accord with my conscience." And he was always faithful to that rule of conduct, as he was to his political ideas, as he was to his friends.

But this doctrinarian, this partisan, was never a sectarian. If he asserted that the cinema should be primarily a great art of the people, he was always ready to support a purely esthetic work which he considered worthy of interest. He liked to find, in films as well as in men, the virtues he embodied more than anyone else: courage and honesty.

In his last book, which was published a few days before his death, there is a preface in which Eisenstein recalls a masquerade improvised during an international conference in the days when we were young. "When I dressed up Moussinac as d'Artagnan," writes the author of *Potemkin,* "I paid hardly any attention to the fact that the qualities of this lovable hero of the novel are also the traits of character of the no less delightful Léon."

Eisenstein, master of images, offered us there the image of Moussinac which his friends would like to retain.

¶ It was alongside Moussinac's name that I first read that of Albert Valentin. In a booklet published by the Presses Universitaires de France in 1927, an article by the former entitled "Cinéma: expression sociale" was followed by the latter's "Introduction à la magie blanche et noire." At the beginning of this essay was a poem, the only regular verses which I know of by Valentin, who was then a very young man fascinated by the silent screen:

> Je m'élance, je tombe et me suive qui m'aime
> Au sein de cette pure étendue où je vois
> Que des ombres sans corps naissent de l'ombre même
> Et tiennent aux regards un langage sans voix. . . .

> (I dart forward, I fall; follow me, if you love me,
> To the heart of that pure white expanse where I see
> Shadows bodiless rising from shadow itself
> And addressing my eyes in a voiceless oration. . . .)

Albert Valentin did not find recompense in the cinema for the passion he had devoted to it and which his talents merited. A writer and friend of Eluard and Aragon, he belonged to the Surrealist group. But his personal standards were such that he very soon stopped writing: all that remains of his work is one piece, a long prose poem entitled *Aux Soleils de minuit* (To the suns of midnight), which was published in several issues of the Brussels magazine *Variétés* but which Valentin never bothered to publish as a book. This text, which André Breton loved, is one of the most moving that the Surrealist era produced.

¶ A child of the age, Paul Gilson grew up in the days when strange white windows were beginning to open onto a new world. Passing through the screen just as his beloved Alice passes through the looking-glass, he found himself so much a part of the great shadowland adventure that he was able to say later: "There is really only one history of the cinema, the one which begins with our memories and gets mixed up with our personal history."

He wrote his history of the cinema in the course of many years, in his critical articles as well as in his essays. But it was not through absentmindedness that this fanatic of the image strayed off into the world of radio and became one of its masters. This medium of expression which offers nothing to the eyes is as unreal as the speechless cinema was in our youth. And there is every reason to believe that Paul never attached much importance to the thing called reality.

He loved the marvelous to such an extent that he made that word the title of one of his books [*Merveilleux*]. In a film that to our eyes was perhaps the most banal possible, he was able to discover the incident, the effect of light, the gesture or the face that satisfied his taste for the extraordinary, his desire for the unusual. He would enter a movie house as if it were one of those inns in picaresque novels, too often finding nothing but what he brought along himself. But, provided as he was with an inexhaustible store of daydreams, he rarely came out disappointed.

He had collaborated on a few films, one of which, *Memoirs of Dead Houses,* seems like an illustration of his poetic work. It is too bad that he did not find the time or the opportunity to do more work for the screen! What beautiful films he could have composed with the help of his dreams! London or some other foggy city, a pale girl, thieves and magicians, mystery, love, humor . . . . We need only read the books he has left us to imagine the groupings and the characters.

In one of his books, *Ciné-Magic,* he opens his "Calendar of Memories" for us, a list of old and new, good and poor films that have delighted him. Now that his great friendly shade has taken its place in our memory amid the shadowy figures he loved so well, he seems to be making a final appointment with us by giving us to understand at the end of this "Calendar" that we will rediscover the marvels of these films and a thousand others along with him, in the paradise of images.

¶ The first generation fascinated by the cinema was no doubt the one which represented the "young cinema" in the era we have just recalled. But hasn't the cinema continued to belong to the young? Today the majority of film viewers are not older than twenty-five and, moreover, it is generally in their first active years that film creators produce the most personal part of their work. The cinema is a young art, and it is with paternal sympathy that I here salute, even in their excesses, those who are ensuring its lasting youthfulness.

One remark, however, dictated by experience and thus in no danger of being heeded: of all the surprises to which the human condition exposes us, the loss of our youth is the least unexpected and the most surprising. Young people claim all privileges for themselves and their agemates. Are they not thus displaying a singular lack of imagination? No fortune is squandered as quickly as that youth they believe they will always possess. "How much wisdom," a moralist would say, "in civilizations in which the young respected maturity! By so doing, they were preparing their own future comfort; they were taking out the most useful insurance for themselves."

At the time I was getting started, a veteran journalist named me in an article about "audacious and turbulent" young people, and I replied: "I do not think I can be reproached with having frequently turned my age to account. Those who boast of their youth seem to me as foolish as those who show off their experience."

As you see, I was taking out just such insurance. Pessimists claim that the cult of youth as practiced today is a premonitory sign of totalitarian regimes. A humorist would add: "Youth is a precious privilege that Nature bestows without using its judgment."

Return to 1900

It was not in the years around 1922 that the French film enjoyed its best period. At that time, while the American, German and Swedish film industries were producing original works each in its turn (the Soviet cinema was to take its place in history shortly afterward), the French cinema seemed lackluster and characterless in comparison. Of course, France had an interesting "avant-garde," but its purely visual experiments could be appreciated only by a few people, and the disagreements between this "avant-garde" and the "commercial" cinema threatened to lead French film production into a blind alley.

1922. How we wish that there were a typically French film style! Perhaps there is one. But it could only be perceived at a distance. We are too close. It seems to us that each of our films is very different from all the others. We cannot make out their family relationship at all clearly. Sharp-tongued observers will say that the character of the French film is its lack of personality, or vice versa.

There is nothing we can do about it; we are Latins and we love eloquence; we make an effort to do away with intertitles, but our scenes are still constructed as if they were to be spoken. They rarely contain the essential "motif" worthy of being developed visually. The Americans found it before we did because they thought less; the Swedes, because they reflected more.

1950. The admiration, of course perfectly justified, that the best friends of cinema then felt for foreign films made them forget that before the First World War there had been a great school of French film which no one spoke about any more and which I myself knew only through dim childhood memories. Thus it was not without surprise (nor, I must confess, a certain satisfaction) that I rediscovered the following lines I published in 1923 and which, if they had not passed completely unnoticed, would have astonished the "avant-garde" circles:

1923. The creators of the first films, at the turn of the century, were not mistaken. The error arose in 1908 with the first adaptations of stage plays. *The Sprinkler Sprinkled,* that ancestor of the film comedy, arose from a conception that was purely cinematic and much more fitting than the one which spawned all the adaptations from Dumas *fils* and Georges Ohnet. The *film d'art* was a mistake. Let us create the film first of all. Art will engender itself. It would be interesting to link up again with the tradition of 1900.

1950. In speaking of the *film d'art* I was probably thinking of that series of films, so easily ridiculed, in which poor Mounet-Sully and Sarah Bernhardt were seen yawning tragically on a white screen impervious to alexandrines; but I was also thinking more or less consciously about those esthetic experiments in which the "avant-garde" and my friends of "the seventh art" seemed to be going astray. This position was more precisely stated in an article I published in 1924 on the occasion of the showing of the first film I authored. Here are some extracts from this little manifesto, whose sole merit is that it was written in an era when people swore only by the German, Swedish or American cinema, and when Méliès, forgotten by everyone along with his films, was selling toys at the Gare Montparnasse:

1924. It can scarcely be denied that the cinema was created to record motion, and yet this is what seems to be forgotten all too often. The principal task of the present generation should be to restore the cinema to what it was at the outset and, in order to do that, to rid it of all the false art that is smothering it. The mistake was to decide too soon that the cinema was an art. If it had been treated only as an industry, art itself would have been the gainer. Would modern automobiles have acquired their beautiful long shapes if their builders had thought about loading them with carriage ornaments before they thought about endowing them with speed? Routine thinkers have chosen to rediscover in films the stereotypes of the arts. The desire for easy success has led most film-makers to draw their inspiration from a Werther-like "Clair de lune" esthetic. It would have been just as disastrous to be inspired by *The Rite of Spring*. The cinema will find "the place and the formula" only within itself.

The slightest industrial progress is more meaningful for the cinema than any artistic innovation. "There are forty thousand movie houses in the world . . . . The largest studio is a thousand feet long." That is what merits interest and prepares the future! Above all the cinema must stay alive. Art will come all by itself, like Little Bo Peep's sheep.

That is why we would like the creator of a film to be not averse to a little humility. Anything he can do is still so far from what can be done, and is so rarely worthy of that admirable instrument, the movie camera! The cinema is not yet an art because the cinematic work is the result of the collaboration of many people. Actors, cameramen, lab men, carpenters, electricians and especially editors and producers work together in a manner that is helpful or harmful to the creator's work. Where is the place for art? I think that we should not think about it or shout for it to appear. We should remain in a state of perfect availability and remember the origins of the cinema before the unfortunate intrusion of the *film d'art*. . . .

Without overlooking the considerable enrichment of technique, it has seemed possible to me to create films—just as at the beginnings of the cinema—with scenarios written directly for the screen and using some of the resources characteristic of the movie camera. I think that the subject of a film should be, before all else, a visual theme. . . .

If there is an esthetic of the cinema, it was discovered at the same time as the movie camera and the film, in France, by the Lumière Brothers. It can be summed up in one word: motion. Outward motion of objects perceived by the eye, to which we would add today the inner motion of the unfolding story. From the union of these two motions there can arise that phenomenon so often spoken of and so seldom perceived: rhythm.

When the Lumière Brothers wished to show the value of their wonderful invention, they did not project onto the screen a dead landscape or a dialogue between two mute characters: they gave us *The Arrival of a Train, A Charge of Cuirassiers* and that *Sprinkler Sprinkled* which was the father of the film comedy. If we want the cinema to grow and thrive, let us respect this forgotten tradition, let us return to this source.

1950. Dare I confess that I am "charmed by this little piece" and that I judge the paradoxes and exaggerations it contains with the indulgence of Philinte?[1] But there is at least one point I no longer agree with. It does not much matter whether the cinema is an art or not, but it is not because the cinematic work is the result of the collaboration of many people, that it is not "artistic" and cannot be personal.

When Eisenstein declared a few years later that he was not the creator of his own films, but that that creator was "the people," he was only adding a tinge of demagogy to a statement that is extremely arguable. Let us not play on words. If *The Battleship Potemkin* was made by the people, then so was *The End of Saint Petersburg*. Now, there is an Eisenstein style in the former and a Pudovkin style in the latter which are very different from each other, and this would not be the case if the same "people" were the creator of these two films.

Let us not be afraid to repeat that the works which count in the history of the cinema, with few exceptions, are due to strongly marked personalities, and that the creative vitality of the American cinema diminished when Hollywood films became the product of a many-headed anonymous collaboration.

1970. "When Eisenstein declared a few years later . . . ." This little sentence stirred vividly that conscientious historian Georges Sadoul. He was not familiar with that statement, and he asked me where I had read it. Now, I had not read it anywhere; I had heard it during an improvised speech Eisenstein made in Paris before the showing of *The General Line* at the Russian Embassy, and I think that his eloquence (he spoke French very well) carried him away at this point and went beyond what he actually thought.

It was in 1929 that the creator of *The Battleship Potemkin* came to France, accompanied by his co-worker Grigori Alexandrov and his chief cameraman, Tissé. The principal reason for that trip was to study the sound film. All three were then to go to the United States. I met him often in the Epinay studios where I was working, and where he was collaborating with

---

[1]Philinte was the understanding friend of Alceste, Molière's surly *Misanthrope*. He indulgently pretended to admire another character's terrible poetry in order to avoid unnecessary friction between them, while Alceste went on to tear the poetry apart needlessly, thus provoking consequent trouble for himself when the other character was offended by his harshness.—ED.

Alexandrov on a trial film, *Sentimental Romance,* a mere pretext for getting acquainted with the new techniques. I remember his enthusiasm and his high spirits when he leaned over our still very primitive editing tables or played with a moviola which he had just discovered. Eyes shining with curiosity and the happiness of being alive, a tousled mop of hair: a laughing lion.

He was then thirty-one, his name was already famous and he seemed to be only at the beginning of a dazzling career. But the time of trials had come for him. In Hollywood, Paramount, which had signed him up, accepted none of his projects and after months of argument his contract was canceled. The film he then undertook in Mexico provoked further disputes with backers who took control of it away from him; he was not allowed to finish cutting *Que viva México* and it was released in fragments. Back in the Soviet Union, he was the object of various attacks, and several screenplays he presented were refused by the Soviet film authorities. Finally he was allowed to make *Alexander Nevsky,* then, a few years later, *Ivan the Terrible.* But the second part of *Ivan* was condemned by a resolution of the Central Committee of the Communist Party. Fought by Stalin's bureaucrats just as he had been rejected by the Hollywood bureaucrats, Eisenstein produced only a portion of the work that was to be expected of his genius. Discouraged and ill, he died in 1948 at the age of fifty.

¶ Another unfulfilled destiny was that of Georges Sadoul, whose name I have just mentioned again. Coming from militant Surrealism, Georges Sadoul became a man of the cinema in the way that other men become monks. A Benedictine of the film, he amassed an enormous documentation in order to construct that *Histoire générale du cinéma* which he left incomplete at his death.

But a bookish documentation did not satisfy him. Like Villemain[1] discussing books, Georges Sadoul could have said that nothing is more useful in discussing a film than having seen it.

---

[1]François Villemain, a nineteenth-century academician widely known for his wit and brilliance, encouraged thoroughness and originality in criticism, urging the students in his extremely popular classes to abandon eighteenth-century critical concepts as stultifying and overly general. He admonished them to steep themselves in the material, the author, and his time in order to understand the work fully.—ED.

He wanted to see everything and he went to see everything. His research, carried out with exemplary fervor and patience, took him to the oldest archives of film libraries and to the remotest countries where a camera ever operated, and he surely saw more films than anyone else.

Thanks to his universal curiosity, our knowledge of the cinema, too long confined to the principal producing nations, broadened to take in the whole world.

In the Beginning Was the Image

1950. It was in *Le Théâtre* that I was led to publish regularly over a two-year period (1923–24) most of the articles from which the extracts on the following pages are taken. By good fortune, film production during this period was extremely interesting not only for its quality—which would be hard to evaluate at present, since nothing is less lasting than the quality of a film—but also for its diversity, the result of a fertile disorder which it would be too easy to contrast with the organized conformity of current production.

I have no illusions about the value of the reflections reproduced here, and I make no attempt either to correct the errors they contain or to soften the sharp tone, typical of youth, which sets them off. The thing that touches me when I reread them (and I am so far removed from the man who wrote them that I can discuss them just as freely as if they were not by me) is the enthusiasm to which they bear witness, an enthusiasm then aroused by the feeling of discovery. The echo of such enthusiasm is rarely heard in our day. I intend no reproach by that statement of fact! At the time of Marco Polo adventurous navigation aroused an interest which cannot be awakened by the regular commercial use of transatlantic routes.

1970. An observation which seemed correct in 1950 but would be less so today. In the age of television and the easily acquired automobile, the cinema has lost almost half its audience in most Western nations. Hollywood can no longer impose its will so firmly, "organized conformity" no longer rules as an absolute monarch, and the return of "fertile disorder" has permitted, for better or worse, the coming of new forms of expression.

Furthermore, many films are produced by countries that did not have a movie industry, hence a desirable variety of inspiration. Finally, to judge by the number of magazines, essays and writings of all sorts devoted to the cinema today, it must be admitted that the passion it stirs in its votaries is not less ardent than the one it inspired in our youth.

This passion is displayed in the selection of articles which follows. Please forgive me if you do not find in them any of those partisan standpoints that became fashionable later, or any of those harsh criticisms that attract the attention of gawkers. My taste did not run to those negative exercises. It is not because, all things considered, there were much fewer poor films then than today, but being free to choose, I felt like writing about only what I liked or things that, for one reason or another, seemed to deserve notice.

1922. *The Cabinet of Doctor Caligari, Torgus, Destiny* and *The Burning Earth* suffice to astonish us. When they appeared, they were not universally liked, but I believe they left no one indifferent. A new formula had been revealed to us.

First of all, the screenplays surprised us: the author had the courage to be sad, to write an "unhappy ending." It would be hard to prove that a story which ends sadly has more artistic value than a cheerful story: our feeling of happy surprise was caused only by an understandable desire for change. The legendary atmosphere, the fog and the night, suddenly cut us off from the blonde American dolls on their millionaire's estates. Faced with a new convention, we understood the already accepted conventions better. But what seemed most new to us in this art was its cerebral qualities.

Up to then the doctrines of the Théâtre Libre seemed to have been created for the cinema.[1] The wall of a real peasant's house had never been erected on the Boulevard de Strasbourg stage. Thanks to the movie camera, real people in real fields were finally going to become a work of art. At last, no more canvas trees, no more painted skies! Most of the catalogued landscapes were swallowed up by our lenses. The drawing rooms in the studios strove to resemble our drawing rooms exactly; klieg lamps emulated daylight; even make-up did homage to truth, as vice does to virtue.

Then all of a sudden, in despite of the realist dogma that, with very few exceptions, seemed unattackable to us, *Caligari* came along and declared that the only interesting truth was subjective truth. We should have been treated a little more gently. We

---

[1] The Théâtre Libre (Free theater) was a nineteenth-century dramatic movement that attempted to recreate reality (usually squalid) on stage by means of realistic blocking, delivery, décor, and other dramaturgical considerations that all denied the blatant artifice contained in the conventions of earlier movements or systems.—ED.

wanted to believe that this doctor with the pointed hat was crazy. But *Destiny* proved to us immediately that such folly was very well thought out. Hence, somewhat of a hubbub.

We must face up to it. The cerebral cinema has been created. We must admit that reshaped nature is at least as expressive as "natural" nature. The sets, the lighting, the actors' performances, even their faces, all artificially arranged, form a whole in the mastery of which the intellect takes delight. This absolute power of the brain is the very danger that menaces films of this type. It is to be feared that feelings of humanity will find no place in them. Works like this are astonishing. For their own good, let us hope that they can become more emotionally engaging.

1950. Those years saw the golden age of the German film. It will be noticed that in film history as in political history (or, more simply, as in a bicycle race) different countries take the lead in turn. France was the first before 1914; from 1915 to 1920 it was America which did most for the progress of the cinema; next, Sweden, then Germany and Russia. America's turn came again at the beginning of the talking picture era, then France's. Since the end of the Second World War it has been the Italian and British schools that have contributed the most original or most novel formulas to the screen.

It may also be observed that these periods of glory experienced by the film production of a country usually coincide with a period in which this country is encountering economic difficulties. Thus, Germany in 1922, at the worst moment of its inflation; Russia right after the revolution; America and France at the moment of the great crisis that began around 1929; after 1945, Italy and England, impoverished by the war.

Without going so far as to say that the quality of the films produced by a country is always inversely proportional to that country's prosperity, isn't it allowable to think that in a period of prosperity, when success is easy (thus, in America from 1940 to 1946), there is a tendency to be lazy and content with the repetition of stale formulas, whereas difficult times call for an effort and a quest for originality?

1970. "We invented Neorealism," said one of its masters, "because we were unable at the time to organize a studio properly." This witty remark conceals a hint of truth, if the condition of Italian technology immediately after the war is duly considered, but it is necessary to add that the light of Italy, the acting talents possessed by the Italian people above all others, and the ease of improvisation natural to the country where the *commedia dell'arte* was born, favored the invention of this style which was to be highly successful and to exert great influence in every country.

January 1923. The Swedes, and Mr. Sjöström in particular, know how to concentrate the action of a film in a few clearly developed scenes. A work of art with such pure and firm lines surprises the lovers of agitated complications; it might serve as an example for more than one of those who think they are "creating art" by teaching the cinema the formulas of an outworn symbolism or impressionism. Here, lucidity of action and starkness of expression reign. There is no cheating. The director presents his work stripped of all those procedures that are termed artistic because they are borrowed from the unwanted left-overs of the other arts. He wishes to arouse emotion only by means of these faces clearly viewed in close-up, only with these true gestures.

To judge by *The Exiles* and *Love's Crucible,* it seems that the Swedish producers wish to broaden their style. Their technique is becoming more like American technique: the scenes shorter, the action more rapid. No doubt they are experiencing the necessity of making themselves understood by audiences everywhere. Those who like the serious, slow rhythm of their films will miss it. *Love's Crucible* is a remarkable work, but it does not have the value of *The Phantom Carriage* or *The Outlaw and His Wife.* Jenny Hasselquist is the main character in this film. It is impossible to forget her broad forehead, her determined gaze, her rigidity, her criminal obstinacy, her brusque starts like those of a threatened animal. No facile effect, no unjustifiable expression . . . . The Swedes—honesty of the image.

1950. *The Treasure of Arne, The Outlaw and His Wife* and *The Phantom Carriage* marked the apogee of Swedish production. In stating that "their technique is becoming more like American technique," I was, without knowing it, announcing the decline of the Swedish film. Let us extract from another article a few lines written in the same period:

> What is more serious is that American producers seem to be looking for the "international" film especially. They ask for works that are easily accessible to every country; everyone knows what childish nonsense has resulted from similar solely commercial preoccupations. The works most worthy of what we expect of the cinema—those from Sweden among others—are all clearly national in character, but this does not prevent them from being understood outside their country of origin.

Since 1930 Swedish production has become sparser and sparser. The talking picture and most of the modern inventions used in the industry have given an added advantage to the large nations at the cost of the smaller.

1970. Since 1950 Swedish production has regained its vigor and its personality. Contrary to what I was saying above, it seems that the obstacles raised in the world by the difference of languages have favored the independence of national productions. Just a few years ago, who talked about Indian films, Bulgarian films or Brazilian films?

The first flowering of the Swedish cinema—as Georges Sadoul has justly noted—was facilitated by the isolation of Sweden between 1914 and 1918. The Second World War produced the same effect.

January 1923. A child and his dog, both abandoned, are adopted by a plumber and his wife. The man is brutal and lazy. The woman loves the child, who wants to take the plumber's place on a call. . . .

But why try to recount this screenplay? It crumbles away when you tell it; you attempt to seize it—nothing more exists of it but a few dancing images.

It has often been said that in a film the screenplay should not be important. Let us confess that we arrived at that formula to console ourselves. We would like the screenplay to be important, but we pretend to scorn it because the commercial conditions for the existence of the cinema force upon us screenplays that are devoid of intrinsic value. Therefore, let us pay no more attention to them and let us be interested only in the visual developments for which they are the pretext. It is no doubt the wiser thing to do . . . .

1970. This is not unlike statements being made in certain film circles today. A lasting confusion between the experimental cinema or amateur cinema (in the most favorable sense of the word) on the one side, and the feature film intended for a wide audience, on the other. For the members of this audience, the thing that counts above all is not the "visual effects" or any other effects, but the story being told to them and the interest they take in it.

. . . I do not mean that screenplays should be more "thought out." On the contrary, I would want them to be composed solely for the eyes of the spectators. But I would like their psychology to be more logical. Or their nonlogic to be more lyrical, as with Chaplin, Mack Sennett or Douglas Fairbanks, who have turned out good screenplays—pretexts for their amazing chases. But try and write them! A good screenplay cannot be told in words. . . .

1950. Of course, of course. . . . But now that a quarter of a century has passed during which I have had to hear a good many screenplays summarized, I would say almost the same thing in different terms: "A good screenplay is one that can be told in a few sentences."

This does not mean that every screenplay that can be told succinctly is good, but that, if a screenplay has good features, they will show up in the briefest summary of it. I hope inexperienced screenplay writers are willing to be convinced of this truth, and will permit me to give them a piece of advice: the shorter a screenplay résumé is, the better its chances of being read by the professional to whom it is submitted. If his first reading of it is favorable, he will not stop there. He will want to know how the idea that aroused his curiosity is developed But no professional has the time or the inclination to read every hundred- or two-hundred-page screenplay sent to him.

. . . Does that mean that the screenplay of *Trouble* is good?

It is not bad, is not very pretentious and offers the opportunity to include some likable images. We are bored every week by so many novels, stage comedies and stage dramas made ridiculous by the screen, which they in turn make ridiculous, that we find some relaxation in *Trouble*. The children's home, the little dog, Jackie dragging the plumber's bag, the leak, the twenty-dollar bill, are all pleasing motifs. And there are two very good things: the scene in which Jackie, hesitating between various ways of awakening the brute he is afraid of, finally gives him a violent kick (this is in the style of Chaplin), and the courtroom scene in which the child gives his testimony so skillfully that we all understand without the aid of a single word. Naturally, the producers saw fit to add awful intertitles. You would think they were afraid to see the cinema acquire any personal force, and that whenever the image is sufficiently expressive they hasten to smother it with unnecessary words. Let us drop the subject. The cinema is strong enough to resist even its craftsmen. But they should not go too far.

This silent testimony of Jackie Coogan reminded me of a very fine scene in *A Midnight Bell*: Charles Ray, alone in a chapel that is said to be haunted, is trying to be brave; he attempts to read, he starts to whistle, he jumps at the slightest noise. He remains that way for at least five minutes, alone on the screen, and never fails to be entertaining. It is a delightful virtuoso accomplishment. . . .

1950. It will be noted that it was possible to suggest words and sound by means of the images (Jackie Coogan's testimony, Charles Ray beginning to *whistle* and jumping at the slightest *noise*); the viewer's imagination did the rest.

This power of suggestion was so strong that more than once I have heard people who are not well acquainted with the history of the cinema declare that a certain old film was a talkie, whereas it was silent. Those people, who incidentally remembered very well the plot of the film, the details of certain episodes and even the names of the cast, thought that they had *heard* the dialogue. This should give food for thought to those who, even today, refuse to admit the supremacy of the visual element in film stories.

1970. An analogous observation can be made about the visual

element itself. How many people think they remember a film as being in color whereas it was really made in black and white! These viewers *imagined* the color in their memory. The same goes for screen ratios: many people hardly remember after a few months whether a film was in the old ratio, or in wide screen, or some even wider process. (See the later chapter "Speed and Shape.")

. . . The most pleasant feature of *Trouble* is the impression of freshness this film gives. Such naïveté—I am not speaking of the child's—surprises us. I do not think that similar films will ever be made in France. We are too cultivated, and our least cultivated film-makers are precisely the ones who want to add the most literature to their works. What literature! A film like *Trouble* can only be the product of a very naïve or a very refined civilization. It may be stated as a fact, moreover, that the American cinema, plain and powerful, is the one that some of our most modern men of letters have liked most—because it was not infected with the literary spirit.

1950. One of the sore spots of the silent cinema was the bad— that is, the unnecessary—intertitle. (Today we have unnecessary dialogue, which is hardly an improvement, but at least it does not interrupt the flow of images, whereas the intertitles, sown in handfuls by awesome specialists, filled the screen with their frozen chatter.) From the same period, let us quote the following observation:

I recently attended a showing of *Pay Day*, Charlie Chaplin's latest film, which you will see soon.

During the entire opening of the film, the audience was gripped by tremendous mechanical laughter, which continued in fits and starts, following the rhythm of the images, as if the brain of the viewers were controlled by the projector.

There were only a few pauses for taking a breath. These moments of relaxation coincided with the appearance on the screen of so-called funny intertitles which the producer had seen fit to add to Chaplin's slapstick. You know the nature of these witticisms; they used to be very successful with the critics once, but this time all they did was to calm down the audience, which had been caught up in the gears of the comedy. They stopped laughing. The cinema had made progress.

1950. It can be noted today that laughter caused by a visual effect is different in nature from that caused by a verbal joke, and that humor perceived by the eye has a more rapid and more potent action than verbal humor.

1923. Simplicity: that is the quality, the chief quality of the best parts of *The Hearth*. The plowshare slicing through the rich earth, the oxen, the smoking hearth, the blurred but luminous landscapes, formed images of calm and powerful lyricism.

The intertitles, almost all neutral and brief, testify to the intelligence of this production. I did not like the reference to the sea nor "life too has its storms." That is strictly literary, and I think that Mr. Boudrioz would be ashamed to write a sentence containing such a facile comparison. All that is symbolic seems weak on the screen. This literary storm does not affect us much when compared with a single human gesture: in front of his dying brother, Bernard, who is still full of jealous rage but is beginning to yield to remorse, becomes confused, lowers his head, picks up a wisp of straw and twists it in his fingers. That is cinema. The film-maker who created that brief vision—and others just as sober and direct—should in the future resort only to pure visual expression. He knows the simple secret of it.

1950. This film, made by Robert Boudrioz in 1919 for Abel Gance's studio at Pathé, was one of the first films to depict rural life. Even today films of that type are rare, especially in the United States, that great farming country where farmers almost never appear on the screen. (Moreover, there is no country whose film production reflects actual existence less than that of the United States.)

"Life too has its storms" was an intertitle preceding a view of the sea in fury, all of this being interpolated into a dramatic conflict that had nothing to do with the sea. This type of metaphor was not rare at the time. In another film, when the villain with an elegant moustache and dubious intentions was courting the pure young maiden and took her by the arm, the screen suddenly showed the image of a caterpillar crawling on a rose!

1970. We may smile at that naïve symbol, but we should stop for a moment and take note that for a while now symbolism has again come into favor in the novel as well as in the theater, and even in the cinema. If the symbol, as Jules Lemaitre said, is "an extended comparison of which we are given only the second term," how many contemporary works conceal from us the first term of the comparison and require us to guess its meaning! It seems that what their authors are showing us represents something different from what we are seeing, by virtue of an analogical correspondence. All right. But in certain cases, why not simply show us the *other* thing? Is it because, once revealed, that thing would lose the appeal that a "dark brightness" lends it?

You will tell me that in poetry . . . . Naturally. André Gide is correct in speaking of "the poetic benefit of the doubt." Nerval informs us that his most beautiful poems "would lose some of their charm if they were explained," and his example suffices to show that what is obscure one day can become luminous the next. But poetry is not dramatic art, which, to judge by its masters in the past, has no use for the equivocal and the hermetic.

"What!" the bluestockings of both sexes will exclaim, "why do you want to understand?" Nowadays *not* to understand is good taste.

¶ "Even today films of that type are rare." Nothing has changed and it is still unusual for the cinema to take its subject matter from country life. For the most part, film characters belong to exceptional categories, just like those of ancient tragedy and standard society drama. On the screen, common people rarely have a chance to star. Thus, in wars, peasants form the obscure masses and their names are mentioned only on the monuments to the dead in their villages.

1923. I would like critics to admit they are not perfect; their humility would be a pledge of their sincerity, and their dicta, if understood to be subject to the error imputable to the human condition, would have more force and less vanity.

For the role of the critic is one of the funniest in the world, and I would laugh at it more if I had the time. Just look at us, little men that we are, busy judging our brothers' works with the gravity indispensable to lofty duties, and declaring this to be good and that to be blameworthy! Doesn't every line of criticism imply "my judgment is the best" (which is in general the basic principle of all human nature, thanks to which we have not yet done amusing ourselves or existing)? Moreover, our moods are inconstant and we often marvel at a work simply because it relaxes us by its contrast to another. Perhaps it is best that things are this way, and that we are allowed to retain the great pleasure of contradicting ourselves. It is up to the reader to exercise all caution.

This preface was not indispensable, but it is convenient for me. Thanks to it, I can lament as much as I please the fact that *Don Juan and Faust* reached the movie houses in the same month as *The System of Doctor Ox*.[1] I lament this because the former film is important and I might have enjoyed it more if I had not taken great delight in seeing the latter within the same short period. I would like to discuss them separately, but they form such a perfect contrast to each other that I cannot destroy the singular harmony created by their opposition.

Don Juan and Faust is an *artistic* film, and one of the best of that type which have come to the screen. Here, "artistic" takes on its true meaning, which is "relating to the arts." *Don Juan and Faust* relates to the arts; there are few images in this film that do not conceal some artistic purpose or allude to some reminiscence of the other visual arts or literature. If that was the author's purpose, he has succeeded perfectly. More than one American producer who believes he is "creating art" and history with the money at his disposal, will see in *Don Juan and Faust* what can be achieved by the taste of this old, impotent Europe. (A parvenu is not laughable when he discusses the business ventures in which he has shown his intelligence and boldness,

---

[1] The English title *The System of Doctor Ox*, a direct translation of the title *Le Système du Docteur Ox* in the French text, is used here merely for convenience. It has not been possible to determine which film is meant. According to a communication from René Clair, the director was Marshall Neilan. —ED.

but he often is laughable when he wants to prove his culture and taste. America is like that sometimes.)

But the artistic success of *Don Juan and Faust* is precisely what causes some misgivings. We see beautiful tableaus. Do we see a film? In its present state the cinema cannot express thoughts and remain visual. What are Don Juan and Faust if not the representative types of two of the most widespread human tendencies? Will their silhouette, their pantomime, tell us the secret of their psychology? Which leaves the plot: inadequate for Faust, who resembles a run-of-the-mill magician, it is full of details which disfigure Don Juan. Is Don Juan this bashful man who needs to take lessons before courting a woman? Is it this man who becomes a seducer after a disappointment in love and remains at bottom a naïve jilted lover? Another step in that direction, and we would see him entering a monastery at the outset of his career because of a thwarted infatuation . . . .

That is the danger presented by films which evoke great literary reminiscences. The image seems to be a childish deformation of the thought behind it. But to criticize *Don Juan and Faust* solely from the literary point of view would be to make a mistake worse than that made by the film author in his choice of subject. In cinema the movement of the action counts most of all.

Here, the screenplay all too often prevented the action from assuming the beautiful rapid pace of the ending. But Don Juan's final party, feverish and magnificent, unfolds in a perfect rhythm. It is the only moment in the film that is completely moving emotionally; it is so thanks to the noblest means . . . .

1950. It is too bad that the intransigent critic of *Don Juan and Faust* was unable to attend the showing of *Beauty and the Devil*, another Faust film created some twenty-five years later by the present writer. This young man would probably have defended his position and, in the name of the conception of the cinema that was dear to him, would have had some misgivings. And no doubt he would have been right.

1970. The stand I took when criticizing *Don Juan and Faust* was not in accord with that adopted by the partisans of the "artistic" cinema, of whom the creator of *Eldorado* was the master.[1] For my part, I could not help thinking that experiments that were too exclusively of an esthetic character were contrary to the nature of the cinema and brought their creators to an impasse. In fact, the "artistic" cinema—Americans use the pejorative form "arty"—hardly outlived the 1925 avant-garde movement.

But in the history of art there is no abandoned formula that cannot return some day in another shape. Since about 1955 an independent cinema has developed, thanks to the curiosity of a new audience and to official or private encouragements that were rarely forthcoming in the past. This cinema is shown in so-called art and experimental houses both in France and in various foreign countries.

Marcel L'Herbier had arrived on the scene too early. For *L'Inhumaine* he had assembled the most brilliant and the most "modern" names of the rising generation: Fernand Léger, Robert Mallet-Stevens, Pierre Mac Orlan, Darius Milhaud . . . . But the film had no audience. It may be claimed that today an equivalent attempt would be successful, or would at least enjoy a critical success like that justly accorded forty years later to *Last Year at Marienbad,* a work whose esthetic and spirit are not so far removed as one might think from the one created in 1923 by Marcel L'Herbier.

. . . I said "rhythm," and in uttering that word I regretted all the misuse it has suffered, because it will eventually become meaningless, at least for films. Nevertheless, I want to keep using it in speaking of *The System of Doctor Ox.*

Here is a film which seems to have been made on a dare, in close imitation of American films: a series of mysterious crimes, two rival newspapers, an innocent heiress, a brave young reporter, mad chases, people moving from plane to plane, from plane to train, from train to plane, from plane to hydroplane, from hydroplane to steamship—those are some of the things it offers. Now, this long childish affair does not merely have the merit of being extremely entertaining from start to finish; it is endowed with an extraordinary vitality of motion which is created not only by the speed of the chases but also by the craft of its editing, its rhythm.

This rhythm is the prerequisite of cinematic lyricism. *Don Juan*

---

[1] Marcel L'Herbier made this "subjectivist" melodrama in 1922.—ED.

and Faust is a lyrical film only by analogy, via the artistic reminiscences it evokes. *The System of Doctor Ox* seems to me at times to attain that true film lyricism which arises from motion alone.

Here is where *Don Juan* and *Doctor Ox* are in perfect contrast: one of them sumptuous and made up of several older arts, the other a naïve fantasy wending its way through the forces of the modern world. Our education, our tastes, lead us to prefer *Don Juan,* which contains more art and intelligence. But *Doctor Ox* is probably closer to the cinema of tomorrow. The very childishness of this type of film is perhaps a proof of its strength: let us not forget that all of our knowledge concerning the cinema can be summed up more or less as follows: we are at the beginning of a great unknown thing. The formula of *Don Juan* is limited; it is made up of elements foreign to the cinema; it makes us think—and it seems that before thinking any more, we should learn how to simply see.

Rotary presses ready to spread the news in a hundred thousand copies, airplanes, telephones, steamships, speed: it is amusing to see American film-makers show all that with a sort of wonderment—which is shared by the audience. This is the state of mind I imagine primitive artists had when standing before their gods, the state of mind the people who admired them had. Our modern arts have sought at times to rediscover naïveté; but this does not consist of stylized sheep and false perspective; it is in the spirit—and no doubt in the spirit of certain films.

Let us not curse this naïve and mystical spirit which is that of the masses, and consequently that of the producers. All the arts have undergone its influence at their beginning. We are in "the medieval age of the cinema." Let us await the Renaissance, but let us not be too impatient; we still have plenty of mistakes to make.

1950. What unjustified optimism! When compared with the present age, that "medieval age of the cinema" appears as rich in various inventions as the Elizabethan age in the history of the theater. It is only necessary to rerelease a very old Chaplin or Sennett film to see young people of today marvel at what they behold as if it were an extraordinary novelty. And yet I hear the fools sneering: "Those old films! Look at those dresses, that make-up, that exaggerated acting!"

They might be referred to Baudelaire's poem "Une Charogne."[1] These old, decomposing films still retain for us that "divine essence" called *inventiveness,* in which our modern films are so notably lacking.

1970. That is especially true of film comedies. The golden age of American comedy ended with the coming of the talking picture.

1923. *La Roue* (Wheels) is the archetype of the film that is Romantic in spirit. As in a Romantic drama, you will find in Mr. Abel Gance's film improbable situations, superficial psychology, a constant attempt to achieve visual effects—and verbal effects as well—and you will find extraordinary lyrical passages and inspired movement: one could say the sublime and the grotesque.[2]

Given a drama so obviously "thought out," so carefully filled with literary ideas and purposes, it is tempting to dispute these thoughts and purposes with the author. No need to take the trouble. If a screenplay should be only a pretext, here it is a cumbersome pretext, sometimes annoying, rarely necessary, but in any case not deserving of lengthy consideration. It is hardly of interest that as screenplay writer Mr. Gance has made a mistake, like most film-makers, even if it is a mistake more serious at times than those we are accustomed to. If I were asked to judge Mr. Gance by the psychological intentions he expresses on the screen

---

[1] In "Carrion," Baudelaire compares his love's future to a rotting carcass they have watched in horrified fascination. In one sense, the poem reduces simply to the biblical "ashes to ashes . . . ." But it is also a parody of Petrarch's and Ronsard's love sonnets in which the poet admonishes his love to pursue a *carpe rosam* course regarding him, for "tomorrow she may die" or be old, wrinkled, faded, and forgotten. The poem's last quatrain reads:

> So, my beauty, tell the vermin
> That will devour you with kisses
> That I have retained the shape and the divine essence
> Of my decomposed loves.　　　　　—ED.

[2] Victor Hugo's theory of the sublime and the grotesque, enunciated in his dramatic manifesto, *The Preface to Cromwell* (1827), became one of the French romantic's main themes. Clair here uses the term ironically to describe Gance's ups and downs, rather than in an accurate historical way.—ED.

and by the titles he writes, I must admit that my judgment would not be in his favor. Right now we are concerned with cinema.

As I see it, the real subject of the film is not its odd plot, but a train, tracks, signals, puffs of steam, a mountain, snow, clouds. From these great visual themes that dominate his film Mr. Gance has drawn splendid developments. We had already seen trains moving along tracks at a velocity heightened by the obliging movie camera, but we had not yet felt ourselves absorbed—orchestra, seats, auditorium and everything around us—by the screen as by a whirlpool. "That is only a feeling," you will tell me. Maybe. But we had not come there to think. To see and feel is enough for us. Fifty years from now you can talk to me again about the cinema of ideas. This unforgettable passage is not the only one that testifies to Mr. Gance's talents. The catastrophe at the beginning of the film, the first accident Sisif tries to cause, the ascent of the cable car into the mountains, the death of Elie, the bringing down of his body, the round dance of the mountaineers, and that grandiose ending amidst veils of cloud: these are sublime lyrical compositions that owe nothing to the other arts. Seeing them, we forget the quotations from Kipling, Aeschylus and Abel Gance throughout the film, which tend to discourage us. And we start to hope.

Oh, if Mr. Abel Gance would only give up making locomotives say yes and no, lending a railroad engineer the thoughts of a hero of antiquity, and quoting his favorite authors! If he were willing to create a pure documentary, since he knows how to give life to a machine part, a hand, a branch, a wisp of smoke! If he were willing to contribute in that way to the creation of the *film* that can only be foreseen today!

Oh, if he were willing to give up literature and place his trust in the cinema!

1950. "As I see it, the real subject of the film is not its odd plot, but a train, tracks . . . ." This contempt for the subject is quite typical of an era when people liked to think that "the primary duty of the present-day film-maker is to introduce the greatest possible number of visual themes, by a sort of ruse, into a screenplay made to satisfy everybody." A conception that would be altogether wrong today, but was pardonable in 1923. (See the later chapter "Pure Cinema and Poetry.")

1970. I agree even today that Abel Gance's literary inspiration was arguable. But that should not cause us to forget that this great visionary was the creator of an original dramatic style, like Griffith before him and like Eisenstein, whose *Battleship Potemkin* came out soon after *La Roue*. Moussinac put it well: at that time Gance was "the only French film-maker who has achieved power and has swept away flowers and slag in a great lyrical gust."

Abel Gance's influence on film technique was great, and it is only right to recall that, among his inventions, the "triple screen," which gave his lyricism room to move about, appeared a quarter of a century before Cinerama.

"Fifty years from now, you can talk to me again about the cinema of ideas," I wrote in 1923. The fifty years are almost over, and in fact you might say that the cinema "of ideas" has arrived, but it does not seem that we always have good reason to congratulate ourselves on it. How many mediocre films give the illusion of importance because their authors include a glimpse of a "message"!

The cult of ideas lends a surprising appeal to the performing arts. Thus, at the Venice festival, a gathering intended to reward purely cinematic values, the announcement of each prize was followed a few years ago by a statement justifying the jury's choice: "A film that affirms the necessity of understanding between men" or "that proves that courage helps men support the greatest trials," and other basic truths toward which the philosophic critics were "holding out their red aprons."[1]

It is not enough officially for the prizewinning film to be the best made or the most interesting; it also had to display some virtue. It is said that these moral justifications were an inheritance of Fascism, and I would not be surprised if they were: all dictatorial or totalitarian regimes believe that artistic activity should serve some purpose or teach some lesson.

What a pity that a criterion like this was not current in the eras before our own! Corneille would have received an award not

---

[1]Clair refers to Victor Hugo's "Ballade XIII," which contains the refrain: "Children, the cattle are coming; hide your red aprons." The refrain might be paraphrased to say "Don't go into a bullpen wearing red." In his distortion of the phrase, Clair suggests that the intellectual critics deliberately jumped into the bullpen to wave red flags at the bull, but that the bull itself was nothing more dangerous than a set of weary truisms.—ED.

A scene from Gance's *La Roue* (1922), with Séverin-Mars as the engineer blinded by steam. (The Museum of Modern Art Film Stills Archive)

A scene from Buchovetzki's *Othello* (1922), with Emil Jannings in the title role and Werner Krauss as Iago.

for the quality of his tragedies, but for having shown, in *Le Cid,* that the worth of a nobleman lies in his fencing ability and, in *Horace,* that it is permissible to kill your sister if she is noticeably deficient in her sense of patriotism.

March 1923. Documentary films are perhaps preparing the advent of that pure film which will exist in its images alone and which will no longer be under the guardianship of any other art. Nothing seems further removed from this type of film, which may never be seen by our generation, than the genre of "adaptations."

Everyone knows that these are adaptations for the cinema of literary works; not so many people know the harm they have done to the art of the film. Fascinated by the name of some novelist or playwright, film-makers have persisted in filming literary works without caring about the cinema. The films were almost always bad, but the public, also attracted by the name, went in and paid— what more can be asked? There is no reason why this interesting industry should cease to exist. Unless the number of films shot outruns the number of books written. But then the same stories could be remade . . . .

Nevertheless, all the objections that can be raised against "adaptations" should not lead us to damn them indiscriminately. An adaptation is absurd and harmful if it merely illustrates with a few images a novel that is projected onto the screen in plentiful intertitles. But it can be interesting, it can be perfectly visual. *Othello* is an example of what an intelligent "adapter" can do. It is too bad, though, that intelligence can be purchased less easily than the rights to adapt a work.

Forget *Othello,* forget Shakespeare's text. Have no fear: care will be taken to recall its spirit to you. Go to see *Othello* as you would go to hear a symphony: it is a symphony of images inspired by the Shakespearean theme. Certain facial expressions of Othello and Iago are literal translations of the text. In other places, the presentation of the scenes, their succession—in short, the inner motion of the film—recall Shakespeare and seem in no way unworthy of him.

This film is not the banal parasite of a great work. It would be a serious misunderstanding of the cinema to be shocked by the liberties it takes with the plot of the drama. It may be imagined that the author, imbued with the spirit of the text, closed the book and thought solely of the images it summoned up. That is the only method of adaptation. Up to the present it seems to have been used rather sparingly.

The high quality of the acting contributes a great deal to the success of this film. Emil Jannings is an Othello who makes no concessions to the practices of the Opéra. Black-skinned, thick-lipped, clumsily sensual, he becomes a stupid child driven by Iago. His worried eyes, his staggering gait, his trembling hands, everything in him expresses jealousy. And in the scenes of loving and doubting, nothing is more moving than his savage gentleness.

D. Buchovetzki, the director of *Othello,* was not afraid to show us an almost clownish Iago who bounds through the palace, suddenly freezes and takes off again for new misdeeds. How were Iago's monologues and treacherous words to be translated to the screen? They are here translated into movements. It is as if Iago were devastating the palace through which he dashes so insanely. Just as in Shakespeare, who performs the same task with a few words.

Othello is an adaptation, but it is also a film composed with so much intelligence that it can win over the enemies of adaptation to a cause that is inherently rather bad.

1950. An odd result of the coming of the talking picture is that the filming of theatrical masterpieces has become more and more difficult. In the past film-makers could try to narrate a Shakespearean tragedy in images, and no one was shocked by the liberties unavoidably taken in this transposition from the original work. But who would dare to add a spoken scene, or even one line of dialogue, to *Romeo and Juliet?*

1970. Such daring is indeed inconceivable. (Whereas certain differences between early editions of Shakespeare lead us to think that there were various alterations of the original text after the author's death.) But if the filming of the masterpieces of the theater is a delicate undertaking, it is not impossible, and it is a pity that the French classic theater lends itself less well to this understanding than the Elizabethan theater.

When we see Laurence Olivier's *Henry V* and *Hamlet* or Orson Welles' Falstaff in *Chimes at Midnight,* we in France cannot repress a feeling of envy and regret. Our great tragic writers are scarcely suited to a cinematic production. Neoclassical rigidity and the unjustifiable law of the three unities have weighed heavily on our authors' inspiration. Men of letters like Chapelain, the Abbé d'Aubignac or Boileau, leaning pedantically on Aristotle's *Poetics,* imposed completely unjustifiable rules upon the theater.[1]

Corneille, who with more freedom might have rivaled Shakespeare, fought all his life against these rules and finally admitted that he could make nothing of them, writing:

> It is certain that there are precepts, since there is an art, but it is not certain what they are. There is agreement about the name but no agreement about the reality, and the general acceptance of the words is coupled with arguments about their meaning. No one doubts that the unities of action, place and time must be observed. But there is no small difficulty in knowing what these unities of time or place are.

An excellent example of the superstition attaching to dogmas even when they are devoid of all content! Our Romantics freed themselves from those very dogmas. But, desirous of imitating Shakespeare, they often only created a pastiche or a parody of him. (Except for Musset, who, writing for an imaginary stage, troubled himself little with rules and fashions.) And alas, we can only subscribe to the opinion of Thomas De Quincey, who said of the Elizabethan theater:

> No literature, not excepting even that of Athens, has ever presented such a multiform theatre, such a carnival display, mask and anti-mask, of impassioned life—breathing, moving, acting, suffering, laughing.* . . . the French [national drama] . . . lies under the signal disadvantage of not having reached its meridian until sixty years (or two generations) after the English. In reality, the great period of the English Drama was exactly clos-

---

[1] Influential seventeenth-century French neo-classical theoreticians who distorted Aristotle's description of classical dramatic procedures to produce a prescriptive, highly formalized and artificial set of regulations for French theater.—ED.

*From the Introductory Narration of Part I of *The Confessions of an English Opium-Eater.*

ing as the French opened: consequently the French lost the prodigious advantage for scenical effects of a romantic and picturesque age. This had vanished when the French theatre culminated; and the natural result was that the fastidiousness of French taste, by this time too powerfully developed, stifled or distorted the free movements of French genius.

The author of *Confessions of an English Opium-Eater,* a great humanist, mentions a play written by either Hardy or Rotrou (he does not remember which of the two) in which there is a truly Shakespearean scene.[1] This leads him to conclude:

> It is remarkable that in the period immediately anterior to that of Corneille, a stronger and more *living* nature was struggling for utterance in French tragedy.

The same remark can be made about poetry before the coming of Malherbe, a fine poet but a terrible schoolmaster. The famous "At last Malherbe came" can well be changed to *"Alas, Malherbe came."*[2] In regard to the French theater, despite the respect its masterpieces inspire, it is not sacrilegious to murmur: "Alas, classicism came."

March 1923. *Robin Hood* has merrily borne on his shoulders the crushing weight of fame that preceded him to our shores. A film like this disarms criticism. What is the use of picking at details, given such a whole? I do not know whether the Middle Ages as seen by the Americans are the real Middle Ages. But costumes or castles are not enough to give us an idea of that era: its spirit would have to be revived for us. Since this cannot be done, I like the interpretation of the Middle Ages given by Fairbanks' film as much as a history book. But minds accustomed to the rules of the theater cannot understand what gives *Robin Hood* its value to us, and they see in it only an enormous piece of childishness.

---

[1] Hardy and Rotrou were both extraordinarily prolific early seventeenth-century French dramatists. Clair adds the note: "It needs to be checked. But the fecundity of these two playwrights is discouraging to the researcher. Hardy alone is credited with the authorship of over five hundred plays."—ED.

[2] The line, an extremely well-known one in France, comes from Boileau's *Art poétique,* and expresses that poet-theoretician's admiration of Malherbe for having brought neo-classical order to French poetry for the first time.

> At last Malherbe came, and first in France
> Made his verses observe a just cadence;
> Taught the strength of a word properly placed,
> And trained the Muse to the rules of duty.   —ED.

Forget the story. Judge *Robin Hood* as you would judge a ballet or a fairy-pantomime. Look at it for just a moment with simple eyes. Pay attention only to the perfection of the motions, of the motion: the cinema was created to record it. *Robin Hood* is an army of banners on the march, steel-clad horses galloping, free men dancing in a forest, sprints through a castle built for giants, leaps that traverse space, streams, forests, countrysides . . . . Do you think that *La Légende des siècles* is closer to reality? It is neither more accurate nor more lyrical.[1]

The unbelievable situations, the prodigious feats to which Douglas Fairbanks accustomed us in his previous films, are here justified and in perfect agreement with the spirit of the film. Robin Hood is battling against a hundred adversaries, as in "Le petit Roi de Galice" (The little king of Galicia). We see:

> *Les cent coupe-jarrets à faces renégates*
> *Coiffés de monteras et chaussés d'alpargates,*
> *Demi-cercle féroce, agile, étincelant;*
> *Et tous font converger leurs piques sur Roland. . . .*
>
> (The hundred bold cutthroats with renegade faces,
> Monteras on their head and alpargata-shod,
> A fierce semicircle, agile and glittering;
> And all pointing their pikes at Roland in their midst.)

And isn't this an image from the film?—

> *Durandal brille et fait refluer devant elle*
> *Les assaillants, poussant des souffles d'aquilon;*
> *Toujours droit sur le roc qui ferme le vallon,*
> *Roland . . .*
>
> (Durandal, flashing forth, now causes to fall back
> The dense attacking throng, emitting north-wind blasts;
> Still steady on the rock that shuts the valley fast,
> Roland . . .)

Are Robin Hood's gallops swifter than those of "L'Aigle du casque" (The eagle of the helmet)?

> *Rien n'arrête leur course; ils vont; ils vont! ils vont;*
> *Ainsi le tourbillon suit la feuille arrachée . . .*

---

[1] Victor Hugo's massive epic poem, *The Legend of the Centuries,* is a highly lyrical, symbolic, fantastically imaginative history of humanity that works basically through mythic, rather than scientific, constructs and concepts. "The Little King of Galicia" and "The Eagle of the Helmet" are sections of *The Legend.*—ED.

(Nothing arrests their dash; they go; they go! they go;
The whirlwind thus pursues the leaf torn from its branch . . .)

Hugo seems to be handling a camera when he describes:

Les bonds prodigieux de cette chasse affreuse,
Le coteau qui surgit, le vallon qui se creuse,
Les précipices, l'antre obscur, l'escarpement . . .

(Those most prodigious leaps during that fearsome chase,
The hill that rises up, the valley hollowed out,
The precipices, pitch-dark cave, and the escarpment . . .)

The chief merit of Hugo's epic piece is certainly its rhythm. The same is true of Douglas Fairbanks' creation. The rhythm of *Robin Hood* makes us forget the imperfections of this type of film. Likewise, it is lucky for Hugo that the reader is carried away by Tiphaine's ride and does not have the time to stop in mid-chase for verses like:

Nul ne le sait; le sort est de mystère plein;

(Nobody knows; for fate of mystery is full;)

which correspond cinematically to very bad camera work.

I am not unaware of the conventionality of a comparison like this. It has only been attempted in order to make certain "intellectuals" understand that a film like *Robin Hood* can be as worthwhile as a poem, and that it is as pointless to argue about the plausibility of the one as of the other. Lyrical motion saves everything.

1950. While we are on the subject, let us pay our respects to the memory of Douglas Fairbanks, who was not only an actor but also an outstanding producer, and who, in his poetic and optimistic films, created an unforgettable "type." The glory and good fortune of Hollywood are due to Chaplin, Griffith, Sennett, Ince, Fairbanks and a few others who were creative men and not the employees of a vast organization controlled by accountants.

1970. In 1950, almost all American production was still controlled by that vast organization in which five big companies, actuated by a spirit of "friendly competition," as they said somewhat ironically, formed a sort of Holy Alliance. This state of affairs has since changed considerably, and the so-called crisis has favored the rise of more or less independent producers and film-makers. (See the later chapter "On Hollywood.")

April 1923. Everyone knows Sessue Hayakawa's talent, that powerful sobriety he revealed to us in *The Cheat*. Here Bessie Love seems to be inspired by him and worthy of that inspiration. Her frightened eyes, her curt gestures, her sad pout, remind us of the best moments of Lillian Gish. The scene with the glass of milk—an insipid idea, in fact an unacceptable weepy bit—becomes, thanks to her, a marvel of simple emotion and truth.[1]

That is where the cinema seems to me to have some advantage over the theater. Certain great stage stars, like Sarah Bernhardt or Lucien Guitry, spent most of their life acting in wretched plays. They performed them sublimely, it is said, and redeemed the imperfection of the scripts. Agreed; but if I venture into a theater, the excellence of the actor does not prevent me on occasion from hearing the badly written dialogue. Nothing like that in the cinema: an admirable show of grief does not serve to adorn a ridiculous line. The expression of a silent face, taken in isolation, can be as beautiful appearing in a bad film as in a masterpiece. Working with mediocre and false material, actors like Sessue Hayakawa and Bessie Love are able to evoke beauty and truth.

The defenders of the theater would have easy sailing if they retorted by laughing at the intertitles of films. In fact it should be recognized that intertitles are often the major blemish of a film and emphasize its weak points. But perhaps we will manage to make the writers of titles understand that the least bad intertitle—there is no best one—is the most neutral and brief, the least "literary," intertitle. Let them read, first Stendhal, then the Napoleonic Code. Let them meditate the sentence: "Everyone sentenced to death will have his head cut off."[2] When every

---

[1]The film with Hayakawa and Love being discussed was released in France as *Le Devin du faubourg* (The neighborhood fortune-teller). It is probably *The Vermilion Pencil* (1922, directed by Norman Dawn), although the same actors were also teamed in *The Swamp* (1921, directed by Colin Campbell). —ED.

[2]The Napoleonic Code, basis of the French legal system, is a marvel of succinct, concise, and simple language. Stendhal claimed that he read it daily and used it as a model for his own style. The phrase Clair quotes, *"tout condamné à mort aura la tête tranchée,"* cannot be translated into English in a manner that reproduces the powerful impact it has in French.—ED.

intertitle combines that much strength with that much brevity, we will spend more pleasant hours in front of the screen.

The intertitle already declares its uselessness in film comedies, where its appearance quashes the laughter aroused by the remarkable inventiveness of the American directors. What "witty" words can compete with Larry Semon's sprint over the top of his train in *Zigoto dans les coulisses,*[1] which we have just seen? We feel in this film a motion comparable to that which animates the most violent lyrical effusions; dazzling flashes of comedy come fast and furious. The film, guided by the spirit of a flickering star, moves at prodigious speed toward the goals that chance destines for it. I know of few conclusions as perfect as the general explosion with which Larry Semon has ended several of his pictures. The problem raised by so much speed and so many surprises, incoherent situations and perils, can only be resolved by some catastrophe.

We can never thank the Americans enough for creating the film comedy. Their dramatic films have far less value. We can still only foresee the day when film tragedy will be as purely visual as a gesture by Chaplin or a sprint by Semon.

1950. Let us not allow such an unfounded assertion to get by. The Americans did not *create* film comedy, which existed at the time of Max Linder and, before him, at the time of the men we call "the French primitives."[2] But the American school, of which the founder was Mack Sennett and the most illustrious representative, Charlie Chaplin, renewed the film comedy so thoroughly that nothing better has ever been done in this area since their golden age.

1923. The film comedy is the type of film in which the cinema has best succeeded in being itself. The dramatic film has sometimes been completely visual. But the sentimental film is almost always tainted with literature; it has recourse to vulgarly emotional intertitles, and transports to the screen the sorriest tricks

---

[1] It is difficult to say exactly which Semon film this was, though the likeliest candidate is *The Show* (1922). Semon's films in 1923, the year of this article, include *No Wedding Bells, The Barnyard, The Midnight Cabaret, The Gown Shop, Lightning Love,* and *Horseshoes.*—ED.

[2] Notably, the Lumière brothers, Méliès, Zecca, and Feuillade.—ED.

of the theater. That does not prevent it from bringing sweet tears to your eyes, you will tell me. All right. It moves us. But it is uninteresting to dwell on nothing but the functions of our lachrymal glands. Intensely funny or dramatic films also move us to tears, but in another fashion, worthy of their severe beauty.

Most films are conceived according to this successful sentimental formula. Should they all be rejected? No. That would also mean rejecting the future of the cinema, which is developing in them and in spite of their spirit.

1950. Although it is difficult to compare the respective merits of dramatic and comic works (see the later chapter "On Comedy"), it can be said that before 1928 the film comedy had chalked up successes that the dramatic film seldom equaled.

Since the film started talking, we have seen just the opposite: with few exceptions, all the films produced after 1928 which merit preservation are dramatic films, while the sap of the film comedy appears to have dried up.

After seeing some old American film comedies, Mr. Louis Chauvet remarked:

> Obviously Charlie Chaplin is an outstanding mime, but we may still wonder, as we observe the infallibility of certain effects, whether the film comedy did not give up half of its power on the day it stopped being silent. Words are too often stupid or vulgar; it is hard for them to be as funny as a gesture. . . . Thus old films become a sort of retrospective of *forgotten secrets*.

1970. It is a pity that amid the throng of new film creators who have arisen in numerous countries in the last ten years or so, very few, alas, have dared to take a chance making comedies.

How many of them have created a stir with gloomy films or films following the routine of the "gangster" genre (crooks, cruelty, holdups, suspense, etc.)! An author's inadequacy or clumsiness is easily masked by the conventions of these various types of film. But in comedy, every weakness is visible, every mistake glaring. People laugh or do not laugh. And no critical subtlety can fool the public on that point.

Therefore, it may seriously be claimed that the "serious" genre is less serious than the comic.

May 1923. And the fifty thousand movie houses of the globe

are filled with a constantly changing crowd to whom the screen speaks of love. Curiosity is aroused at the thought of the very young generations that are being raised on the cinema. The film awakens the desire to travel in the most peaceful heart— that stalk of grass in the corner of the screen which was growing in Oceania on the day that a transient lens seized its trembling form; that vessel in front of a large, white, sleeping city; that ravine in Chile; that wisp of smoke in the Caucasus—the film offers us the most beautiful human forms, exuding charm for our sake, smiling for us, and the well-behaved young man has the time to be in love with twenty ephemeral goddesses before reaching the age at which it has been decided he will get engaged to his parents' friends' daughter. How many jealousies, desires and mental upheavals! (It is not quite clear just what the ferocious little eye of the lens sees. The cinema is a dangerous invention: its madcap celluloid ribbons are long enough to put several girdles round about the earth. Just think that it would only take a match at any point whatsoever . . . . It is all the same to me, but if I were one of the calm, level-headed people, I would watch out. Soon it will be too late: the lens will have absorbed all of us.)

Vanina, which had its first run at the Ciné-Opéra three months ago, is now back on several screens. Thus we were able to see a beautiful film over again and to find out how many imbeciles it takes to make up an audience. A double advantage.

People sometimes bemoan the fact that the cinema is forced to be an art of the people. I am ready to believe that this purely commercial necessity is the cinema's best hope for progress. For no provincial or neighborhood audience displays as much systematic hostility and self-confident stupidity when shown a new picture as the audience of an "elegant" house. . . .

1950. That "elegant" house was the Colisée, at that time the only movie theater on the Avenue des Champs-Elysées (which then had only two cafés: Fouquet's, which still exists, and Rigollet's, which has vanished). Aside from a few large hotels, the Avenue des Champs-Elysées in 1923 looked more like it did at the end of the Second Empire than the way it does today.

In the lounge of the Colisée was a bar where almost every

night you were sure to find Louis Delluc, who lived a few steps away. He remained all evening in the darkness of the bar, his large head, like that of a melancholy bird, bowed over a glass of English beer, and interrupted his reverie only to go from time to time and cast a glance at the screen, which could be seen from the entrance to the lounge. We conversed with him in low tones so as not to disturb the orchestra. His brief remarks, punctuated by long silences, would contain nuances of resigned humor and a bittersweet nonchalance, like that of a very intelligent old man who is too familiar with the ways of the world to still enjoy talking about them. He died in the spring of 1924 at the age of thirty-four, leaving us an important critical *œuvre* and the sketch of a cinematic *œuvre* which he had had neither the time nor the means to complete.

The program at the Colisée changed every week, on Friday. The new film shown that evening was invariably greeted with laughter, jokes shouted out loud, or whistles. It was fashionable for the moviegoers from the "high-class neighborhoods" to come to the Colisée on Friday evenings to make fun of the films.

1923. . . . Those who find this somber and feverish work ridiculous must be the same people who go into ecstasies at the "truly Parisian" wit of the revues and new old plays at the Boulevard theaters.[1] How I prefer the healthy atmosphere of the working-class audiences, who would not understand the "fine points" of that nineteenth-century wit, and who simply admire the vigor of the hero, the smile of the girl, the chases, the scaling of walls and the lips meeting in close-up!

Vanina, it seems, is based on a Stendhal story. An unimportant detail. It does not contain too much literature, but condenses into one night a romantic adventure which unfurls before our eyes. Certain scenes could easily have become ridiculous—imagine *Vanina* handled by Italian directors—but this danger was averted with rare felicity. See the young hero dashing into the palace by torchlight, conspirators all around him; he opens a door, sees the woman he loves and drops his sword at her feet. Even the imbeciles I have just mentioned were

---

[1] That is, the theaters that cater to popular or middle-class tastes.—ED.

unable to laugh at that gesture, emphatic as it was. The reason is that this scene, like the entire film, is endowed with perfect motion—that rhythm of images whose laws are undefinable and which manifests itself so clearly that a practiced eye can recognize the worth of a film director after only a minute of viewing. I think that musicians and poets—at least those who would be intelligent enough to forget the laws peculiar to music and poetry—would make better film editors than the professional movie-makers: they would stand a better chance of acquiring that sense of rhythm which shows up so seldom in French films and so often in American films, even the poorest.

Vanina is a *film*. Its creator understood cinema. That is a rare merit.

When will all directors decide to spend ten minutes thinking about the nature of the cinema, about its meaning, about what is logically its future, instead of unthinkingly filming stage farces and melodramas with their feeble lens?

1950. *"Vanina, it seems,* is based on a Stendhal story. An unimportant detail." Once again, beloved things are sacrificed in order to shock the timid souls who do not yet understand that the cinema claims all rights.

"Imagine *Vanina* handled by Italian directors." At the time the style of Italian silent films was famous for its theatrical exaggeration. No one would have believed that some day the best realist films of the postwar period would be produced in Italy.

1923. Certain spectators have said: "It's very good. But the screenplay is nonexistent." And certain specialists: "It's very good. But there's nothing very new in it."

They are no doubt right, and it is difficult to justify the emotion we experience when viewing this film. All I can say more precisely is that *The Girl I Loved* gives me the feeling of something perfect in itself, and takes its place among the most memorable moments of this young art: *The Adventurer, Broken Blossoms, The Outlaw and His Wife* and a few others, among which should be mentioned Griffith's *True Heart Susie,* which *The Girl I Loved* resembles in many more ways than in the sim-

"Free men dancing in a forest" (p. 61): a scene from *Robin Hood* (1922), with Douglas Fairbanks in the title role (second from left) and Alan Hale as Little John (far right). (The Museum of Modern Art Film Stills Archive)

Charles Ray in *The Girl I Loved* (1923).
(The Museum of Modern Art Film Stills Archive)

ilarity of their titles.[1]   (But this film by Ray shows a sense of moderation of which America is sparing. Perhaps that is what most strikes our French minds, and perhaps also what has prevented this film from being very successful in its country of origin.)

These moments of cinema—let us call them that because their value is only momentary and because the cinema is still nothing more than a development—represent perfection in a genre that they themselves define, for our arsenal of words can scarcely form definitions except by allusions to other artistic genres, confusion with which would be dangerous. (A person may hate the "sentimental" novel, but still like a film which reflects its spirit. Criticism itself should be expressible in images. The more visual a film is, the harder it becomes to discuss it.)

The Girl I Loved is taken from a poem by the American poet James Whitcomb Riley. It was adapted for the screen by Albert Ray and directed by J. de Grasse. Nevertheless, it is Charles Ray who seems to be its principal creator, since he has already given an inkling of this film several times in various other films of his before giving it its full treatment here.

The screenplay is taken from a poem. Is that why the film contains so much poetry? No, poetry on the screen arises from the image in itself and not from the literary spirit that inspired it. A poetic spirit prevails throughout this work because it is endowed with perfect motion.

Motion. I do not mean motion recorded by the image itself, but motion of the images in relation to one another. *Motion,* the primary basis of cinematic lyricism, whose rules, though still mysterious, are becoming more precise every day.

Except for that admirable scene of the horse bolting, which proves that Mr. Gance's rhythmic inventions in *La Roue* were conceived of at the same time in America, everything one sees in *The Girl I Loved* moves very slowly in front of the lens. And yet the film is endowed with intense motion, the expression of the incessant motion of that inner life which finds one of its first and most poetic expressions in *The Girl I Loved.*

---

[1]The similarity exists in the French titles. Ray's *The Girl I Loved* was released in France as *Premier Amour* (First love) , while Griffith's *True Heart Susie* was retitled *Le Pauvre Amour* (Poor love).—ED.

Poetry! Just when, in literature, it seemed to be dying at the hands of the heirs of Rimbaud and Mallarmé, poetry is reborn, with its still hesitant rhythms and its pristine purity, on the great white canvas toward which the men of the whole world turn.

1950. Charles Ray brought to the American film a quality that was often lacking in Hollywood's best productions: charm. He introduced to the screen the character of a bashful young man in love, as funny as he was touching, which has never been revived since the death of its creator.

It is likely that Charles Ray was not merely a talented actor, but that, like Douglas Fairbanks, he was the guiding spirit of the films he appeared in. The unity of inspiration of these films cannot be explained otherwise. This assumption seems confirmed by the decision he made, when he was at the peak of his popularity, to become the producer of his own films. It was in this capacity that he made *The Girl I Loved,* an unforgettable film that was a failure in the United States. Another film which he produced in the same circumstances ruined him. Within a few months, Charles Ray, one of the most famous screen actors in the world, became an unknown pauper.

It has been said that Hollywood, which was already beginning to monopolize its power, never forgave Charles Ray for his desire to be independent and did everything possible to end his career. Unfounded as this accusation seems, it is nonetheless true that Charles Ray was never again seen on the screen except in walk-on parts, and that a conspiracy would not have been more effective than the consignment to silence which seems to have been used against him.

1924. It is not too late to talk about *Cœur fidèle* (Faithful heart) , which was shown in a few theaters last month. This film does not date from just yesterday, but because of the ineptitude of our methods of distribution, it has not yet been seen by a wide audience. But it dates from tomorrow. We shall see it again.

Before formulating our criticism, let us say that you must see *Cœur fidèle* if you wish to be acquainted with the resources of the cinema today. Its plot is banal, a sort of *Broken Blossoms* seen through French eyes. But you know what importance should be attached to the subject of a film: the same, more or less, that is attached to the subject of a symphony. All we ask of a plot is to supply us with subjects for visual emotion, and to hold our attention.

The factor which distinguishes *Cœur fidèle* from so many other films is its having been composed for the screen, for the joy of "intelligent" eyes, so to speak. From the appearance of the very first images, the film sense is in evidence—no doubt more rational than instinctive, but undeniably there. The lens turns in every direction, moves around objects and people, seeks the expressive image, the surprising camera angle. This exploration of the perspectives of the world is thrilling: it is inconceivable that so many directors have persisted in multiplying matte shots and the tricks of still photography when they could have awakened so much curiosity with a slight tilt of their camera.

The study of the proper camera angle, the only angle right for a given image or scene, is far from having been exhausted. The Americans, who took the first steps in that direction, seem to have stopped short in fear of what still remained to be discovered. *Cœur fidèle,* among other films—and among other French films, I must add—points us once again in the direction of that study, progress in which is inseparable from progress in cinematic expression.

Mr. Jean Epstein, the director of *Cœur fidèle,* is obviously concerned with the question of rhythm. People talk a lot about cinematic rhythm, and the question seems to be the most important one the cinema has to answer at present. It must be said that up to now no complete answer has been proposed. It appears that rhythm sometimes crops up spontaneously in a film —especially in American films—but too often it remains sketchy and disappoints us. When it is intentional—and it is in *Cœur fidèle*—it is created by means of the reappearance of earlier images; at first this is very effective, but it soon becomes a burden to the overall movement and quite justly annoys the majority of the audience, who cannot make out what the author is driving at, and get impatient. Periodic repetition of earlier images—like assonance or rhyme in prosody—seems to be the only effective rhythmic element the film now has at its disposal. But rhyme and assonance do not bring back the same word in the sentence, whereas the repetition of images summons up more or less the same vision. Something else, which can only be guessed at now, must be found. The absolute mathematical solution has the drawback of not taking into account the sentimental value of the recalled image. No doubt it is necessary to combine harmoniously the sentimental rhythm of the action and the mathematical rhythm of the number of images . . . . But forgive me for letting myself be carried away by this question, which will perhaps seem to be of interest to only a very few readers. I advise these readers once again to go and see *Cœur fidèle* and its carnival, a beautiful scene of visual intoxication, an emotional dance in the dimension of space, in which the visage of Dionysiac poetry is reborn.

Cœur fidèle can be criticized for lacking unity of action. The film too often goes astray into technical experiments which the action does not demand. That is the difference between the advanced technique of our school and American technique, which is completely at the service of the progress of the story. That is also the explanation of the difference in the audience's attitude toward American films, in which the expressions are immediately accessible, and ours, which require an effort of the intelligence alone. That is the cause of many a mass dissatisfaction . . . . But let us not dwell on this. A quality director will be able to find the means to reconcile both schools for the greater good of the cinema. If a film is worthy of the cinema, that is already a most agreeable miracle! *Cœur fidèle* is worthy of it in more than one respect. Those who compare the young and still barbarous cinema with all of literature and all the arts, will not understand this. But let them subject our contemporary old drama to this comparison! The cinema will seem to them in contrast to be an inexhaustible source of poetry.

Apropros of *Cœur fidèle,* certain details in it have led some people to speak of an unpleasant return to realism. I think that the cinema need fear nothing of the sort. The suppleness of cinematic expression, which passes in a flash from objective to subjective, simultaneously evoking the abstract and the concrete, will not permit film to confine itself to an esthetic as narrow as that of realism. No matter if the view of a gloomy cabaret or a poverty-stricken room is photographically exact. The screen gives a soul to the cabaret, the room, a bottle, a wall. It is this soul alone that counts in our eyes. We move from the object to its soul as easily as our being passes from a sight to a thought. The screen opens onto a new world, one vibrant with even more synesthetic responses than our own. There is no detail of reality which is not immediately extended here into the domain of the wondrous.

1950. I do not agree with this: "All we ask of a plot is to supply us with subjects for visual emotion, and to hold our attention." It seems to me that holding the viewer's attention should come first, and "visual emotion" second.

But I give myself a good mark for the distinction I made between French technique and American, "which is completely at the service of the progress of the story." This difference, though palpably lessened, still exists today, and the viewer could still blame some of the best French films for dwelling here and there on self-indulgent points of style without too much concern for the action. This remark, which sounds trite today, was not lacking in novelty in 1924, when the entire so-called avant-garde was devoted to almost purely esthetic experiments.

1929. A young telephone operator lives alone amid the crowd of a big city. On a day off she meets a young factory worker who is suffering from loneliness like herself. They speak to each other, they get along with each other, they are happy. But an incident separates them before they have even had a chance to tell each other their names.

How will they manage to see each other again? They look for each other in the crowd, but in vain. Their whole future collapses, as does that precious past, just a few moments old . . . . No, they meet again, and that very night. They live in the same building. They were neighbors and did not know each other.

That is a screenplay résumé which I do not advise beginners or even well-known film writers to submit to one of those firms that manufacture the French film. The reception would be a cold one. I can hear the unanswerable objections this subject would not fail to raise. Certainly, this story offers no opportunity for slipping in those scenes of "high life," those nightclubs, those chorus girls, those "society" receptions, those masquerade parties, those jazz musicians, those mansions and those "modern" furnishings without which a film has no chance of pleasing the public, if the authorities are to be believed. It's not about the romance of the world's greatest actress or of the richest prince or financier; it is just the modest story, devoid of startling theatrics, of a factory worker and a telephone operator. We are certainly not about to see this film produced in France. Nevertheless, this film exists. It is called *Lonesome*. It was made in the United States.

It must be admitted. The Americans can still surprise us, and not only with material that produces cheap surprises: a mass of riches, incredible technological means, the huge crowds at their disposal, their resourceful publicity. No, we know this side of their genius all too well, and surely only provincials who are habitually far removed from any screen, and people who never go to the movies, would still be awestruck by *Ben-Hur* and so many other sagging heaps of plaster.

The Americans can still surprise us, and by a quality usually denied them: intelligence. I am not unaware that a statement like this may upset preconceived ideas and easy formulas (a nation without culture, grown-up children, "king dollar," etc.). But we are talking about cinema, and the intelligence in regard to things filmic which is often apparent in American films is not the smallest surprise that was in store for us.

If we consider two recent films, *A Girl in Every Port* and *Lonesome,* we cannot continue to claim that the sole reason for the superiority of the American film is the might of its financial resources. There is something else behind these films besides dollars. There is the intelligence of the authors and the producers. These films prove to us that certain heads of American firms can be interested in original works, can encourage the efforts of inquiring minds and look for success not merely in the mass-production line. This tendency is a symptom of vitality that we would like to find in European production.

Here, the crisis of the cinema is continuing, and it is in the choice of "subjects" that the fatally wrong path the French film has taken appears most clearly. There is no production firm, no author, that is not looking desperately for film subjects. But this search will be disappointing as long as they keep straying in the same wrong direction. All of theater and the novel have been squeezed completely dry by the cinema, and there is no use still trying to get something out of their empty peel. Nor is there any use asking for screenplays written for the screen. Who today could manage to develop an original idea within the ridiculous framework of conventions which has been forced upon the art of images? Even before its production has begun, a film work is paralyzed by "commercial" rules, altered at the wishes of various foreign purchasers, castrated by the tyranny of censorship. It can see the light of day only on the condition that it shock no one. Thus, it loses its good qualities little by little and finally is in danger of pleasing no one.

A few recent American films (*White Shadows in the South Seas, Underworld, A Girl in Every Port* and *Lonesome,* among others) show us that American producers are not hampered by our fears, and that intelligence and boldness are not so rare in that land as people here like to say.

1950. This article, published in 1929 in *Pour Vous,* as was the next article, allows us to measure the distance that has been covered since that date both by the American film and the European film. Today it is the English, French or Italian film that New York critics hold up as a model to Hollywood producers, in terms more or less similar to those used above. For example, it was Europe that produced *Brief Encounter* and *Paisà,* and it is in the United States that it is almost impossible to develop an original idea within the framework of imposed conventions.

1970. Let us rectify this rectification. Since 1950 the "imposed conventions" have weighed less and less heavily on American films. Hollywood could allow itself the luxury of a production hemmed in by various tabus as long as business was prosperous. When takings are cut in half, the devil take morality! Any subject that promises a profit is good. Furthermore, the hegemony of the big companies having come to an end, American production has become more varied and, on occasion, more original.

1929. We are no longer unaware that the cinema owes part of the fascination it exerts to the taste of most mortals for affairs of love. The final kiss, in which so many screen dramas find their solution, is no empty rite. It gives a sort of physical recompense to those viewers who have no other resource than to delegate to the young hero the right, earned by an hour of passionate expectancy, of clasping the heroine in his arms. And yet this recompense, as unreal as those ghosts just now erased from the screen, is not sufficient to calm the desire that the thousand faces of the young woman have aroused. It is midnight. It is the hour of the cloakroom and the crumpled hatcheck. The audience must go home with that desire born of the vision of a shadow, a desire no reality can satisfy.

Dear shadows! They have awakened in us a form of love which could scarcely be imagined before the invention of the moving film. Was there, then, something new to be discovered in this area? The screen has opened its white door onto a harem of visions beside which every three-dimensional body seems imperfect. We rediscover in these images the atmosphere of amorous daydream typical of adolescence. It is not so much a question of love as of desire. If it is admitted that the law of constraint can help an art find its perfect form, we must thank the modest censors who allow us to see on the screen all the images of love except those in which love finds its satisfaction. Thanks to the zeal of these virtuous men, the cinema shields its faithful from wretched satiety, and devotes the innocence of its ghosts solely to the awakening of desire.

It is not surprising that a film conceived under the sign of desire should touch the heart of a clientele so perfectly accustomed to the various forms of this emotion. *Homecoming* is a film in which amorous desire takes the place of unity of action from start to finish. From those first images in which two prisoners are speaking of a far-off woman, to that final image in which the man left behind understands that he will at last possess the wife of the man who is departing, desire is present to such an extent that the most alert spectators are somewhat embarrassed and feel like snickering. This film, in which nothing happens that is not chaste, is disturbingly outspoken. Watching certain scenes, you get the impression that you are "not wanted," and you feel like withdrawing discreetly in order to let the characters in the story argue out such affecting questions all by themselves. The image in which the husband tries to reclaim his weeping wife and feels her lips pulling away from his, lips moist with tears but unwilling to grant even a kiss of pity—only someone who has never known love can fail to be overcome by what that image contains: that open bed, the drama of thwarted desire, and those beautiful female arms. The cinema has already shown us so many unhappy couples that it is becoming difficult to give us a new kind of emotion. Now, never has a moving image contained so much heartrendering sensuality, so much tragic immodesty.

1970. . . . "We must thank the modest censors who allow us to see on the screen all the images of love except those in which love finds its satisfaction." It was impossible to foresee that that epigram written long ago would later prove worthy of consideration and would inspire a feeling close to nostalgia. (See the later chapter "On the Morals of Our Day.")

1950. "Politicians," one of them once remarked, "make only one speech throughout their career, merely changing the form of it more or less, to suit the circumstances." I might apply that epigram to myself. In rereading the preceding pages, it seems to me that I often rewrote the same article with different titles. The persistence with which the same ideas are expressed apropos of different films proves that I did not have the makings of a critic, and that, led by chance to perform the duties of one, I was less interested in offering opinions on the pictures I was discussing than in elaborating a theory of the cinema for my own use or, more simply, in clarifying my own ideas. Hence those repetitions and contradictions which the reader will not fail to have noticed.

It is not easy to be a film critic, at least if you are not content merely to tell the story and stealthily hand out a little praise or a little blame. The critics who have a personal conception of the cinema—that is, those who count—are forced to make an extremely meritorious effort if they wish neither to repeat themselves nor to join the company of those who have nothing to say and whose talent consists in performing variations on this absence of thought.

Speaking of this type of critic, I cannot resist quoting here a passage from a letter recently sent to me by a writer who, though a follower of the paths of pataphysics, has good reason to know what is going on in the screen world:[1]

How pleasant, fruitful and reassuring is the task of the film critic! What solid defenses he has to fall back on! Consider, if you please, the vast field of disparagement open to the plow, I mean to the heavy oxen of his common sense. Is the subject good? Then the direction is miserable . . . (subdivision: the subject is good, but badly developed—the dialogue is bad—the shooting script lets the subject down, etc.). Is the direction excellent? Then it is a pity to see so much talent wasted on such skimpy or such abominable subjects . . . (subdivisions: the esthetic reasons which make the subject displeasing to the critic, then the ethical reasons, then the political reasons, etc.). Does the subject have pretensions? Then the film is pretentious. Does the subject have no pretensions? Then it is not the sort of film that will add to the glory of our poor old French cinema, etc. And all this time I have remained on the intellectual plane, but how many resources are offered by technique! The subject may be good and well handled, but unfortunately the photography is dull—or too brilliant—or the sound inadequate (or dry, or flabby, or brittle, or blurred, or muffled, or shrill, etc.). Not to speak of the music, which . . . , or of the editing, which, too tight, or on the contrary, too loose . . . . The great catastrophe occurs when everything works out right, because then the film is too good, too perfect. Where is that little grain of error, that unsophisticated touch, that hint of improvisation—in a word, that foul-up—which characterizes works of genius? Although, of course, it is well known, and more's the pity, that certain films which are full of pleasant clumsy promise would be improved if they were worked over a little more, that they were not given enough technical attention, etc., etc. Naturally, all of this is subject to revision in the light of the acting performances: whether the director has lazily depended on the adulterated talent of commercial stars, or has imprudently attempted an unfortunate experiment with youngsters not up to the mark. According to the particular case, one point or another will not be mentioned at all. A given film will be, for the critic, nothing but a screenplay he dislikes, whereas another film will be merely an opportunity to spout a little trade jargon while discussing what he considers faulty technique.

---

[1]Pataphysics is the supposed "science of imaginary solutions" fancifully spawned by Alfred Jarry, creator of the pre-surrealist *Ubu Roi*. The College of Pataphysics exists even today, mostly in the minds of its members, among whom Clair proudly claims his place.—ED.

If I am to be sincere, I must make a few corrections in this most amusing "critique of critiques." A film critic would have to see more than one film per day if he wanted to keep up with everything appearing on the screen: an obligation like that would engender disgust in any normally constituted man. Even if the critic reviews only about a hundred films a year, even if he writes only one article a week, it would be surprising if after a few seasons the sharpness of his judgment were not blunted. I confess, I would have been incapable of harnessing myself to that job continually, and I do not fail to have respect for those who overcome its difficulties, when they fulfill it creditably.

There is nothing more varied than opinions about a film. Paul Eluard writes:

> In the days when we went to the movies very often with a few friends, a curious phenomenon occurred. We were usually pretty much in agreement on everything. But never about the cinema. We never had such endless and inconclusive discussions as those about the films we had just seen.

This "curious phenomenon" occurred not only among the Surrealist crew; it occurred and still occurs among all film viewers no matter what affinities of education or taste link them together. The nature of the cinema is such that the modes of judgment we usually employ with respect to the arts and literature are not suited to the works it produces.

That is why the task of the film critic is not an easy one, and that is also why this task is far from unnecessary. Between creators (you may take this word in its simplest meaning, if you wish) who cannot survive without the immediate approval of a vast audience, and a vast audience that wants only to be entertained and pays no attention to the quality of the films presented to it, criticism can play a very important role. Imperfect as it is, if it succeeds from time to time in pointing out the merits of a film that is in danger of going unnoticed, its existence is justified.

1970. "Criticism can play a very important role." We may very well wonder whether on occasion the critics are not in danger of lessening the importance of this role by their own doings. One of them, Michel Aubriant, recently wrote:

There is a gap at present between critics and moviegoers. I am not happy to make this observation. These two groups no longer speak the same language. And yet everyone agrees: the cinema is an art of the people. But we see the critics striving to turn their readers away from films intended for a wide audience.

It is true that a number of critics write only for themselves or their colleagues, according to the fashion of the season. The coterie spirit, which would be excusable in little magazines, is in evidence all over, even in major publications. When critics no longer care about serving the public, establishing a bond between film-maker and moviegoer, honestly helping the latter to choose among the films being offered to him and helping the former to be heard, they surrender the influence they ought to exert and their reviews become pointless exercises.

The great fear of many critics is that the reader might think they did not understand or like something other people claim to like or understand. Now, as René Barjavel has said so well: "As soon as you are afraid of being taken for an imbecile, you become one." By making a selection of the jargon of a certain class of film critics and the gobbledygook of a certain class of art critics, it would be possible to compile, for the delectation of our grandnephews, the most astonishing nonsense anthology of our day.

A scene from Epstein's *Cœur fidèle* (1923; p. 70). The prostitute (Madeline Erickson) gives the hoodlum (Edmond van Daele) the news that precipitates the climax. (The Museum of Modern Art Film Stills Archive)

From *A Day's Pleasure* (1919): "he extracts from the folding chair he is trying to set up . . . all the humor that can possibly be extracted . . . (p. 88)." (The Museum of Modern Art Film Stills Archive)

Three Masters

1923. Mack Sennett is one of the great personalities of the cinema. It was he who in 1915, along with D. W. Griffith and Thomas Ince, founded the Triangle Company, where present-day film was born. It was he who created the genre of slapstick comedy, those poems of the imagination in which clowns, bathing beauties, an automobile, a little dog, a jug of milk, the sky, the sea and some explosive are the interchangeable elements every combination of which arouses laughter and amazement. The swift, fresh lyricism of Mack Sennett reveals to us a weightless world in which the laws of gravity seem to have been replaced by the joy of motion. His short comedies announce to us the reign of lyric fantasy which will no doubt be the triumph of the cinema.

Does Mack Sennett think he has completed his task? He is said to be devoting his time to dramatic comedy, and we are sorry for it, because the screen does not have too many real poets. *Suzanna*,[1] which has just been presented to us, is a good film, but its true excellence can be recognized only by lovers of the image. Most of the audience can see in it only a film similar to so many others, with a conventional subject that is scarcely apt to arouse interest.

Once again, let us try to forget the theme offered us, and let us look with simple eyes. Let us recall the scenes of the masquerade, their delicate lighting, the youthfulness of the characters and their graceful movements; the entire ending of the film, in which Mabel Normand runs away (in the night she seems to be clothed in moonbeams); the amazing close-ups: a white arm issuing from the darkness, reaching out, being lowered, and revealing the neck and the face it encircled; the father's eyes wet with tears and the girl's hair which seems to come out of the screen.

Here one rediscovers the poet, the master of light and shadow whose work does not seem to be guided by a concern for the story, but by the quest for rhythmic effects that create visual

---

[1]*Suzanna* (directed by F. Richard Jones) was the latest Sennett-produced Mabel Normand film released before this 1923 article of René Clair) although it may not be the film Clair is here discussing; the title in the French text is *Rêve de seize ans* (Dream of a sixteen-year-old.)—ED.

emotion. Do not talk to me about three-dimensional cinema if you mean by that films in which the characters will be the flat cutout figures of the stereoscope. True three-dimensional film is seen when we are shown the work of an artist in love with living forms, one who can make them move in front of us or make us move around them by means of his sensitive and inquisitive lens. A double motion of images and viewers, an ever-moving pair of scales whose beam is the white screen, thanks to which we see the slightest visions of the world being infinitely recreated.

1950. A few years later, ruined by the failure of his latest films and by unlucky speculations, Mack Sennett stopped producing pictures. It should be noted that most of the businessmen and financiers of the early eras of the cinema made a fortune (in France: Gaumont, the Pathé Brothers, Aubert; in the United States: Zukor, the Schenck Brothers, Goldwyn, Mayer, and so on), whereas most of the creators ended their life in straitened circumstances (in France: Méliès; in the United States: D. W. Griffith, Mack Sennett, and so on).

When I was in Hollywood a few years ago, I wanted very much to meet Mack Sennett. I expected to see a very old, worn-out man, and found myself face to face with a big sturdy fellow with lively eyes and an alert mind, seemingly undiscouraged by his financial ruin.

And yet he would wander around all day long, still hoping to find work in that Hollywood where he had possessed enormous properties on which hotels, banks and movie houses stand today. And nobody knew him any more.

Europeans seem strangely sentimental to the people there when they express surprise at the indifference of that industry which manipulates millions of dollars, but did not have the decency to give its true founders—Mack Sennett or D. W. Griffith —a modest place on its boards of directors. The religion of material success and its corollary, contempt for failure, are the most shameless faults counterbalancing the solid good qualities of the American character.

1923. We have just seen a rerelease of *A Day's Pleasure,* a Charlie Chaplin film which is not one of his best but which contains wonderful passages. Every Chaplin film gives us back the sense of cinema that some ambitious productions make us lose.

It was recently discovered that a tree, a house or a locomotive possessed a personality as interesting to the camera lens as a human being. The aspects of these things and their participation give rise to dramatic effects of rare power. Have people stopped to think that Chaplin drew comic effects from them by an exactly similar procedure?

Chaplin—and it is in this way that he seems to have discovered the original power of the cinema—proceeds by visual motifs, which he exploits as completely as Wagner does a musical phrase. Look at *A Day's Pleasure:* he extracts from the folding chair he is trying to set up, from his little volcanic car, from a pile of smoking asphalt, all the humor that can possibly be extracted without harming the balance of his farce.

Lock Charlie into a cellar, a store or an empty room, and I wager he will be able to find something in his prison to bring about the explosion of laughter with which his worldwide audience greets him.

1924. We should not be afraid to repeat comforting commonplaces: Charlie Chaplin is the man who has given us the works most worthy of the cinema. The sentimental and the dramatic film are still weak, stifled by the proximity of the theater and of fiction. The film comedy was born almost spontaneously and up to now has furnished the best expression of the cinema. Now, the creator of the film comedy is Charlie Chaplin. (I am not forgetting Mack Sennett, but Chaplin went further than he did.)

A Woman of Paris offers us the opportunity to see a dramatic film created by the greatest comic author of our time. The test was a frightening one. Charlie Chaplin's genius has passed it triumphantly. *A Woman of Paris* may not be as "pure" a work, from the viewpoint of cinematic art, as *The Adventurer* or *The Immigrant,* but that is due to the difference we have pointed out between the dramatic formula and the comic formula. The latter permits all sorts of implausibilities, the most poetic illogicalities; the former has not yet won all its freedom.

Certainly, it would be easy to criticize the screenplay. It scarcely corresponds to its title,[1] the action is disjointed, it is not free of implausibilities (the cut-off telephone conversation, the meeting of Marie and Jean brought about by a mistake, the scene between mother and son overheard by Marie because of a door standing ajar). But once again, what does the screenplay matter! This film is not a minutely engineered drama. We are interested not so much in the plausibility of certain events as in the psychological truth, which here appears in a merciless light. Perhaps for the first time the characters of the drama are no longer those marionettes with stylized souls normally presented to us on the screen: the good man, the bad man, the ingenue, the villain. They are complex and subject to the workings of fate. The scene in which Pierre Revel wins back Marie with a few words reminds us, by its slightly confused gracefulness and its apparent lack of logic, of certain pages in Stendhal. The psychological excellence of *A Woman of Paris* is evident at the end of the film, when the spectator admits he is unable to judge the characters of the drama according to the conventional morality of the screen and the melodrama. None of them is entirely vicious or entirely good. Their behavior depends a little upon their will, but a great deal upon chance. They are human beings.

Moreover, these characters are very well played. Edna Purviance, Carl Miller and especially Adolphe Menjou—one of the few French actors on the American screen—seem inimitable to us. Let us pay our respects to their talent, but let us not forget that when the acting in a film, down to the smallest walk-on part, is perfect, it is the director who deserves a good part of the credit. Chaplin, who does not appear on the screen, is visible in the performance of every character. Whether comic or dramatic, his films are steeped in humanity. His taste for psychological truth is such that it somtimes carries him beyond the lines of his story (the scene in which Marie throws her pearl necklace out the window with great dignity . . . then runs out and picks it up). But this quest for psychological truth is so rare on the screen that it appears here as a real innovation.

---

[1]The French title is *L'Opinion publique.*—ED.

The technical execution of *A Woman of Paris* is very simple, and not much different from that of films produced ten years ago. Nevertheless this work is perhaps the most novel of the season. This leads us to reflect on the excessiveness of the purely technical experiments which have interested us so deeply in France. Of course, technical experiments are among the most important factors in the progress of the art of images, and we have been glad to note the lead taken by the French school in this area. But Chaplin reminds us that form is not everything. Let us remember his lesson.

1950. Over a quarter of a century has passed since Chaplin created that film, a quarter of a century during which about fifteen thousand films have been conceived and completed, and *A Woman of Paris* is still an extraordinarily unusual work today. The innovation mentioned above—psychological truth— is still an innovation now, so few are the films in which the characters do not seem to have been taken out of the conventionality closet.

The above article names Stendhal in this regard; today I would add the name of Tolstoy (which is not surprising in view of the influence the earlier writer had on the later one). In Tolstoy just as much as in Stendhal, there are few characters who can be "judged according to conventional morality," whom the author does not seem to be trying to understand completely without blaming them for their acts. This is the case in *A Woman of Paris,* whose mute heroes seem to be revealing themselves to us more openly than any of the talking characters we have seen since.

1970. In 1921, Louis Delluc wrote: *"Chaplin gives the impression that he will develop at a dizzying rate* and will never be boring. At the very most, we must expect him *to do something tragic."* This "something tragic" foreseen by Delluc was audaciously combined with comedy in *A Woman of Paris,* made in 1923, four years before the arrival of the "talkies." There are some great silent films about which it is possible to be sorry that they came too soon and could not take advantage of the contributions of sound and speech. Dreyer's *Joan of Arc* is one of those, and so is *A Woman of Paris.* Perhaps because it was a dramatic comedy, whereas speech would have added nothing to the same creator's pure comedies.

How is it possible to make people today understand the revolution caused by *A Woman of Paris,* now that its influence has spread to so many later films? Lubitsch was the first beneficiary of that influence. It may be said that there is not one Lubitsch, but two: one before and one after the appearance of *A Woman of Paris.* Chaplin's masterpiece created a style that inspired Lubitsch, and its mark is to be found in his best comedies.

This assertion does not lessen the glory of the creator of *Trouble in Paradise.* It is no cause for shame to have had preceptors. To consider oneself free of all influences is the privilege of the ignorant. From *Lady Windermere's Fan* to *To Be or Not to Be,* what delightful inventiveness and talent for comedy! Too bad Lubitsch has not had disciples of his own!

1950. Charlie Chaplin was the greatest film *author.*[1] But in the past not many people suspected it. Even his warmest admirers, dazzled by his acting performance, were not sufficiently aware that in a major film like *The Gold Rush* or in a sketch like *The Pilgrim,* his skill in construction was just as excellent as his richness of comic invention. Below are some excerpts from an article entitled: "An unknown personality—Charlie Chaplin the author."

1929. Nothing more can be said about Chaplin that is correct and still not banal, yet all that has been said about him is still insufficient. The masses do not know that Chaplin is the greatest author, the greatest creator of fiction, living today. His acting talent has obscured his genius as an author. Most critics and writers see in him primarily the "brilliant mime" or the "sublime clown," epithets which lessen his stature.

Chaplin is not merely that; he is an actor and one of the best. But other great actors are sometimes his match. As an

---

[1]Clair uses the term *"auteur"* to describe a film director long before Truffaut and the *Cahiers du cinéma* critics "discovered" the word and the concept regarding the authorial control brought to a film by its director, regardless of the contributions made by scenarists, actors, and the many other artists whose work influences the film's final form.—ED.

author, he is unique, and no film author can be compared to him.

Chaplin the actor is the most famous man in the world. Chaplin the author is not recognized. The public—that is, everybody aside from a few initiates—does not know how a film is written and the term "author" means nothing to it. If Chaplin did not appear in person in his films, would his name be known to more than one out of a thousand of his present admirers?

We recently were able to see *A Woman of Paris* again. When this film dating from 1922 is shown today, why is its magnificent old age not made public? Can the moviegoer who smiles at Edna Purviance's dresses because they are no longer in fashion, admire the newness of this old film if he is not informed in advance how old it is? A few years in the cinema are equivalent to a century for another art form. The passage of time permits us to give this drama the place it deserves in the development of the art of images. *The Cheat* in 1916, *A Woman of Paris* in 1922—almost all the achievements of the American dramatic cinema are contained within those titles and dates. *A Woman of Paris* was not as successful as Chaplin's other films, but the American silent cinema was renewed by that failure. . . .

A Woman of Paris, in which Chaplin does not appear, disconcerted more than one of his admirers. They were fascinated by Chaplin the actor; in this film Chaplin proved that he was an author first and foremost. It does not matter whether he is his own interpreter or other actors lend him their faces: he is everywhere, he creates every character. He appears behind every scene in this film in which his figure is not shown.

Have I looked at these scenes ten or twelve times? I still admire their perfect measure, their ease, the way they hang together. They are still touching, and always in a new way. So many other films arouse emotion (comic or dramatic) only by surprises, a method which works only once! *A Woman of Paris* has no surprises. The story is moved along gently by a fate that is more touching than any sudden revelations. Every detail of these well-known scenes can be foretold. But their excellence is inexhaustible.

Chaplin . . . . None of the homage paid him is adequate,

since the same words are used to praise so many fashionable authors, brainless directors and stars created by publicity. People are still being unfair to him. They forget too often what he is, what they owe him. Why don't they treat themselves more often to the rare pleasure of admiring someone unreservedly and unrestrainedly?

Chaplin inspires our confidence and reawakens our passion for the cinema. He proves to us that mind can be the master of this industry, this mechanism, these balance-sheets in dollars. He makes us forget the business end of the cinema, its puppets, its financiers, its laws and its bondage. We will never be able to proclaim loudly enough the love he inspires in us, our humility before his work, and our gratitude.

1950. I have just seen again *City Lights,* a film Chaplin made nearly twenty years ago. I must confess that I seldom go to the movies nowadays. Most films bore me and I have the greatest difficulty understanding what is going on. Someone always has to explain the plot to me afterwards. I understand only the films I like, and vice versa. But when it comes to those films, my memory, which often fails me, works like a charm. I remember every image in them. And yet I did not remember that the last scene of *City Lights* was so perfectly beautiful, despite a melodramatic situation which would have bordered on the ridiculous except for a miracle.

Judge for yourself: the poor tramp gets out of prison, to which his love for the poor blind girl had led him. Thanks to the pauper's sacrifice, the girl has been able to undergo a fabulously expensive operation, which has restored her sight. Now she "recognizes" the man she had believed to be young, handsome and rich.

I do not dare imagine what would have become of this scene if it had been directed by anyone but its author, or—even worse—if it had had dialogue written for it by some of our present-day specialists. As it stands, nothing can be compared to it. The shots that make it up, its pace, even its lighting, are all perfect and all bear the stamp—so rare, so moving when recognized—of genius.

A dramatic moment from *A Woman of Paris* (1923), with the three principals, Edna Purviance, Carl Miller and Adolphe Menjou. (The Museum of Modern Art Film Stills Archive)

From *Limelight* (1952), with Chaplin and Claire Bloom. (The Museum of Modern Art Film Stills Archive)

¶ The first study of Charlie Chaplin published in France was written by Louis Delluc, who died in 1924. This study begins with the following words:

> For a cinematic creator, Charlie Chaplin's face has the same importance that the traditional bust of Beethoven has for a musician or musicologist. I hope that this declaration will automatically eliminate unwanted readers and that we will be left with people who are able to understand one another.

This pronouncement by Louis Delluc, written in 1921, has lost nothing of its value. Some thirty years later, on the appearance of *Limelight,* we perceive that the unique nature of Chaplin's work continues to escape objective analysis, and that it can be discussed only among people "who are able to understand one another."

What was true when Delluc wrote it nearly thirty years ago, is still true today. We have just had the proof of it in the last few days in seeing *Limelight.* Those who like *Limelight* and Chaplin—fortunately, they form the great majority—have much more trouble defining the reasons for their admiration than do those in the minority, who do not share it. Between them and us, debate is useless.

A professor of cinematic dramaturgy might say that *Limelight* is a nearly perfect example of what should not be done, that the story of a paralyzed ballerina cured solely by the power of persuasion is laughable, that the story of the has-been actor is reminiscent of "Laugh, clown, laugh," and that in a play or a novel the weaknesses of a plot like that would cry out.

All that is true, or rather would be for anyone but Chaplin. If you read the synopsis of the action of his film without having seen what he has done with it, you have difficulty believing that a masterpiece can be based on a theme that looks so feeble. But if you see the film, you no longer recognize the theme which sounded so awful when summarized. Where are those weaknesses which seemed so glaring? The glare of genius has dispelled them.

It is surprising that none of the innumerable articles devoted to *Limelight* has mentioned the film's obvious resemblance to *City Lights.* In both pictures a weak girl is saved by some poor devil who sacrifices himself for his protégée's happiness. In both films the consistency of Chaplin's themes is in evidence, and melodrama can be averted only by a miracle. But the miracle takes place.

"Miracle" implies "faith" or "state of grace." Grace cannot be explained. I admire those critics who subtly discover so many things in *Limelight* that are not in it. As I see it, what is evident in both these pictures is a certain emotional quality whose sweetness had not been offered to us by anyone but Chaplin.

We feel this emotional quality taking shape in his first comedy successes; it grew in *Shoulder Arms* and the films after that until, in *City Lights,* Chaplin appeared for the first time in sentimental scenes that were more important than the purely comic scenes. Twenty years later, in *Limelight,* comedy no longer appears except at rare intervals, as if to justify the astonishing prediction made by Louis Delluc.

If Chaplin had never existed, or if in December 1913 he had not crossed the threshold of the Keystone Studios, if he had never made a film, no doubt the cinema as a whole, as we know it, would have been the same, because Chaplin's work is so profoundly original that it is scarcely linked with the development of the art on which it shed its luster. The gigantic industry would have unleashed the same torrent of images onto the world, and the same stereotyped heroes would have been offered to the same mass worship.

But *we* would not have been altogether the same people we are today. We would have been without a friend, without that dialogue which he and we entered into with confidence—that is, he and millions of anonymous people, those who, as Delluc said, are able to understand one another.

1970. Eternal shifting of values! Today it is the correct thing in some circles to belittle Chaplin's work and its author himself. I admit that his autobiography has done him harm, that his eccentricities and his mode of existence are not in line with the tramp image he created, "but this type of criticism," as Marcel Proust said when attacking Sainte-Beuve, "touches upon precisely all those points at which the true personality of the poet is not involved."[1] If Vigny had questionable dealings with

---

[1]Proust wrote *Against Sainte-Beuve* to discredit the whole school of biographically oriented criticism that the romantic writer founded.—ED.

the police of the Second Empire, I am sorry for it. But—assuming that the accusation is well founded—it was not this dubious character who wrote "La Maison du berger" (The shepherd's house) ; it was the other, his brilliant double. "Every man has his double," says the German legend which made such a tragic impression upon Nerval. Which is the more real, the man whom only his contemporaries knew, or the works that expressed his transcendent truth and that survive him?

Chaplin's originality has been dulled by time. Of course. That is true of all great creators whose inventions have so strongly influenced the work of their followers that they have become everybody's property and finally look like commonplaces. Recently people have been pleased to discover Buster Keaton, whom young people did not know or did not know well. I am far from belittling that admirable character, and I consider *Our Hospitality* to be one of the masterpieces of American cinema. But just suppose that all of Keaton's films had been seen again and again for a long time by the habitués of film societies, and that people suddenly discovered the work of Chaplin, unknown until then—what cries of enthusiasm would be uttered!

1923. Reflection is necessary for full appreciation of the value of D. W. Griffith's *One Exciting Night*. First of all, it is a very entertaining film. Reflection is not needed for that. It is very pleasant to see an entertaining film, and for the hour that *One Exciting Night* runs you can laugh, be surprised and be frightened without thinking about anything but the story of the film. What a pleasure! How childish the great philosophical constructions, social conflicts and greeting-card psychological dramas seem next to this detective and ghost story, which can appear childish only to the "brains" incapable of understanding the cinema.

But is that all? And has Griffith only produced a work comparable to the little humorous detective novels? A very uneven work, some parts of which partake of the film serial style?

We must always be on our guard with a man like this. His best works are blemished by annoying mannerisms, and his less good ones are still full of remarkable visual expressions. His faults are as glaring as his good qualities: he preaches, he delights in facile sentimentality, he makes numerous concessions to his audience, which he himself said had the mentality of a two-year-old child. But he possesses the sense of the cinema in the highest degree. It is in his films that the most beautiful rhythms ever to enliven a series of images have appeared. It is in certain parts of Griffith's work that we have seen the destiny of the dramatic film.

Let us attach little importance to the plot of *One Exciting Night,* even though it is very well constructed and causes us to jump with surprise many times as it unfolds. This film, which to those in a hurry to formulate an opinion resembles all other detective films, contains an extremely important innovation. For the first time, the spectators are brought into the action of the film to such an extent that they live every hour of this mysterious night[1] just as the characters of the drama do. Both audience and characters are perplexed by these shades passing by, these fleeing figures, these doors that are opened and immediately closed again, these disembodied hands, these cardboard ghosts. For the first time, after the final explanation, the confession of the guilty party, the marriage of the innocent young couple, in this reassuring atmosphere, we are still troubled by doubts, by memories of unexplained events. Griffith has not felt obliged to give us an exact account of everything that happened. He tells us what the first cause of the drama was, but leaves in the dark all the little occurrences that arose from chance, the confusion of his characters, and our imaginings.

Too often in the cinema the spectators have the impression, which becomes tiresome in the long run, of being gods who know the cause of everything, the future as well as the past. Nothing is concealed from them. Everything is explained to them, and sometimes in advance. Griffith's audacity and skill, in this *One Exciting Night,* consisted in not leaving us outside the drama, but bringing us into it and having it enact itself within us. He achieved this result by means of a wonderfully controlled editing job. The images appear for a few moments; they suggest more than they tell; other images come in just when the first ones begin to explain something to us. That is cinema.

---

[1] The French title was *La Nuit mystérieuse* (The mysterious night).—ED.

That, also, is truth. We never know all the causes of the simplest event. We could spend our whole life trying to find a logical explanation for what we see in a single day, and not succeed. Let us allow the illogical to play a part in dramas. It is the only way to be logical with ourselves.

Carol Dempster is charming; an obliging storm allows us to enjoy the shape of her praiseworthy legs. Her partner has the merit of not looking like an actor. When will we be rid of these actors who look like nothing but actors? Nothing is more annoying, except perhaps those novels in which the main character is a writer.

I prefer not to remember the tinted roses which make certain tableaus in the film look like a touching birthday card. The storm at the end, which is incidentally very well handled, reminds us that Griffith is a humorist and that no one can parody him as well as he can himself.

1950. Among D. W. Griffith's last films, *One Exciting Night* was the last to assure us that his genius would survive. Griffith's contribution to the cinema in its infancy is immeasurable, now that all his inventions have been so completely assimilated by his pupils that they have become the common property of film art.

And yet the boldness of Griffith's work still, at times, discourages imitation. Who nowadays would dare to conceive a design as vast as the one he set for himself in *Intolerance?* In that film four stories from four periods of history were told side by side, their themes crisscrossing until their four endings blossomed out on the screen all at once. Thus, the chariots raced toward the destruction of Babylon at the same time that a train carried off one of the heroes of the contemporary story across the plains of America, and each of the stories being told was progressing toward its inevitable conclusion at the same rate of speed. I have seen an ordinary audience in a movie house burst into applause at that moment, because the rhythm of the work was so right, and that incredibly daring gamble had been carried off so well.

One Exciting Night is one of Griffith's minor works. But even this minor work has led to so much else! Detective films and pseudo-psychological mysteries, the type known as "suspense" films in English—an inferior genre if there ever was one, and one that has been worn to a frazzle but is still an attention-getting cliché—have contributed hardly anything new since *One Exciting Night,* which created the recipe for them.

1970. How fragile is the glory conferred by the screen! One might think that Griffith long ruled over the American cinema. Now, it was in 1915 *(The Birth of a Nation)* that he began to be known all over the world. By 1925, he had lost most of his fame. By 1930 his name belonged to the past.

¶ In 1935, "an evening of thin mist in London" (as Guillaume the Unloved sings), the sight of a white sail passing by in the light of dusk that was descending on the Thames reminded me of one of the first images in *Broken Blossoms.*[1] A little later, walking in the Chinese quarter, which some friends had offered to show me, I thought I had already walked through these poverty-stricken streets and I seemed to recognize them. The house with sad windows, the lonely policemen and the haloed street lamps—it was the set of *Broken Blossoms* that was taking shape around us. A few minutes more and perhaps, at the hour when London ghosts begin to glide between walls of unknown date, the girl with big terrified eyes, the gentle Chinese boy and the savage boxer would pass one by one down that street where reality seemed to be yielding to the pressure of memory.

The bright light coming from a shop window dispelled the reverie into which a few outward appearances had cast me, but as I followed my friends into a more or less Asiatic restaurant, I kept thinking about Griffith's film, whose paled images had come back to life in my memory all along the path we had just taken.

"And Griffith, what is he doing now?"

No one knew. No one had heard anything about him for a long time. Probably he was not working any more. Perhaps he was living in retirement in some small town in the United States. Perhaps he was even in Hollywood, that capital of illu-

---

[1]The line comes from Guillaume Apollinaire's poem "The Song of an Un-loved Man," in which the poet experiences encounters involving deceptive appearances due to the fog, his lonely frame of mind, and the foreign surroundings.—ED.

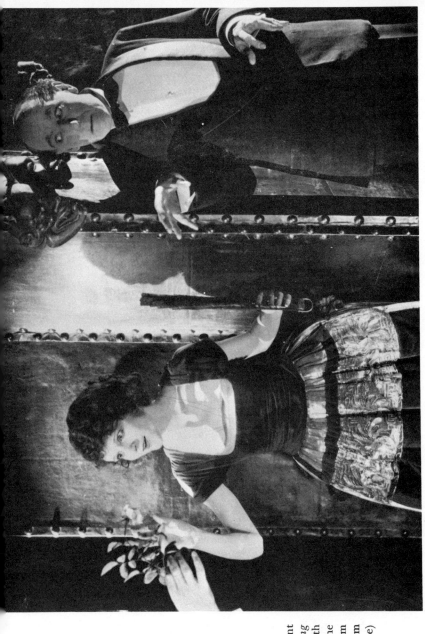

A suspenseful moment from *One Exciting Night* (1922), with Carol Dempster as the heroine. (The Museum of Modern Art Film Stills Archive)

"It was the set of *Broken Blossoms* that was taking shape around us" (p. 94): Lillian Gish as the sad Limehouse girl (1919). (The Museum of Modern Art Film Stills Archive)

sion where worldwide glory is created in a few weeks but where those who outlive their good fortune are as completely forgotten as the dead.

Night had fallen, and we were finishing our meal in the rear of a large empty dining room, the entire length of which separated us from the door that opened onto the deserted street, when that door opened. Emerging from the shadow, a man advanced toward the bar that was near the entrance and leaned his elbow on it in the pose habitual to solitary drinkers. When he turned his head toward us and the light struck his large-featured face, the impression of being in a dream, which had left me at the door of the restaurant, invaded me again. Were the reminiscences awakened by certain views in a district of London working so violently on my imagination that I now thought I was face to face with that Griffith whose features I knew only from the portraits I had seen of him?

My companions, whom I informed of my confusion, bantered me goodhumoredly. The power of a dream is not so great that the creator of *Broken Blossoms* could suddenly appear in that offbeat section of London on that very night because I had just been thinking about him. I agreed, but I could not tear my eyes away from the man who was drinking a whisky at the bar and not paying the least attention to his surroundings. If it was not Griffith himself, it was a character so much like him that his appearing at that very moment was as extraordinary as if a ghost had materialized. Alone in the middle of the room, he seemed to be a living challenge to plausibility, and no matter what explanation could be given for his presence, it catered to the taste every rational mind has for the miraculous.

Eager to satisfy the somewhat ironic curiosity of those with me, who thought I was at the mercy of a hallucination, I advanced toward the man. The nearer I came to him, the more he resembled the man I thought I had recognized.

"I beg your pardon. Aren't you Mr. Griffith?"

He turned his piercing eyes toward me, and in an instant ghost and man assumed the same face. It was he.

He accepted our invitation to sit with us, and told us that he had come from America to discuss a film project (which incidentally never got anywhere) and had disembarked in London that very day; but he told us nothing about what I especially wished to know: why he had been impelled to come alone, that very night, into that out-of-the-way area.

He drank another whisky, laughed several times with a resounding laugh, as if he wanted to prove that he could still laugh, and after reciting a few lines of Shakespeare with his beautiful preacher's voice, he got up suddenly. He crossed the empty room, opened the door and plunged into that darkness from which, it seemed to me a few minutes later, only my imagination had summoned him up.

You might have said that he was departing into the fog in quest of his vanished youth and genius, and that, like Thomas De Quincey dreaming of his poor Ann, he was searching in the deep night of London and of his past for the little girl of *Broken Blossoms* whose trembling hand attempts to move her lips into the form of a smile.

Pure Cinema and Poetry

There was a lot of talk about purity around 1925. Abbé Bremond[1] had ignited the battle over "pure poetry"; I don't recall whether the arguments exchanged during that affair touched on the purity of the theater, sculpture or choreography, but I know that "pure cinema" was on the agenda. What was involved here? A desperate but not unnecessary revolt against "anecdotal and descriptive" cinema.

> Now that cinema-as-art is dying, swallowed up by its double, cinema-as-industry, it may seem absurd to exalt the image as an "end in itself," the "abstract" film: pure cinema.* But it is in eras of decadence that we must display the most radical extremism. . . . Rimbaud and Cézanne, who cleaned off the filth that covered the word and the object, and their Dadaist and Cubist successors, have sufficiently freed us from the subject so that we can appreciate the most deliberately anecdotal works as a reaction. But this nonchalant attitude we adopt in regard to arts which have existed for some tens of centuries cannot be maintained in the presence of a mode of expression that is barely out of the egg, but already bastardized, deformed, strangled.

For his part, my brother Henri Chomette, who was quite interested in the matter, discussed it in these terms:

> No sooner had the cinema freed the image from its original immobility than it began to express itself in disappointing formulas.† False humor, Italian melodrama, the serial, and "natural" color came along to doom our new hopes. Later, the spectator—anxious for information about the theater but depending on chance for the choice of films to see—discovered *The Cheat,* Chaplin, Mack Sennett and *Nanook.* And his understandable discouragement gave way to a temporary reconciliation.
>
> At present—except in the eyes of the French legislator, who still classes it along with "traveling shows"—the cinema has been able to win its least favorable judges back to its side. Yet, although it is a new-born force with numerous possibilities, it

---

[1]The Abbé Bremond was a renegade Jesuit scholar whose *La Poésie pure* (1927) was directed against intellectualism and rationalism, insisting rather that poetry is born of a purely intuitive instinct similar to religious mystical intuitions.—ED.

*Georges Charensol, in *Les Cahiers du mois,* 1925.

†Henri Chomette, in *Les Cahiers du mois,* 1925.

is still showing signs of only one of its potentials: the representation of known things.

In short, the only role it plays in regard to the eye is partially comparable to that of the phonograph in regard to the ear: recording and reproducing.

Of course, stop-action filming reveals to us events which our eyes did not perceive or did not perceive clearly (the opening of a rose)—but at least we had an idea about the sum of these events. Of course, trick shots give us unprecedented illusions (elimination of gravity, or of the opacity of a body through double exposure)—but only by sticking to objects familiar to our reason, concrete and well-known objects. Do you wish to escape from the real and conjure up something imagined—a soul, for example? You will have to make use of a body, which has become transparent—but is still a recognizable human body. A conventional representation, but representation.

Thus, all the present uses of cinema can be reduced to films of a single world, the representative, which can be divided into two groups: documentary—mere reproduction in motion—and dramatic (comedies, dramas, fairy-pantomimes, etc.), the origin and essence of which can be found in older types of performing arts (drama, pantomime, vaudeville, etc.).

But the cinema is not limited to the representative world. It can create. It has already created a sort of rhythm (which I did not mention when speaking about current films because its value in them is extremely diluted by the meaning of the image).

Thanks to this rhythm, the cinema can draw from itself a new potentiality, which, leaving behind the logic of events and the reality of objects, engenders a series of visions that are unknown —inconceivable outside the union of the lens and the moving reel of film. Intrinsic cinema—or, if you will, pure cinema— since it is separate from all other elements, whether dramatic or documentary—that is what certain works by our most personal directors permit us to foresee. That is what offers the purely cinematic imagination its true field and will give rise to what has been called—by Mme. Germaine Dulac, I believe—the "visual symphony."

Virtuosity, perhaps, but just like a harmonious concert of instruments, it will move our sensibilities as well as our intelligence. For why should the screen be denied that faculty for enchantment which is granted to the orchestra?

Universal kaleidoscope, generator of all moving visions from the least strange to the most immaterial, why should the cinema not create the kingdom of light, rhythms and forms alongside that of sound?

¶ And yet Alexandre Arnoux was distrustful and declared

the horror he felt at the "purity" that was always dinning in his ears:

> Pure poetry, pure music, the pure novel disgust me. Only the impure moves me, allows me to make contact with it and become part of it; only the impure does not belong to a race that is not mine. My emotions have need of a certain coarseness, and I am not fond of eating substances that are chemically pure and reduced to formulas; I am not fond of begetting by means of abstract copulation. I follow Pascal's advice and await my future life before acting the angel. While waiting, I keep my feet on the ground and refuse to purify to infinity and extract quintessences till nothing is left.

But Arnoux, who was one of the most lucid and sensitive critics of the cinema, liked it too much to be satisfied with this humorous grumbling. And on another occasion, following the lightning-like fancy which makes his writings a ballet of ideas, he was led to write the following passage:

> Some day people will have to understand that the ultimate goal of the cinema is not to blind us with checks, millions of dollars, bad rhetoric and *tableaux vivants,* but to discover mysteriously an unknown corner of the sky, a naïvely supernatural image. The shadow of a cloud passing over a meadow, a leaf yielding to the wind, a piston moving regularly back and forth—that is enough, if we know how to entrust it to the instrument that records it and how to reproduce it in a proper rhythm of transitions. We keep coming back to Cézanne's three apples. Three apples, and in front of them, in cinema as in painting, three things that cannot be bought: an eye, an intelligence, a sensitivity. Nothing else is needed; and yet those three things are almost never brought together.

¶ All in all, the partisans of pure cinema were not saying much more than that. For my part, I did not think that the problem with which these partisans were occupied merited all the discussion it was raising:

The cinema is primarily an industry. The existence of "pure cinema" comparable to "pure" music seems today too much subject to chance to merit serious examination.

The question of pure cinema is directly connected with that of "cinema: art or industry?" To answer this last question, it would first be necessary to have a precise definition of the con-

cept of art. Now, our era is not favorable to such precise form-
ulations. Next, it would be necessary for the cinema's conditions
of material existence to be drastically altered. A film does not
exist on paper. The most detailed screenplay will never be able
to foresee every detail of the execution of the work (exact camera angle, lighting, exposure, acting, etc.). A film exists only on
the screen. Now, between the brain that conceives it and the
screen that reflects it, there is the entire industrial organization
and its need for money.

Therefore, it seems pointless to predict the existence of a
"pure cinema" so long as the cinema's conditions of material
existence remain unchanged or the mind of the public has not
developed.

Nevertheless, there are already signs of the pure cinema. It
can be found in fragmentary fashion in a number of films; it
seems in fact that a film fragment becomes pure cinema as soon
as a sensation is aroused in the viewer by purely visual means.
A broad definition, of course, but adequate for our era. That
is why the primary duty of the present-day film-maker is to introduce the greatest number of purely visual themes by a sort
of ruse, into a screenplay made to satisfy everybody. Therefore,
the literary value of a screenplay is completely unimportant.

¶ The same point of view led to the statement: "In front of
the lens, *Andromaque* and *The Charterhouse of Parma* lose all
their value" (which is still more or less true today despite the
power of speech the film has acquired). But if the *literary* value
of a subject is still unimportant, it is still true that in the cinema,
today as yesterday, the problem of the screenplay is the most
important of all, and that a screenplay "made to please everybody" is not so easily found as a hastily written sentence would
lead one to think.

To have done with the pure cinema, let us add that if the
intention behind it was to define a poetics of the screen, the
question was not as superficial as it appeared:

1923. In a recent film based on a famous Romantic poem,
most of the intertitles were lines excerpted from the adapted
work. We were not a little surprised to observe that many of
these famous lines seemed unusually weak when projected onto

the screen between two images. These isolated notes from the grand verbal orchestra were almost without value. I suppose that an image taken out of the film and placed in the middle of the poem would also lose all its force. It seems that the poetry of books and the poetry of the screen are incompatible.

The only poetry that can exist in the cinema is that created by the image itself. It is a singularly new poetry whose rules are not determined. The flowers and sunsets with which some film-makers attempt to awaken poetic feeling are clichés of the same order as the "noble chargers" and the "torch of the night" of outmoded literature. Here, poetry arises from the rhythm of the visions. The pure lyricism of Sjöström and Griffith—the Chinese boy in *Broken Blossoms* leaning against the wall of a building, the high snowclad peak of *The Outlaw and His Wife* —has already been shown to us. For my part, I know of nothing which conjures up the idea of heroï-comic lyricism, or just plain lyricism, as well as the madcap dashes of Douglas Fairbanks, the implausible flights of Mack Sennett's bathing beauties or Charlie Chaplin's enormous sprints in no particular direction when pursued by a policeman or fate; these sprints continue simply because they have begun. Many effusions of lyric poets have no other reason for existing. . . .

Nanook, Storming the Alps with Skis and *The Eternal Silence* prove that the interest of an audience can be held for a long time without the aid of a worked-out screenplay. The images are enough. It can be entertaining to predict the future. There will perhaps come a day when a simple series of images, with no definable link but united by a secret harmony, will arouse an emotion analogous to that aroused by music. Perhaps the public will go farther toward understanding the cinema than the boldest critics can predict. Every precise esthetic is in danger of being too limited. . . .

The pleasing thing about the cinema is that it is an art—if it is only an art—solely dedicated to the present. It is destined to lose every trace of its past as long as celluloid is mortal. And perhaps that is a good thing. An art without experience, without a museum, will be unusually alive, supple, attached to humanity and, like it, transitory. And open to any future. . . .

Fiction? Reality? In writing *Six Characters in Search of an Author*, that critical drama, Pirandello brutally shook our current conception of the already ailing art of the theater. Did he really wish to make us believe that someone could drown in a cardboard well? That was going a bit far. We followed him, but from now on we will be on our guard as soon as the curtain goes up on a stage.

Fiction? Reality? Just try to separate fiction from reality on the screen, where they are both merely flitting shadows.

I believe that the film is only at the beginning of its conquest of the inner world. The succession of images, infinitely supple, now as precise as a phrase in literature and now as vague as a phrase in music, will make possible the expression of the most complex feelings and the remotest sensations. Will not the film be able to suggest to the general public more easily than the word the things they cannot understand or accept in the theories of Freud or the novels of Proust?

¶ At the time when people hoped that the cinema would become a new instrument of poetic creation, Surrealism was attempting to renew poetry in its own manner. An article in 1925 on this twofold subject gave me the inspiration for the following reflection:

The relationships between Surrealism and the cinema have been well examined by Mr. J. Goudal in the *Revue Hebdomadaire*. It would take too long to discuss his ideas here, but one point is worth a brief comment. Mr. Goudal writes: "The application of Surrealist ideas to the cinema is free from the objections that can be raised to Surrealism in literature." All right. But other objections occur. If Surrealism has its own technique, so does the cinema. The thing that interests me in Surrealism is the element of purity and nonartistry it unveils. In order to translate the purest Surrealist conception into images, it would be necessary to subject it to cinematic techniques, and this would put that "pure psychic automatism" in danger of losing much of its purity.[1]

For that reason, I cannot believe that the cinema is the best medium of expression for Surrealism. Nevertheless, the cinema and Surrealism are far from remaining strangers to each other.

[1]The self-explanatory phrase comes from André Breton's famous *Surrealist Manifesto.*—ED.

Here, I agree with Mr. Goudal, who emphasizes the hallucinatory nature of the cinema and the uselessness of any logical commentary on the events which the screen shows. If the cinema cannot be a perfect medium of expression for Surrealism, it still remains an incomparable field of Surrealist activity for the mind of the spectator. Buster Keaton's remarkable *Sherlock Jr.* has supplied a sort of dramatic critique of that characteristic of the cinema comparable to the one supplied for the theater by Pirandello's *Six Characters in Search of an Author.*

¶ But Surrealism was still only a movement of initiates whose activity was very important in the history of our era, but was not perceptible to the general public which was reached so easily by the cinema.

The screen speaks of love to a hundred fifty million human beings every week. It is a strange custom, that of having so many films end with a kiss or with the promise of sex. The greatest creators of moving images have complied with it. And we may wonder whether these representations of love are not one of the essential charms of the cinema, one of the secrets of the enchantment it works on the masses . . . .

On the screen appear beings who are immaterial, transparent and bathed in light. Film companies have chosen the prettiest women and the handsomest men for the games of the modern populace. And every evening, with the magnification of its various shots, the screen offers us a glorification of the human face and the whole human body, which is made larger by the lens and seems to be on the scale of the bodies of the ancient demigods.

Do not smile. The public's taste for these optical illusions is not a fad created by fashion or publicity. It is possible to see in it the rebirth of poetry. In this era when verbal poetry is losing the charm it exerted on the masses and is becoming "a matter for initiates" (how many people were reading Lamartine and Hugo in the nineteenth century, and how many read the modern poets today?), a new form of poetic expression has arisen and can reach every heart beating on earth.

It shows up in those successions of images which often defy logic, but which also often cause a breath of amorous lyricism to blow through the darkened theaters. A poetry of the people is there, seeking its way. . . .

There are still good people who blame us for the lyrical tone we adopt when speaking of the cinema. Those people are not following attentively the progress of that enormous mechanism which is still in its infancy. We like the cinema not so much for what it is as for what it will be. Marcel Proust wondered "whether music were not the unique form of what the communication of souls would have been if language had not been invented, words formed and ideas analyzed." No, not unique. Marcel Proust would not have written that if he had known the possibilities of a visual art, the cinema.

¶ "We like the cinema not so much for what it is as for what it will be." It is hard to believe today that in 1925, when those lines were written, people thought that the cinema would remain silent. The quotation from Marcel Proust would have been meaningless after the success of *The Jazz Singer* two years later.

On the eve of this metamorphosis, we had just noticed that films—like civilizations—were mortal. It was in 1925 that the cinema first looked back at its own past. The event took place at the Cinéma des Ursulines, which opened with a program including *The Joyless Street, Entr'acte* and *Five Minutes in the Prewar Cinema,* causing Parisian first-nighters to run to a little movie house located behind the Panthéon. Those "five minutes," in which pre-1914 newsreels and various dramas of the same era were shown, made most of the audience double up with laughter and led others to some useful reflections. Did we have the right to laugh at these primitive works? Was not time going to gnaw at tomorrow's films as it had at yesterday's, stripping them of all plausibility and leaving only a silly skeleton?

It was not without melancholy that I then noted:

The cinema lives under the sign of relativity. Its authors, its actors, its works and the ideas they suggest pass by swiftly. It would seem as if the cinematograph, a machine for capturing minutes of life, had tried to defy time and that time was taking a terrible revenge by speeding up everything relating to the screen.

Writing in Images

1923. The last vision is obliterated and disappears from the darkened screen. "Good night." We leave. A few minutes ago the audience was moved. The emotion faded out with the last feet of the film.

At the cloakroom, people begin giving their opinions. "Not bad, this film, but what an unbelievable story!"

That is the usual fault found by an audience that is primarily attuned to "the story." Of course, screen writers have often turned a movie house into an academy of implausibility. Nevertheless there should be some mutual understanding.

Do you think that the subjects of stage plays are always more believable than those of films? Take a close look at them. They would often appear just as fragile if they did not have a strengthening factor which the screen lacks: words. Every line spoken comments on the plot and justifies it. Words can save the worst causes, as in the courtroom.

In the cinema all we have is the image. The printed intertitles are a frigid commentary. Only the living image seizes our attention. We see characters acting as if they were under the spell of a fate that strikes them dumb. Watch people dancing through a pane of glass that shuts out the sound of the music: the silent dancers look like maniacs.

Is that an inherent shortcoming of the screen? No. The Swedes have already shown us the depth of simple stories. Let us not try to progress too quickly. Later on, film-makers will control the economy of their images: the public will understand that a sort of cinematic syntax is gradually taking shape. The image will express more and express it better.

Even today, how many sentences would be necessary to translate correctly the face of Lillian Gish in the snowstorm or a certain glance of Charlie Chaplin!

1926. I would like to ask the intellectuals, who are often the severest critics in an audience, not to judge a film by the value of its screenplay alone, as they do too often. The cinema, a twenty-five-year-old art, cannot always treat "profound" subjects. The fact is that the literary value of a screenplay has scarcely any influence on the value of the film. Good films are often based on themes that would make poor novels. Consider the plot of *Children's Faces* or of *Broken Blossoms*. These stories, banal for literature, are fine themes for the cinema. Too many moviegoers, if they yield to the power of the screen, summarize their impression afterward in a narrative that lacks the charm of the images. Now, only the image is of importance.

Apropos of this, let us point out that the state of mind peculiar to the spectator of a film is not without analogy to the condition of a man dreaming. The darkness of the theater, the numbness caused by the music, the parade of shadows over the luminous canvas, everything conspires to plunge the audience into that state of half-dream in which the suggestive power of the images exerts a hold comparable to that of the visions which people our slumber. In the morning, the incoherence of our dreams makes us smile and we are surprised at having been puppets in so many adventures incomprehensible to our waking mind. I have often seen a movie audience experience a feeling comparable to that of a man awakening. They have been at the mercy of astonishing visions, they have been drawn into the vicissitudes of an unexpected story development; they have surrendered themselves to the irresistible current of the images; and when the lights go on, they are amazed at having yielded to the promptings of those crazy shadows. They are amused at their own credulity. Their critical sense returns. The contact with the most ordinary reality restores their logical habits of thought. At that moment it is not unusual for them to feel a certain scorn for the adventure whose least detail they were following with passion a few minutes earlier. Let us not complain about this transitory ingratitude. It is a homage to the film's suggestive power. An art which can carry thought so far away from its customary realm is not a mediocre art.

1950. It will be observed later that speech and sound, adding an element of reality to the film presentation, have made the viewer lose the feeling of dream which the sight of the silent shadows created in him. (See the later chapter "A Visit to the Monster.")

1923. The original painter and original artist proceed in the manner of oculists. To be treated by their painting or prose is not always pleasant. When the treatment is over, the practitioner says to us: "Now look." And there! the world (which was created not once, but as often as an original artist has appeared on the scene) appears entirely different to us from the old one, but perfectly clear.

Thus spoke Marcel Proust, who created for us a world entirely different from the old one. This sentence explains to us why new artists encounter so much misunderstanding and hostility: it is because it is unpleasant to submit to an eye treatment when you think your vision is already perfect. People began to see clearly by the Baudelaire or Rimbaud method when Baudelaire and Rimbaud were already dead.

Now, the thing that is amazing in this new world that is the cinema, is that it reaches the masses almost unerringly—despite its novelties. Chaplin's genius reaches the masses and the elite and—contrary to what is customary in the other arts—the masterpieces of the screen are almost always its greatest successes. Is this not an index of the perfect health enjoyed by this new thing that is the cinema?

1950. The author of *Remembrance of Things Past* never, to my recollection, mentioned the existence of film in his books. (What a pity! He would have described a movie theater so well, in the same way that, in a metaphor several pages long, he transforms the Paris Opéra into a submarine grotto.) Proust's work completed its blossoming in 1923, after the death of its author, whom I met only once, at the home of Lucien Daudet, in 1918. (He showed up unexpectedly about midnight, as was his custom, leaving a fiacre waiting in front of the door.) It was Lucien Daudet who had spoken to me, at the front in 1917, about his friend's writings. As soon as I got back to Paris I got hold of *Swann's Way* in a lending library, and after reading the book, which then cost three or four francs, I returned it without thinking of purchasing it. It was a copy of the Grasset edition (the only one that existed at the time), which is now one of the rarities of contemporary bibliophilism!

1970. A very pleasant fact for those who liked Proust right from the start, and something very unusual in the history of literature: Proust's work has weathered a half-century without being sent to "purgatory" and without losing any of its novelty. Why can't the same be said about a film?!

1928. Let us understand each other: to be the author of a film does not necessarily mean conceiving the theme of the film —what the public calls the "story"—oneself. If that were so, the author of Racine's tragedies would be not Racine, but Tacitus, Euripides, Segrais or even Henriette of England. . . . The "story" is not the essential element. Look at what Racine and Pradon did with the same theme.[1] Have the plot of *A Woman of Paris* developed by just any screenplay writer: instead of a masterpiece you will have an uninteresting disaster-page news item. The author of a film is the man who turns the screenplay into a shooting script, directs the actual shooting and does the editing of the scenes that have been shot.

In my opinion, these last two operations should depend entirely on the first. To prepare a shooting script does not simply mean writing shot numbers in front of technical directions; it means presenting an action, developing it in well-ordered scenes, expressing the sentences of the plot by means of the transition from one shot to another, finding details of visual expression that are clearer than a sentence, prearranging the camera angles and the approximate duration of the series of images—in short (if we wish to continue our comparison and return to the most perfect of our tragedy writers), to do the work which Racine undertook when he said: "My tragedy is done; now all I have to do is write it." . . .

Soon the value of a cinematic work will depend primarily on what is done at its author's desk. The symbolic attribute of the film author will be the fountain pen and no longer the megaphone. King Vidor claims that a film should be written with the camera and not with the pen. All right, but this is playing on words. To make itself known, inspiration does not need studio sets, the smell of paint and the blows of the carpenters' ham-

---

[1] Racine's enemies encouraged Nicolas Pradon to stage a rival version of *Phèdre* to ruin the reception of Racine's play. Despite their formidable initial machinations, Racine's version eventually enjoyed a successful run and a long life, while Pradon's play lasted for only nineteen performances. Time has only emphasized the tremendous difference in quality between Racine's genius and Pradon's derivative imitation.—ED.

mers. You might just as well say that a playwright can only write his play in the prompter's box.

1970. This brings up the eternal question: "Who is the author of a film?" A question that can be answered only in the case where a single authority has had effective control of all the operations that created a film. Otherwise, there is no general rule and every case is a particular case.

Most films are the result of a collaboration in which it is difficult to separate the responsibilities or hand out the praise. That is why the formula "Un film de . . ." (A film by . . .) followed by a single name—a formula used by publicity departments and most of our critics—is incorrect much of the time. In English, the terminology is precise: "Screenplay by . . . Produced by . . . Directed by . . . ." In that way you know more or less what's what. But only more or less.

For example: when I saw *Scarface,* I was struck by a particularly expressive shot: young Scarface wants to demonstrate the effectiveness of a tommygun. With one blast he mows down a row of billiard cues standing up against a wall (as he will do with a rival gang on Valentine's Day). This good visual idea, as I later learned from the screenplay writers, Ben Hecht and Charles MacArthur, figured explicitly in their script. Who is the author? The men who conceived that image or the man who got it down on film?

1927. A playwright has just published some advice to filmmakers. He says, not without understandable irony, that he respects the "sacred mystery" of the studios, but he makes it understood that our films will be better when we ask for help from the "specialists"—the playwrights.

This author points out, and rightly so, the error of directors who make a film out of a series of tableaus framed by intertitles, without any concern for dramatic construction and the springs of the action. If, he says, the film-makers want to "construct" a film, they should take advantage of the experience that theatrical writers have acquired.

The diagnosis is accurate, but the remedy suggested worries me. It is obvious that cinematic dramaturgy is in its infancy.

But have patience. The dramatic film has just been born, and up to now the efforts of the best men have been concerned with giving cinematic expression its indispensable technical means. Now that has been done, and unless mechanical and chemical progress is made in the near future, the study of technical means of expression will no longer offer us anything new. From this point on, this study is no longer the object of our best efforts. The most difficult thing remains to be done: to construct the architecture of a cinematic action, which does not yet exist, except in comedies. In the realm of drama, the best films offer us only hints of it. The dramatic film, led astray by the disastrous wave of "adaptations," has been constructed on the model of dramatic or fictional works by brains accustomed to verbal expression alone.

"But what else can be done?"

We shall soon know.

"But in the meantime?"

I can only have a premonition. It is only a film-maker of genius who can answer you some day through his film work. And, to make you understand what I expect of the cinematic drama, I can only proceed by comparisons: suppose that the theater had never existed and that people had never known anything but the form of the monologue or the narration. Suppose that someone suddenly came upon the form of the play, the method of presenting an action by means of the actors' words alone, by means of concentration of the scenes, and no longer in accordance with the necessity for plot exposition. The revolution caused in men's minds would not be greater than it will be on the day that the film drama will come to be.

1950. First skirmishes with the playwrights and—although the film was still silent—for reasons quite like those that were to give rise to a livelier battle when "filmed theater" threatened to invade the screen. (See the chapter "In Self-Defense.")

1923. "If," say the men of letters, "they agreed to pay us properly, we would work for the cinema, and then you would see some interesting screenplays . . . ."

Nothing is further from the truth. Merely paying a novelist

well will not make him play the harp or build a house correctly. The arts of the mason and the harpist—or of the screenplay writer—have their own rules which are only distantly related to the art of literature. The men of letters should first forget their trade of assembling words and learn that of creating images. How many of them will be capable of such detachment?

The confusion between literature and the cinema is unfortunately not confined to literary men alone. Didn't a publishing house which organized a screenplay contest form a jury composed mainly of men of letters, some of whom are even members of the Académie Française? How can these brains, accustomed to verbal creation, appreciate visual ideas? They will instinctively choose the best subjects for novels or plays. The best screenplays—those of Chaplin and Fairbanks—would seem childish to them; they would scorn them, because they are unaware that the cinema is still in its infancy and that the intelligence of a film-maker is to be judged partially by what he refuses to attempt.

Grandeur and Servitude

"The most important factor in one's entire life is the choice of one's profession, and it is a matter of chance."

This sentence of Pascal, applied to "cinema people," inspired reflections lacking in indulgence:

1927. Is it good to reflect? No. "The cinema," says Cendrars, "is a drug."

The addict does not reflect. If he talks about his craving, it is only in order to justify it. He does not reflect: he pleads a cause.

When a creator of films speaks to moviegoers who are somewhat enlightened, he excuses himself. Do you think he does not always understand the meaning of those indulgent compliments bestowed on him? You say nice things to us, but you are thinking: "Can't he do better, since he's lucky enough to have that wonderful device at his disposal? He and his colleagues claim to be authors, but all they can squeeze out of that extraordinary invention, the cinema, is these mediocre series of images, whereas everything still remains to be discovered!"

You are right. More than one film-maker thought along the same lines in the past, when he was only a spectator, before he knew either the studios or those shops in which film is sold by the yard; when he was still unaware what "cinema people" say before, during and after the making of a film. Now he keeps quiet. The indignation that overpowered him at first is calming down. His most cherished projects seem to him like dreams of another world. In his eyes routine gradually begins to take on the appearance of reasonable tradition. He is learning how to behave himself, as they say. At this point the cinema people come up to him and say: "Now you are a great director." Thanks.

To tell the truth, not many cinema addicts are to be found in the "cinema corporation." But there are a few all the same,

---

The chapter title implicitly refers to Vigny's fictionalized autobiographical novel, *Grandeur et servitude militaires,* in which he details moments of greatness and moments of bondage brought about by the idiosyncrasies of nineteenth-century military life.—ED.

and their craving has not taken away all their lucidity. The cinema, which they know very well, disgusts them. But they cannot do without it. They are the ones who suffer the most from its defects. They are also the ones who love it the most. They often say they are ready to break that detestable bond which ties them to it. But they do nothing of the kind. They keep hoping, in spite of everything. . . .

For a long time the cinema was considered an imitation of the theater. Most film industrialists will be delighted if some day the cinema, in color, in three dimensions and talking, allows them to distribute the successes of the Michodière or the Athénée[1] to the provinces in a hundred copies. On that day their dream will be fulfilled: the cinema will be dead.

Many "cinema people" come from the theater in one form or another. They retain a tremendous respect for that theater, which often wanted nothing to do with them. To those are added the illiterate members of the corporation, who, in their touching ignorance, see the theater as a temple of intellect, or in any case as a performing-art form infinitely superior to this magic lantern which they themselves present with smiles and excuses.

Theater people and cinema people influenced by the theater continue to regard the screen with the same indulgent interest Mr. Antoine[2] had in cafés-concerts, from which he would sometimes hire a performer: "Obviously it isn't art, but there's something in it . . . ."

It is impossible, for example, to see Murnau's *Sunrise* without reading Mr. Henry Bernstein's opinion of the film by way of a preface.[3] Can you picture a character who would come out before the first act of *Secret* and read us Mr. Murnau's opinion of Mr. Bernstein's play? That would seem like an unusual and ridiculous procedure to the director of the Gymnase Theater. It seems perfectly natural to the heads of Fox Film, and this makes their way of thinking clear: the screen is a poor relation of the stage; playwrights are "intellectuals" who do film authors

[1]Two Parisian legitimate theaters.—ED.

[2]André Antoine, founder and principal actor of the Théâtre Libre.—ED.

[3]The film was preceded by a projected printed critical commentary, much in the fashion of the prefatory titles the Museum of Modern Art attaches to the prints it circulates in America.—ED.

—be they Chaplin, Stroheim or Murnau—great honor when they deign to pay attention to them . . . .

1970. You can see: times certainly have changed, and nowadays it would not seem at all out of place for a noted film-maker to give his opinion on a play. Today more books and essays are devoted to the cinema than to the stage.

In the past, it is said, the theater was primarily a "middle-class" entertainment enterprise. Perhaps. But is the cinema of our day always intended for the masses? Is it not in some way taking the place of what the middle-class theater was yesterday? It is the descendants of those who once applauded Porto-Riche and Alfred Capus[1] who talk the most, at dinner parties, about the films that "must be seen."

¶ The name of Erich von Stroheim has just come up; this is a name which cannot decently be mentioned without stopping to salute a man whose work is of major importance and whose life was a symbol.

To gauge the full importance of his work it is necessary to go back through the years and put yourself in the era when it appeared. This is the case for all the authentic creations in the history of the cinema. Time lessens their power to shock; physical changes deface them; the inspirations they awoke and the imitations made of them tend to rob them of their claim to originality. But the work of Erich von Stroheim, mutilated as it is, still shines with the glow of its unusual novelty.

The system that formerly held sway in Hollywood threw out the film-maker who, with Chaplin, was the greatest of those whose style influenced the American film. It is in the light of that fact that the life of Erich von Stroheim is symbolic, because the battle between the individual and the machine is far from over. The career of this creator lasted only about ten years. After that, he was only an actor and, excellent as he was in this capacity, we cannot help thinking about the films he might have made himself, films we shall never see.

His first films had been enormously successful, and their author

---

[1] Turn-of-the-century playwrights whose work, now virtually forgotten, once held a certain vogue in France.—ED.

was reigning over an industry that was unwilling to submit to his dictates. But it was a dangerous game. To keep it up, each success would have had to be followed by an even greater one. At the least sign of slipping, the crash would be brutal and mediocrity would take its revenge.

On the day when a young employee of the Universal Company named Irving Thalberg took it upon himself to interrupt the shooting of *Merry-Go-Round,* which Stroheim was directing, and to assign a director of his choice to finish it, a new era began. The age of the great individuals, thanks to whom the American cinema had reached full flowering, was coming to an end and making way for the quasi-anonymous reign of the producers, administrators and bankers. And Hollywood was to develop an organization so perfect that it would be able henceforth to defend itself with all its might against any possible intrusion of genius.

Genius! In the language of cinema, what is the worth of this word, prostituted by ambiguity and the confusion of values? An author of genius is one who creates without imitating and who draws from his own substance the best and most *unexpected* part of his work.

How many people are there in the history of the cinema who can fit this definition? No matter how many there are, Erich von Stroheim is at the head of the list. He owes nothing to anyone. We are all in the debt of this man who died in poverty.

What has not been said about Erich von Stroheim! That the name he made famous was not his, that he invented the particle "von," that he was the author of his own legend, that he had never been the Austrian officer whose unforgettable figure he incarnated in his films . . . . All of that, which is possible, hardly interests us. His nobility, like his past, even if he fabricated it, is truer for us than if he had had the proof of it in some parchment. What he himself was is less real than what he created.

In Hollywood, I saw him at a party in his home, in which he played to perfection his role of a European host: kissing of hands, monocle, politeness and considerateness. Now, everyone knew that he drank a lot and we might expect some uproar before the evening was over. But that night he drank nothing but water and behaved like the most perfect of all the aristocrats whose manners he had observed, being an attentive director. Perhaps he was not a nobleman, but he had been able to make a lord of himself.

A few days before his death, the French government made him a Knight of the Legion of Honor. The decoration was presented to him in a house he had rented near Paris, in the presence of many guests, and it was at that celebration, where champagne was drunk around a dying man—in the baroque atmosphere of his own films—that he played his last role.

Unable to move, he was lying on a sort of stretcher placed in the center of the drawing room. When the cross was pinned to his black silk pajama shirt, he managed to sit up on his resting place, and he gave a military salute. This gesture, which, though pompous, caused no one to smile, gave a final confirmation to his legend; for his last audience he became once again the Viennese officer who had perhaps existed only in the land of his imagination.

1927. I could never finish totaling up the serious or childish ways in which those who make their living from the cinema have betrayed it . . . . The intellectual poverty of cinema people makes me shudder when I think that these are the men guiding the destinies of such a young art, and one to which we attach so much importance. They have seen nothing, read nothing, understood nothing. It is useless to seek in their speeches or actions the trace of any general idea that can be discussed, or at least the excuse for their ignorance and mistaken notions. Nothing is to be found there but hucksters' spiels, dangerous and futureless schemes. They live and think from day to day, and fear nothing so much as that their trade might develop and that progress might kick them out of their jobs . . . . They would be pitiful if they were not so strong, because of their numbers, and so impudent.

Let us add to these bitter reflections from which excerpts have just been given, this note taken from an article entitled "Millions," which dates from the same period, but could have been written only yesterday. Nothing has changed, except the real value of the millions that are discussed:

René Clair and Erich von Stroheim at the celebration of Stroheim's Legion of Honor. (Photo courtesy Denise Vernac)

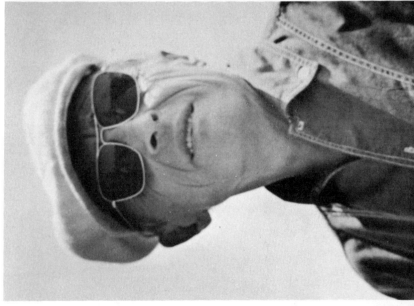

Two camera portraits of René Clair. (René Clair collection)

1927. Every year several "big films" appear on the screen. This is the name given to films on which at least five million has been spent (francs or dollars, no matter—since five million francs are rarer in France than five million dollars in the U.S.). The last record seemed to have been established by *Metropolis,* a German film which ran to five or six million gold marks. But the United States did not let Europe keep the record long; they have called our attention to *Ben-Hur* and to the sum spent on it: a hundred fifty million, they say, in our currency.

The press is ecstatic; seeing the screen filled with sagging plaster and made-up crowds, some good people discover the grandeur of the cinema. The creators of these films, who are at times talented men, are immediately consecrated as great men. (In the cinema, a film-maker's value increases in direct proportion to the number of millions he spends.) Thus, everybody is happy. Who goes next?

It is because of similar practices that the cinema (at least what a few of us call the cinema) is heading for a gilded end. People smiled when I spoke about the end of the cinema. I was hardly trying to be amusing: the cinema will die of money.

Art and money, creative intelligence and the rules of finance, are here at grips with one another. Take care! To guide our art toward "lavish" productions, to accustom the masses to shows of which the chief quality is expensiveness, is equivalent to committing suicide. It means making the film more of a slave to money every day, whereas the laws of money are already smothering it. A film-maker who can only demonstrate his genius or talent by spending millions is often confessing his weakness by so doing, but he is furthermore often betraying the higher interests of the cinema in that way. The more need we have of the aid of financiers, the more we shall have to abandon to them what little remains of our independence.

1970. Hard times having weakened the power of the financiers, the independence of film-makers is less limited today than in 1927. Besides, the *nouveau cinéma,* as it has been called for about ten years, has shown a greater concern for originality than for expensive perfection.[1] A film made on a modest budget, even if the photography is of doubtful quality, has a chance of finding an audience, which was almost impossible in the past. But big-budget films must resort too often to i iternational co-productions. This sort of undertaking, which has rarely produced good results, was already being discussed in the last years of the silent film.

1927. A European combine? An international combine? Very well. But only providing this combine deals with the distribution of each film and not its production. The success of American films, that of German films only yesterday and the more recent success of Russian films, all prove to us that the genius of each nation must be respected. If you talk to us about business, we will ask you to tell us what success has been obtained by those insipid, conventional and soulless machines called "internationally co-produced" films.

A good automobile can be made out of parts manufactured in different countries, but not a good poem. The film is an automobile and a poem at the same time. And the two parts of its nature, its body and soul, cannot be separated without danger.

¶ The following paragraphs present the main points of an essay entitled "The Cinema Versus the Mind":

1927. As of now, the cinema, an enormous worldwide mechanism, has become stronger than the human mind that created it. And the creative spirit, the spirit of development, is dragged along by the routine of its gears. It is in this sense that we can say that the cinema, the real one and not the ideal one, the one we are experiencing and not the one we desire, is rising up against the mind. . . .

A big industrialist or a big businessman can manage his industry or business successfully. But we do not ask his opinion of Shakespeare or Lautréamont. The cinema is managed by businessmen whose turnover permits them to control even the spirit

---

[1]The term "new cinema" replaces the earlier "new wave" in French designations of cinematic movements or generations.—ED.

of the film and its development. These businessmen do not want to occupy themselves solely with figures. Like everybody else, they have artistic preferences, and naturally they think their preferences are the best. They impose them. The men who could really make the film a work of art must obey the directives of those who are only really competent in business. . . .

It is pointless to protest against these conditions, which are those of the film's existence today. Of course, the mind leaves a little of itself in this industrial product, and the little that sneaks in vanishes when the celluloid does. Film records the imaginings of the mind only at the price of expensive labors, then drags them with it into its physical death.[1] We will not live to see the revolution—will it ever occur?—that will be caused by raw film as cheap as the novelist's white paper, and developed film as durable as the sculptor's marble.

Therefore the cinema must do without the relative freedom enjoyed by the other arts. It must also abandon the claims of those arts which have striven for lasting or eternal forms. Let us resign ourselves to being merely craftsmen producing ephemeral works. If we feel some sadness at times on seeing these imperfect works disappear in a few seasons, let us constantly remind ourselves that our films are only test pieces. Our task is to prepare the materials that the cinema of the future will use. Our works do not count. The only work of art in which we believe is the development of the cinema, which is taking place thanks to all those who love it. It is a work on which the film creators of the whole world are collaborating, and while our individual works will all perish, this universal work will not.

No doubt we ourselves shall never see the cinema grow out

---

[1]At the time of Clair's observations, it was common practice to melt down films to recover their silver particles, once their commercial potential was considered to have been realized. Two of Clair's own early films, dating from this very moment, probably suffered that fate. In addition, until the end of the Second World War, most 35mm prints were made on nitrate-base stock, which was both unstable and highly explosive. Under very unfavorable conditions, the stock could begin to decompose in a few years' time. Even under excellent storage conditions, prints made before the time Clair wrote these words are now almost all in some advanced state of disintegration. The revolution Clair speaks of in the next sentence came about with the acceptance of acetate-base stock during the war. That stock is highly stable, and no period has yet even been predicted for its durability under proper storage conditions. —ED.

of its awkward age. No doubt—and we must face up to this—we will be the sacrificed generation, the screen craftsmen who were the first to catch a glimpse, but only a glimpse, of what our successors will accomplish. . . .

Industrialization may destroy tomorrow all the hopes that the discovery of the world of images awakened in us. All that would be necessary is an invention shrewdly exploited by skillful businessmen and well received by the bad taste of the public. I am not speaking of color cinema (though it may prove dangerously contagious), but, for example, *of the talking picture, a fearful monster, an unnatural creation,* thanks to which the screen would become a poor theater, the poor man's theater, whose plays—production and text—would be printed in hundreds of copies . . . . (You will shudder to learn that certain American industrialists, among the most dangerous, see in the talking picture the show of the future and are working at this very moment to fulfill this frightening prophecy.)

1970. Since this essay is not of a particularly entertaining nature, I thought it best to reproduce only a few passages of it here, and among these I was careful not to omit the above outburst directed against the talking picture, so that my readers could have a little laugh.

Let us not count on the education of the public as a factor in resisting the misdeeds of industrialization. We know these phrases: "We must wait. The public will improve itself. We must not push it too quickly. It must get accustomed to novelties, etc., etc." We are tired of these palliative formulas that have been used for too long to calm down justified rebellions. It is in this way that the best minds are reduced to a state of resignation that is allegedly temporary, but actually fatal. This type of argument, a narcosis of artistic activity, must be considered as the most dangerous. Brutal opposition is preferable to this attempt at conciliation. The broad public has never followed the development of an art quickly enough to be useful to that development in any way whatsoever. On the day that the broad public accepts and enjoys what seems to us to be an innovation, that innovation will probably be outmoded, at least for a mind that denies the cinema the right to be smugly satisfied with its past and its present.

1970. The lack of esteem for the public displayed here contradicts to some extent the trust placed in it elsewhere.

Yes, but is a man never to change his mind? Self-contradiction has this advantage: if you are wrong in one place, you have a good chance of being right in another place.

Let us not be deceived. For a long time to come, the cinema will not find its proper balance or a classic form. For a long time yet, it will be the battlefield on which the hostile inertia of mediocrity and the creative intelligence will struggle most desperately. The broad public likes order in its pleasures, and the cinema will still be a revolution for a long time.

On the other hand, it is too easy to make the public responsible for the present state of the cinema. The people really responsible are those who have perverted the public, who have accustomed it to foolish amusements, who have thought only of their immediate and most easily made profits, while serving up to the masses that vulgar poison which has made them as ill as they are today. Why have they wanted to make the cinema only an instrument of popular amusement, in the narrowest sense of the word? . . .

The spirit of the cinema will always be ahead of its mechanical organization. Some people, observing this phenomenon, have come to the conclusion that an avant-garde exists, and see the question as only an insignificant academic argument between rival factions. They do not see that all the cinema worth mentioning is nothing but an avant-garde, because only the progress of the film can interest us.

There are two types of film-makers: those who are satisfied with existing formulas and stick to their brief past, and those who see a constant evolution in the cinema and stake their fortunes on progress. A few seasons ago, certain improvements attracted the attention of some of these experimenters; it must be frankly admitted that they abused them at times. But can they fairly be blamed for some experimental excesses, while all around them so many others were committing sins of excess routine? Their adversaries did not stop to consider this, and gave the blanket name of "avant-garde" (lazy minds love open-and-shut classifications) to films that were merely pushing technical experiments that everybody uses today.

But if the term "avant-garde" is taken in its true sense and applied to those who are ahead of the rest in making progress, many of us will strive to earn our place in that number. The true avant-garde exists. Charlie Chaplin, who revolutionized the American dramatic cinema with his first drama, is at the head of it. . . .

Today there is no longer a school divided by purely technical disagreements. There are, on the one side, film-makers who derive from a subject a succession of more or less theatrical images framed by numerous intertitles and, on the other, those who attempt to present an action by means that are purely visual and more expressive than long sentences.

The first group can go on building the most lavish sets and hiring the best actors—they will never do more than illustrate a story that would be better understood if it were written in a book. The others, starting off with a subject that is sometimes insignificant, will create a drama that no other mode of artistic expression could have made more moving. When the first group have reconstructed Notre-Dame in front of the camera, they think they have fulfilled the loftiest destiny of the cinema. They have not done much more than a book illustrator would do for an edition of Hugo's novel. The others attach more importance to that bureau drawer from which there emerges a dress collar —and an entire drama—in *A Woman of Paris*.[1]

But do not jump to conclusions. The "avant-garde" will not always mean the search for psychological details any more than it is still the search for technical effects that it seemed to be yesterday. It will always be in advance of the definitions within which the laggards would like to imprison it. The avant-garde is an inquisitive mind applied to an area in which there are still many thrilling discoveries to be made. If this meaning is given to the term, then only this vilified avant-garde interests me.

---

[1] The heroine, who has become a kept woman in Paris, accidentally meets her former village sweetheart. When she shows him her gowns, a collar belonging to the playboy who maintains her falls from among them onto the floor. —ED.

1970. ". . . a succession of more or less theatrical images framed by numerous intertitles." Before long people were going to speak about images accompanied by too much dialogue. At the very hour that these lines were written, the screen was beginning to stammer in the United States and Germany. The time of silence was past. Soon it would be possible to say: ". . . we remember so many marvelous and melancholy hopes with the regret that people feel for what might have been."*

This last sentence seems to outline the tragic destiny of Robert Brasillach, who has left one of the most moving testimonials to the love the cinema could then inspire in a young man.

When Robert Brasillach arrived in Paris at the age of sixteen, Chaplin had just given us *The Gold Rush* and Eisenstein, *The Battleship Potemkin,* Hollywood had not yet stifled the genius of Stroheim, Sternberg was enjoying his first success, Flaherty was composing *Moana,* Abel Gance was starting *Napoleon,* and American comedies were continuing to raise laughter in the four corners of the world.† Is was the "classic era of the silent film," an era comparable to the Elizabethan age in the theater. Soon everything people had taken for granted was to be called into question. The talking picture was to be born.

It was at the Ecole Normale, "at that time one of the most surprising sanctuaries of poetic anarchy,"‡ that Brasillach met Maurice Bardèche.[1] The cinema attracted them, they frequented the earliest film societies, which showed the experiments of "pure cinema," Dadaist and Surrealist films, and Soviet productions, which the pompous and empty-headed censors would not allow to be distributed publicly. Later on, chance put into their hands a run of the magazine *Cinea,* which had been founded by Louis Delluc and which was then being edited by

---

*Maurice Bardèche and Robert Brasillach, *Histoire du cinéma.*

†This section is an excerpt from a preface by René Clair to *Histoire du cinéma* (in the *Complete Works* of Robert Brasillach, Club de l'Honnête Homme, 1963) .

‡Robert Brasillach, *Notre Avant-guerre* (The prewar period as we saw it) .
[1]The Ecole Normale Supérieure is France's most prestigious secondary school, attracting the country's most gifted students to its Paris halls.—ED.

Jean Tedesco and published with the title *Cinea—Ciné pour tous*.[1] In it they found numerous documents of a very recent past which already seemed fabulously distant. It was a great discovery.

The shades of this past—fairground booths, film sold by the yard, glass-roofed studios—had just recently been conjured up. The "prewar" films screened at the Ursulines had raised laughter. But after having a good laugh, people had realized that the primitives of the moving image deserved more than that. It was recalled that Lumière and Méliès had existed. It was noticed that the former had been the forerunner of the realistic cinema, that the latter had created the fiction film and the film of poetic freedom, that a French school of comedy had preceded the American school, that all these ancestors were unjustly forgotten, and that the humble beginnings of the new art had shown the essential lines of its destiny.

In 1935, on the occasion of the cinema's fortieth birthday, Bardèche and Brasillach published their *Histoire du cinéma*. It is not unnecessary to recall this date, because we believe that time has justified any presumptuousness that appears in the title of the book. At that time the authors were personally familiar with only ten years of this history, but it so happens that those ten years—the transition from silent to talking pictures—are of capital importance and that no other era has equaled them for their variety of experiments, the freshness of their inventions and their abundance of fine achievements. Here, the reader is given permission to smile and to consider that memory is a magnifying glass that gives everything connected with our youth outsized proportions.

This *History of the Cinema* also tells the history of a youthful period. These pages contain the breath of an era when film was the big thing, when young people raced from the movie houses on the Left Bank to those on the Boulevards with the same zeal that impelled them to read Proust, Céline, Aragon or Bernanos, when they were so impassioned that they did not worry about looking serious, and when they practiced the only nonconformity that is not a fraud: the freedom of thinking for oneself.

There was no lack of arguments at the time, and this book

---

[1] *Cinea—Cinema for Everybody.*—ED.

lets us hear their distant echoes. But if you do not always agree with the authors, you cannot fail to be charmed by their enthusiasm and high spirits. They like to like things, and they do not take the time to find fault with things they do not enjoy. Their work does not contain any of those formal oppositions or childish ostracisms forced on members of a coterie or a party. Furthermore, since they know what they mean, they write clearly and do not resort to obscurity in order to appear profound. These graduates of the Ecole Normale are not concerned with displaying their knowledge, and their political tendencies do not lead their judgments astray. All that, at the time I write this, is scarcely in fashion.*

The thing they disapprove of is the middle-class film, the heritage of bygone drama and tiresome fiction, everything that threatens to gangrene an art which has nothing to do with the past. Therefore, when they talk about Soviet films they are ecstatic. With the exception of Chaplin, "the humiliated and happy little man who is the only popular hero our age has created," their warmest admiration is for Eisenstein: "No one has leveled a more precise and resolute camera at the universe. . . . Abstraction and sensuality are combined in his work as in that of the greatest creators. He would have been a creator elsewhere, in America, in Germany. In Russia he found his atmosphere and his era."

If these historians had adopted a motto, it would have been: "Poetry first." But where is the place for the poet in the gigantic cinema machine? They give him his place, and it is at the top: "Like every art, the cinema is style—that is, an individual work of art expressed according to an individual variety. It does not seem that the discoveries made in the cinema since 1929 or those that are yet to be made will be able to make us change our mind. . . ."

¶ Were "style" and the "individual work of art" going to survive the coming of sound? Our fears may be surprising today, but in that year 1929—as will be seen later—many of us said, like the authors of *Histoire du cinéma*: "We who have seen an art being born may also have seen it die."

---

*"We were not without intellectual friendly feelings for Communism in that period," *op. cit.*

And the Word Came

The thing Voltaire called "His Sacred Majesty, Chance" concerned itself with the cinema from its birth and continued to contribute to its development. Marey,[1] the Lumière Brothers and Edison thought they had invented only a scientific toy, but this toy, though they had not intended it, gave rise to a new art. Later on, the Warner Brothers, whose business was shaky, risked their all on the talking picture, which was an old idea as hackneyed as the newspapers' sea serpent. After this wager had been won, all the film industries in the world, though no one predicted it, adopted sound. Later still, in hopes of easing its financial difficulties, the Fox corporation introduced as something new the Hypergonar lens, which had been around for a long time. It caught people's fancy and, though no one desired it, every screen got wider.

When a few theaters in the United States began screening talking films, the news was first received in Europe with skepticism, then with alarm, as if it reported an epidemic affecting a faraway country and the whole breadth of the Atlantic might not be enough to protect Europe.

But in 1928, Jesse F. Lasky, president of the American firm Famous Players, while passing through Europe, publicly confirmed the rumors that had reached us and had warned us that the days of the cinema as we knew it were numbered. The first successes of the sound and talking picture were so great that they guaranteed the new invention would conquer the world. For those who had shared our expectations, such news meant nothing else than the end of the cinema.

An amusing anthology could be made of the opinions expressed at that time in the cinema world. They can be summed up as follows: while most intellectuals and artists were frightened at the danger threatening not only an art, but also a universal medium of expression, an alchemy of images, the industrialists and businessmen favored a novelty that held out the promise of bigger profits. The critic Emile Vuillermoz summed up the debate in a few lines:

---

[1]Marey conducted experiments in the nineteenth century that contributed to the eventual realization of motion pictures.—ED.

The primordial misunderstanding is still going on. Every time science furnishes our film industrialists with a new means of taking a step forward, they use it for taking three steps backward. They have only one ambition, to copy and reconstitute the old show business formulas more cheaply and to mass-produce them. For these people, the cinema is still photographed theater. When they have acquired color, it will give them pleasure to be able to offer that exact shade of the costumes and sets of a Boulevard play, and when they have acquired phonotography, they will be delighted to add to that the voice of a popular performer. Every means they are given to escape into the unknown, they will use to make their imitative instinct more servile. Now, the cinema can rise to the dignity of an art *only by transposition*. Three-dimensionality, color and sound could theoretically make this tendency even more powerful: *in practice, they will make it more and more difficult.** They will give the unimaginative laborers convenient new procedures for making tracings. This so-called progress is in danger of bogging down the seventh art.

This is because the present masters of the cinema are like painters who try for nothing in a painting but a likeness and the illusion of reality, or composers who use an orchestra only for reproducing as exactly as possible the noise of a passing train, a closing door or a carpenter's plane tearing shavings off a fir plank. Is this the ideal on which a mode of artistic expression can be based?

A similar opinion was expressed by many friends of the cinema. Among these, let us quote Pierre Scize:

> Given the fact that the masses are drawn to the mediocre as irresistibly as water plunges toward the sea; given the further fact that the film industry and business are unable, on pain of death, to relinquish quenching the mob's thirst for vulgarity, anything can be feared from the talking picture. The retrogression it is bringing us seems fatal, unavoidable.

As for me, I wrote in much the same terms:

Mr. Lasky announces the coming of the talking picture. Is that all? And should we put on gloomy faces because we are informed of "progress?"

It is always unpleasant to be forced to take a public stand against progress. Thiers was "run over" by the locomotive whose budding virtues he contested.[1] Therefore we must be cautious.

---

*Italics mine.

[1] Thiers was a nineteenth-century French statesman who vehemently but unsuccessfully opposed extension of the French railway system.—ED.

It is not the invention of the talking picture that frightens us, it is the deplorable use our industrialists will not fail to make of it.

The sound film or, more precisely, the synchronization between the reproduction of images and sounds, could be useful in the musical accompaniment of films, in newsreels, in educational cinema, etc. It is not even out of the question that an art peculiar to the talking film might be created, an art the object and laws of which we cannot foresee any more than those of the film in general were foreseen around 1900.

But it would be mistaking our "cinema people" to let our hopes run toward those horizons.

¶ It was in London that the talking picture, after conquering America, began the conquest of Europe. Alexandre Arnoux, then editor-in-chief of *Pour Vous,* went to London. The excerpt below from the article he brought back merits quotation. It expresses the astonishment of a civilized man who had believed in the "promises of a wonderful art," promises which "a savage invention" was threatening to destroy. Let us join him as he attends one of the first talking-picture performances:

> Right at the start the general effect is rather disconcerting. Since the loudspeaker installed behind the screen never changes its locus of sound propagation, the voice always comes from the same spot no matter which character is speaking. The synchronization is perfect, of course, but it confuses and annoys the listener. If this annoyance is analyzed, it is soon seen that by the very fact that it has been achieved, the concordance of lip movements and spoken syllables strengthens our demands for credibility and forces us to locate the sound in space—in fact, makes this absolutely indispensable. Otherwise, we are faced with a strange comedy, in which the actors are closely miming the lines with their mouths, while a mysterious ventriloquistic chorus leader, rigid and motionless in the center of the screen, at a certain depth, takes charge of the audible part of their silent speeches.
>
> To palliate this shortcoming, no doubt, and perhaps also because of technical difficulties, the director has avoided, as much as possible, changing shots and looking for varied camera angles, at least during conversations. This leads to extreme cinematic monotony, a clumsy continuity and a static quality which brings us back directly to the theater and a text declaimed in front of

the footlights. As soon as an actor is released from the necessity to speak, the interest surges back. We may wonder whether speech does not rob expression of more elements than it brings to it. . . .

I am making an effort to be impartial. Perhaps I am not succeeding very well. How can a man travel and see things without bringing along himself and his prejudices? I love the cinema deeply. Its interplay of black and white, its silence, its linked rhythms of images, its relegation of speech, that old human bondage, to the background, seem to me the promises of a wonderful art. And now a savage invention has come along to destroy everything. I may be pardoned for some bitterness and unfairness. After so much work and so many hopes, to return at the end to a formula as outworn as the theater, to submit once again to the tyranny of words and noise, which is further aggravated by a mechanical intermediary! And yet . . . .

We cannot remain indifferent. We are present at a death or a birth, no one can yet tell which. Something decisive is going on in the world of the screen and of sound. We must open our eyes and ears. Who twenty years ago, watching those ridiculous reels so trammeled by stage conventions, would have predicted the film of today, *The Circus* and *An Italian Straw Hat, The Passion of Joan of Arc* and *Underworld?* A second birth, or death? That is the question facing the cinema.

¶ This article, which even today contains food for thought ("we may wonder whether speech does not rob expression of more elements than it brings to it"), gave us few reasons to be hopeful. I made an effort to discover some myself when I commented on it:

1929. Second birth, or death? If chance—a few grains of sand in the industrial machine—does not come along to foil the plans of the financiers of the cinema, *we must place our wager on death, or at least on a long sleep that resembles it.* What is the cinema for us? A new medium of expression, a new poetry and dramaturgy. What is it for them? Fifty thousand theaters all over the world that must be supplied with a show—film, music, variety acts or a sheep with five legs—capable of making the spectator's money pour into the box office. It is only by chance that our interests and theirs have sometimes coincided. The stand taken by American finance, and soon by European finance, on the question of talking pictures finally enlightens us in this regard. What if the cinema, this new medium of expression, should die before it has given the hundredth part of what the human mind could well expect of it? That worry is certainly the least of those occupying the present masters of the cinema. Profits first.

Should we despair? If we consider the probable development of the industrial arts, we might possibly find some reason for placing our trust in the unforeseen. *The talking picture, in its present inferior form or in its improved form of tomorrow, will certainly be only one of the phases of a development the end of which we cannot foresee.* Television will appear and all the problems will be raised again. Are we sure that television will not inspire a new technology, that it will not give rise to new means of expression which we are unable to imagine today? If the talking picture looks like the audial getting even with the visual, *will not television be a new triumph for the visual* and the definitive basis for an art of images?

Film, color film, talking film, three-dimensional film, televison: these are the new media of expression science offers us. Still others will arise. The struggle between industry and the spirit of artistic creation is just beginning. Industry will want to subjugate these media to the sole purpose of finding new sources of profits in them. The mind will try to use them as new modes of expression. We have no way of foreseeing the outcome of this struggle, and it may never have an outcome. If, on the one hand, the triumphant power of industry seems to be without immediate limits, on the other hand we have no reason to lose all hope in the resources and adaptability of the creative mind, without whose aid the industrial arts would be bereft of soul, and shortly afterward, of life.

1970. "We must place our wager on death, or at least on a long sleep that resembles it." This sentence, the last words of which I have italicized above, contained a prediction which proved to be completely false for some years. During the early period of the sound and talking picture, the spirit of invention was stimulated by the novelty of the technology.

But there is at least one true view in the preceding. The confusion we found ourselves in at that time made us open our eyes. The revolution caused by the talking picture permitted us to foresee for the first time that the cinema was only at the beginning of a development "the end of which we cannot foresee." That was a new idea and one that, to my knowledge, had hardly ever been expressed in silent film days.

Reader of today, do not make fun of our naïveté. The cinema as you know it is itself only one of the phases of the development the end of which cannot be foreseen.

A Visit to the Monster

I

Long after the trip to London during which he observed the first effects of the "savage invention," Alexandre Arnoux, smiling at the recollection of our fears and gloom, was to write: "In my opinion, there is no greater sin than indulging in nostalgia."

I was committing this sin in advance when I, too, went to London to confront the newborn monster. In the letters I sent to that same *Pour Vous*, I expressed feelings that can scarcely be understood now. But if you just think about it for a moment, you will realize that the adventure in which we were then engaged is certainly unique in the history of arts and technology. Media of expression develop gradually in the course of centuries; for example, music did not pass suddenly from Gregorian chant to the symphony orchestra. But we were being asked to change our tools and our language in a few months. Hence, our hesitation, trouble of mind, and regrets.

May 1929. No man, no firm, no financial coalition could today halt the victorious advance of the talking picture. The American cinema industrialists say they were following the will of the public, and the public expressed its desire for the "talkies."

But if this public were suddenly to lose interest in this new toy, the same compliant industrialists would no longer surrender to their wishes. In the meantime the talking picture has become one of the big business ventures of the era. Banks and electrical companies as powerful as empires are tied to its destiny.

So many billions have been gambled on this undertaking that from now on they will go to any extreme to assure its success. . . .

1970. That was a completely mistaken assertion, which showed a total ignorance of the rules of American industry, which, more than any other, is subject to the verdict of the public.

If the talking picture had not pleased that public, Hollywood would very likely have beaten a retreat, no matter how great its losses were. That is what happens, for instance, in a publicity campaign for a film. If the first results after the release of a film are poor, the rules of the game demand cutting off the publicity expenditures without delay, any outlay from that time on being considered an additional loss. If, on the contrary, the results are excellent, the publicity budget is immediately increased. In movie houses as in stores, for Americans the customer is always right.

. . . The talking picture exists, and the skeptics who claim that its reign will be brief will not live long enough to see the end of it. The time has passed for those who love the art of images to lament the effects of this barbarian invasion. Instead, we must cut our losses.

But the talking film is not everything; the sound film exists too. It is the sound film that carries the last hopes of the partisans of wordless cinema. They hope it will help them ward off the danger that the coming of the "talkies" represents. They want to believe that these noises and sounds accompanying the moving image will amuse the masses sufficiently and keep it from demanding dialogue, that they will give it an illusion of "reality" less dangerous for the art of images than the talking picture.

There is reason to fear that this solution will only half satisfy the general public. If almost everyone is in agreement on the value of mechanically reproduced music, indissolubly tied to the image, which is so much preferable to the improvised scores of movie orchestras, the same is not true for the noises that are added to the action. The usefulness of these noises is too often questionable. On first hearing, they are surprising and entertaining. Soon they grow tiring. When you have heard a certain number of sound films and the time of wonderment has passed, you discover, not without surprise, that the world of noises seems much more limited than you would have believed earlier. . . .

1950. The cinema and the radio have merely repeated the sound effects discovered in the very first experiments. Whereas *organized* sound (music or the human voice) lends itself to an infinite number of combinations, the number of *natural* sounds that can be used for dramatic ends is extremely small.

In the first days of the sound film, practically every sound the microphone could pick up was recorded. It was soon noticed that the direct reproduction of reality gave the most unreal impression possible, and that sounds had to be *chosen* just as images were. (If you are carrying on a conversation of some interest on a street where noisy cars are going by, your eye pays no more attention to the shape of these cars than your ear does to the noise they make.)

It is because of this relative poverty of the catalogue of noises that music is used so frequently and, I must say, so arbitrarily in most films. There, too, the progress made in the last twenty years is quite modest. It was hoped that the sound cinema would give rise to an entirely new type of music, conceived for the microphone and the loudspeaker, and so intimately tied in with the film that it would be almost impossible to separate them. Now, it has to be admitted that, outside of a few exceptional cases, nothing like this has happened and that the music written for films is not outstanding for its basic originality. The score of *Entr'acte* that Erik Satie wrote in 1924 to accompany a silent film is more "cinematic" than many scores written today for sound films.

. . . No doubt experiment has only begun, but it is still surprising that in so little time the sound film has already produced clichés. As soon as you have "heard" twenty of these films, you can already observe that the effects of the sound cinema seem a little tired and that it is time to look for new ones: the jazz rehearsal, the tearful song, the striking clock, the cuckoo calling the hours, the applause in the nightclub, the automobile motor and the dishes breaking are all very nice, of course, but tend to become somewhat fatiguing after you have heard them ten times in ten different films.

A distinction should be made between sound effects that are entertaining merely because of their novelty (which people will tire of quickly) and those that aid in the understanding of the action and serve to awaken an emotion that the view of the image alone would not have awakened; this latter type is the most rare and this rarity must cause some worry. Right from its cinematic birth, the world of images seemed much, much richer. . . . (And yet if the *imitation* of "real" sounds is disappointing and seems limited, it is possible that the *interpretation* of sounds will have a better future. Sound cartoons, made up of "real" noises, give an interesting indication of this development.)

If new sound effects are not found and judiciously used, there is reason to fear that the partisans of the film with sound but no words will be disappointed before long. In that case we would be left with the talking picture only, and that prospect is not at all delightful.

In London it can be observed that the Americans were not exaggerating when they told us about the extraordinary attraction the talking picture has for the masses. From noon to eleven at night, one group of spectators replaces another and the houses are always full. A few months ago the sound of American slang elicited smiles, but today no one is surprised at it any more, and tomorrow it may affect the speech of Londoners.

Three legitimate theaters have closed their doors in this past month and reopened as talking picture houses (one of them was showing a very bad film: no matter how little one may like the theater, one could not help missing the lively glow of the footlights at the sight of that empty orchestra pit covered with flowers like a dead woman, that dark stage, that lugubrious temple in which pallid faces were exchanging stentorian secrets in the night). The other theaters are struggling painfully and are trying to keep their audiences by lowering the price of admission. The newspapers devote long articles to the "talkies" almost every day, criticizing, fighting, praising, and announcing new inventions, unusual projects and new firms.

If you wish to understand the problem of the talking picture, and to see why the talking picture will be predominantly a product of American industry, you must remember that of the approximately forty thousand screens in the world, the United States possesses twenty thousand and the other English-speaking countries four or five thousand. Therefore, twenty-five thousand movie houses, in principle, can show American talking pictures without modifying them. Now, these houses are well supplied with pounds and dollars. . . .

In Europe, the variety of languages will prevent the production of big talking pictures whose cost price cannot be amortized. No doubt the Europeans and the Americans themselves will try to get around this difficulty and produce talking pictures in several languages. But that is a problem for tomorrow, and there is no indication that it is to be solved in the near future. . . .

1950. The problem is still not solved, and the Tower of Babel continues to be the symbol of the talking picture.

Everyone knows the disadvantages of subtitles in foreign talking pictures, which compel the viewer to read sentences and keep him from seeing what is happening on the screen at the same time. As for dubbing, Jean Renoir is quite correct in saying that if the people who perpetrate this crime had lived in a rational period like the Middle Ages, they would have been burnt in the public square for givng a body a voice that does not belong to it, which strongly resembles a misdeed of witchcraft. (It is surprising that actors, who generally show so much concern for their glory and take such pains to safeguard "the dignity of the acting profession," passively accept a degrading practice that is the very negation of their craft.)

The "talkie" has given rise to many another oddity. For example, a Hollywood producer will spend a fortune—let us say, for a war film—building a German town and a French town. And on these sets, where nothing has been spared to achieve "local color" and the authenticity of the smallest detail, both the alleged Germans and the so-called Frenchmen will speak . . . English in unison. This contrast between the concern for realism and the convention that destroys its effect is an absurdity worthy of Alphonse Allais.[1]

This observation could be answered by saying that the theater has set the example for this absurdity, and that Corneille's Spaniards and Racine's Turks spoke the language of Mme. de Sévigné. This answer is meaningless to anyone who has reflected on the nature of the theater and that of the cinema. The theater does not claim to be presenting the view of a real action, but *the completely conventional figuration of an action* unfolding according to the rules of a game in which the spectator joins. It is unimportant within this fictitious framework of sets

---

[1]Allais was a nineteenth-century humorist. See also note on page 247.—ED.

whether the language of the characters is not the one they would use in reality.

In the cinema, if so much care is expended on the construction of the sets, it is in order that there will be no perceptible difference between the photographic reproduction of a real street and that of a street constructed for the needs of the film. The action shown on the screen in most films is meant to give the impression of what that same action would be *if it had really occurred and had been photographed.*

The performing arts are made up of conventions, I know. But it is still necessary that in any given genre the conventions do not contradict each other.

. . . It is unnecessary to pay attention to the bad talking pictures, which are not rare; *Give and Take* and *The Strange Cargo* are perfect examples of these.

Here, the image is reduced precisely to the role of the illustration of a phonograph record, and the sole aim of the whole show is to resemble as closely as possible the play of which it is the "cinematic" reproduction. In three or four settings there take place endless scenes of dialogue which are merely boring if you do not understand English, but unbearable if you do. The witticisms which adorn this dialogue give us a foretaste of what the French talking picture will be in the hands of those among our producers who have already proved in silent films how much they love the worst kind of theater.

If these people were not incorrigible, we could not urge them strongly enough, before they undertake a French talking production, to see *The Broadway Melody,* which is all talking, *Show Boat,* which is sound and partly talking, and those extraordinary sound cartoons which today represent unquestionably the finest achievement of the new cinema.

II

May 1929. *The Broadway Melody* is the film that is enjoying the greatest success in London at this time. It is a recently released American production that represents a summa of the improvements made in the talking picture since the showing of *The Jazz Singer*. For anyone with even the slightest knowledge of the complicated technique of sound recording, a film like this is amazing. The director, Harry Beaumont, and his co-workers (there are about fifteen of them, all named at the beginning of the film, in addition to the actors) seem to have given themselves the pleasure of playing with every difficulty of camera work and sound recording. The actors move around, walk, run, talk, shout and sigh, and the equipment reproduces their movements and voices with a suppleness that would be like a miracle if we did not know that science and meticulous organization will lead us to see many more wonders like these. Here, nothing is left to chance. The craftsmen of this film have worked with the precision of engineers, and it is a lesson for those who believe that the production of a film can still tolerate that disorder which is called inspiration.

With *The Broadway Melody* the talking picture has found its form for the first time: neither cinema nor theater, but a new genre. The immobility of the shots—that flaw of the talking picture—has disappeared. The camera is as mobile, the shots as varied, as in a good silent film. The acting is excellent, and Bessie Love speaking manages to outdo the silent Bessie Love we admired so often in the past. The sound effects are used with intelligence, and if some of them still seem superfluous, others can be held up as models.

For example, the sound of a car door being shut and the car pulling away, which is heard while, on the screen, the anguished face of Bessie Love watches this unseen departure from a window. This brief scene—in which all the effect is concentrated on the actress's face, and which the silent film would have had to break up into several shots—owes its success to the "unity of place" obtained by the use of sound.[1]

In another scene, Bessie Love is in bed, sad and pensive; you feel that she is about to cry: she puckers up her face, but it disappears into the shadow of a fadeout, and from the screen,

[1] The unity of place was one of the three unities prescribed by neo-classical theoreticians for the composition of acceptable drama. According to them, a play had to confine itself to a single location in order to maintain dramatic integrity and credibility. Clair here distorts the concept to suit his own purpose. —ED.

which has turned black, issues the sound of a single sob.

In these two examples it will be noted that at the right moment sound has replaced the image. It seems that it is in this economy of its means of expression that the sound cinema has a chance to find original effects. It is unimportant to *hear* the sound of applause if you *see* hands clapping. When the period of these coarse and unnecessary sound effects has gone by, talented film-makers will probably follow in the sound film the lesson Charlie Chaplin gives in the silent film when he suggests the arrival of a train by the shadow of the cars passing over a face. (But will the public, and especially the producers, be satisfied with such a discreet use of sound? Will they not prefer the imitation of *every sound* to the intelligent choice of certain useful sounds?)

Even in the dialogues of the talking picture, it seems that at the moment a sentence is spoken it is often more interesting to see the face of the listener than that of the speaker. The American film-makers have probably made this observation, because it can be noticed that the best of them take advantage of it frequently and not unskillfully. This is important and indicates that, in the talking picture, they have finished with the first phase, which consisted of showing, with childish persistence, that the actor's mouth was opening exactly at the moment of sound emission—in short, that the mechanism was working properly.

It is the *alternate* use of the image of a subject and the sound produced by this subject—and not their *simultaneous* use—that creates the best effects in the sound and talking picture. This first rule to emerge from the chaos of the brand-new technique may possibly become one of the laws of the technique of tomorrow.

Close Harmony, younger brother of *The Broadway Melody,* also offers scenes taking place backstage in a musical comedy theater. (They will not be the last! Like nobility, sound obliges. . . .) There is nothing special to be noted about this middling film, except a fight scene in a nightclub in which the battle of the two men remains invisible (they are hidden by the spectators crowding around them), but is suggested by shouts and noises.

As in *The Broadway Melody,* the performances are very good: Charles Rogers speaks, dances, sings and plays every instrument in a jazz band one after another. The other performers are flexible and their vocal acting is as natural as their mute acting was in silent films. The absence of theatrical affectations in their voices leads me to think that stage actors are not more suitable than the others to play roles in talking pictures. Film actors who have never spoken will perhaps do better than they in this new genre. But it is especially in the musical theater— to judge by the American example—that the talking cinema will find its best performers.

The two above-mentioned films are both "100% all talking," as the phrase goes here. *Show Boat* is something different. This big film was probably not intended to be a talking picture. But during the twelve months it took to make it, the success of the "talkies" was established and *Show Boat* was converted to fit the fashion. This conversion results in a hybrid film in which silent scenes (the characters expressing their thoughts in written intertitles) alternate with sung and spoken scenes. The mixture is not as shocking as might be imagined, although in theory this formula is as indefensible as that of the *opéra-comique.*[1] But it has given us two remarkable scenes.

The first takes place in the auditorium of the little theater on the show boat. An actor and an actress are on stage. They declaim their roles in a solemn voice, but in lower tones make a real declaration of love to each other and arrange a rendez-vous after the performance. All this takes place in full view of the deeply affected audience and of the manager, who is imitating the song of a nightingale in the wings. You can imagine what a skillful director has done with the alternation of the affected declamation and the sincere whisper, the interplay of long and close shots. Neither the silent cinema nor the theater could have created that effect.

Later in the film, a poorly clad woman singer is performing in a little café. The film-maker wanted to show this woman's rise to success in capsule form. While the song is continuing, the

[1]The *opéra-comique* mixes songs and music with spoken dialogue. As we see from Clair's remarks, neo-classical insistence on purity of genres lingers on in French culture, centuries after it was actually canon—even after Romantic drama waged its major campaign against it and theoretically won.—ED.

"With *Broadway Melody* the talking picture has found its form for the first time" (p. 138): Anita Page, Bessie Love and Charles King were the stars (1929). (The Museum of Modern Art Film Stills Archive)

A backstage scene, mingling artifice and reality, from the 1929 *Show Boat*. (The Museum of Modern Art Film Stills Archive)

singer becomes invisible and swift visions take us all the way to a large concert hall in which the same singer, dressed in an evening gown, finishes the last bars of the song that we have been hearing all along.

A skillful shooting script, a proper use of the new facilities, flexibility of technique, and there you have two successful achievements.

1950. This technique has not changed appreciably since *The Broadway Melody* and the best films made in the same era. Walter Ruttmann's *Melody of the World* (1929), despite some naïve and pompous moments, could still be shown to future film-makers as an example of the "proper use of the new facilities."

Georges Charensol, speaking of the Parisian première in 1950 of *Gone with the Wind,* which was produced in 1938, made the following remark: "Today rereleases of the successful films of the period just before the war are by no means confined to film societies, and many of the people who applaud them are unaware that they are already old pictures."

That is a measure of the slowing rate of progress in cinematic technique since the early years of the sound film.

If the best friends of the silent film undertake an impartial study of talking and sound pictures, they lose their self-confidence right away.

In its best form, the talking picture is no longer photographed theater; it is itself. Then, in its variety of sounds and its orchestration of human voices, it seems richer than the silent cinema. But isn't its richness false and its luxury ruinous? The screen is losing more than it is gaining by this "progress." It is conquering the world of voices but losing the world of dreams over which the silent cinema reigned. I observed the spectators leaving after hearing a talking picture. They seemed to be leaving a vaudeville theater. They were not plunged into that comfortable numbness which a trip to the land of pure images used to bestow on us. They were talking, laughing and humming the last refrain they had heard. *They had not lost the sense of reality.*

III

May 1929. The talking picture, triumphant in the United States, has begun its conquest of Europe with England. Next winter it will be our turn. Soon the principal cities of the whole world will hear the shadows on the screen speak, and it can be predicted that the public will go wild for this novelty here just as elsewhere. If this infatuation lasts, what will become of the thing that, until today, the cinema was for us?

In theory, the talking picture can give rise to masterpieces. Imagine the new Shakespeare who will play on this instrument. . . . But in reality, unless great changes take place in the economic organization of the cinema, the talking picture is doomed to remain an inferior genre. If it is produced on a low budget, it will sacrifice the image to words and will be satisfied with dialogue; it will be that photographed theater—or that illustration of phonograph records—of which we shall see some disheartening specimens before long.

If it is expensive, its producers will have to assure its distribution to an immense and mixed audience whose tastes will have to be taken into consideration, and for whose sake it will be necessary to avoid any bold ideas which might not be understood and might thus compromise the financial future of the undertaking.

Certainly these conditions are not different from those governing the existence of the silent cinema. But let us note one important difference: in the silent film, the fate of the images *left an opening to chance,* and still afforded an opportunity for genius and talent. Despite the prearrangements of the producers, despite all the precautions money could take against the genius of a film-maker, it was still possible to *cheat*. And it may very well be said that most of the worthwhile pictures saw the light of day only because of this cheating. When the producers handed Sternberg the ordinary crime-news story of *Underworld,* and gave Feyder the serial plot of *Thérèse Raquin,* they did not know that from these poor themes were going to emerge the poignant tragedies we know. . . .

1970. "The serial plot of *Thérèse Raquin . . . .*" That was written somewhat in haste. No doubt I meant that the story told by Zola, if removed from the book and divested of the spell the art of the novelist casts over it, becomes nothing more than the theme of a newspaper serial.

Jacques Feyder, who composed a succession of gripping images on this theme, does not occupy today the place his work and his example should have earned him. One of his first films, *Atlantis,* was a worldwide success. This good fortune did not dazzle him. Refusing to stick to the genre of the filmed novel, which had made him known, he manifested the most varied inspiration in films—dramatic and comic, fantastic and realistic—which all bear the mark of his style. He taught the generation that followed his that the public should be neither fawned on nor contemned, and he was one of the few in France who, in the course of many vicissitudes, did their best to defend the everprecarious independence of a film author.

Another independent: Josef von Sternberg, whose name is mentioned above along with that of Jacques Feyder. Sternberg's name is so closely linked to Marlene Dietrich's that people tend to forget that before *The Blue Angel* he had made several silent films, at least two of which are masterpieces: *Underworld* and *The Docks of New York*—called in France (one wonders why!) *Les damnés de l'océan.* In the latter film there is an unforgettable scene: the drunken marriage of George Bancroft and Betty Compson in a sailor's dive by a reluctant parson. I can still hear the shouts and singing of that silent crowd.

I can do no more than mention here *The Sea Gull* [not Chekhov's] that Sternberg directed in 1926 and that was produced by Charles Chaplin. "The film was previewed only once in Beverly Hills, after which Chaplin decided, for reasons of his own, not to release it. In the late Twenties, John Grierson, one of the few people who saw it, called it, 'The most beautiful film ever shot in Hollywood.' "*

Sternberg's independence and his justified sense of his own worth no doubt harmed him more than the Dietrich myth,

---

*Herman G. Weinberg, *Josef von Sternberg* (Dutton and Co., New York) .

which has often been said to have led its creator onto a false path injurious to his career.

. . . With the sound film, the text will be decided on in advance, read, weighed, prearranged according to the established rules. The best images may be spoiled by bad dialogue and the clichés of stage farce and melodrama which it will be hard to escape. The text—intended for the least lively minds—will be the great blemish of the talking picture. In the best moments of *Show Boat* and *The Broadway Melody,* how many beautiful visions were burdened with a text unacceptable to those who find only boredom in mediocre plays and cheap fiction!

"Remember your father, remember your past, remember our old boat, etc.," the old prompter in *Show Boat* said, in a dramatic tone, to the weeping Laura La Plante.

I stuffed up my ears, and then saw on the screen only two troubled people whose words I no longer heard: the vulgar scene became touching.

This new victory of outworn verbiage, this return to the old bondage to words that Alexandre Arnoux mentioned: that is the danger toward which we are being led by an invention that is admirable in itself but the effects of which can be disastrous. A few felicitous scenes selected from a large number of films are not enough to allay our fears. Yesterday poetry, which seemed to be losing its powers over literature and exhausted words, was being reborn, with its still hesitant rhythms and its pristine purity, on the great white canvas toward which the men of the whole world were leaning. Now this canvas is emitting a voice, sentences and words so often heard before . . . . Can the talking picture be poetic? There is reason to fear that the precision of the verbal expression will drive poetry off the screen just as it drives off the atmosphere of daydream. The imaginary words we used to put into the the mouths of those silent beings in those dialogues of images will always be more beautiful than any actual sentences. *The heroes of the screen spoke to the imagination with the complicity of silence.* Tomorrow they will talk nonsense into our ears and we will be unable to shut it out.

In accordance with the will of the industrialists of film, for whom the apex of art will always be the most complete imitation of reality, the cinema is going to lose that charm it derived from its unreal nature. Speaking of Talma and of truth in the theater, Chateaubriand wrote a sentence that can be applied to the situation of the film, now that it has gained the power of speech: "Once we bend to this truth of physical or material form, we find ourselves compelled to reproduce it, since the public, itself grown materialist, demands it."[1]

Nevertheless, it would not be impossible to endow the image with speech without abandoning the achievements of the silent cinema. Imagine a film in which the spoken text took the place of the written text of the intertitles, remained the servant of the image and made its appearance only as an "auxiliary" means of expression; a brief, neutral text to which no efforts toward visual expression would be sacrificed. Only a little intelligence and good will would be needed for an agreement to be reached on this compromise. But will people stick to this solution? Won't they yield to the temptation of using the artifices of dialogue, ready-made phrases, that chatter which drove us away from the theater and made us seek refuge in front of the screen, where "silence alone is great?"[2]

In view of the sound film—despite the inevitable mistakes made at the outset—we are still allowed to hope. In view of the talking picture—despite its first successful accomplishments—we remain worried.

In the midst of the general enthusiasm that greeted the talking picture in America, while the most mediocre artisans in the cinema were acclaiming the new god, thanks to whom their mediocrity will be less obvious, two voices were raised in protest: Charlie Chaplin and Erich von Stroheim took a stand against the "talkies." The protest by these two men, whose genius is loved and whose independence is recognized by everyone who understands the cinema, seems symbolic. It should give

---

[1]Talma was a great neo-classical actor of the late eighteenth and early nineteenth centuries. He introduced such revolutionary "realistic" innovations into staging as the use of period costumes for historical tragedies. His brilliant, comparatively realistic portrayals of tragic heroes are said to have kept the neo-classical theater alive long after its natural life span, and the death of the tradition significantly coincided with the death of the master actor.—ED.

[2]A line from Vigny's poem "Death of the Wolf," in which the poet admires the stoic silence of a dying wolf: "Only silence is great; all the rest is weakness." —ED.

pause to those whom the mere enjoyment of novelty leads to blind optimism.

1970. At the time I was writing these letters from London, I was unaware that in the Soviet Union, Eisenstein, Pudovkin and Alexandrov were publishing a manifesto against the talking picture, and furthermore that in the United States, Murnau and King Vidor, among others, were following Chaplin and Stroheim in taking the same stand. Thus, without consulting one another, the principal masters of the cinema of the time were joining in an opposition that seemed as legitimate to them as it did to me. In their manifesto, the Soviet film-makers, while approving the use of sound—music and sound effects—declared that "any addition of words to a filmed scene, in the style of the theater, would kill its directorial qualities, because it would clash with the ensemble, which proceeds primarily by juxtaposing separate scenes." Georges Sadoul, in quoting this sentence, correctly adds: "Which was defining editing as the essence of the cinematic art."

¶ Editing is in fact a procedure peculiar to the cinema which has no equivalent in any other medium of expression or art form.

One day I was in a projection room with a five-year-old child who had never seen a film of any kind. On the screen, a lady was singing in a drawing room, and the succession of images was as follows:

LONG SHOT: The drawing room; the singer is standing near a piano. A greyhound is lying in front of the fireplace.

CLOSE-UP: The singer.

CLOSE-UP: The dog watching her.

At this last image, the child uttered a cry of surprise: "Oh! Look! The lady has turned into a dog."

Nothing could be more logical and sensible than that exclamation. I would have been quite confused if I had been compelled to reply. Editing is an *extraordinary* convention to which our eye is so well accustomed that we no longer see what is unusual in it. But for a new eye, one image replacing another in a flash does in fact give the impression of a magical substitution or a lightning-like metamorphosis.

All the time that our eyes are open to the light, they never record anything but an uninterrupted succession of images. Now, editing permits the eye of the camera to effectuate arbitrary cuts in time and space in a fraction of a second. In the past, Méliès would film tableaus from start to finish as if his lens had replaced a spectator in the theater. Thanks to the first craftsmen who juxtaposed and intercut various scenes or shots taken at different distances, that which had been up to then only photography in motion became the language of cinema.

And yet the infinite advantages this procedure offers can become disadvantages if it is used unthinkingly or immoderately. Disorderly editing can give rise to a confusion that makes the viewer wonder: "Where are we? When is this taking place?" I am well aware that a certain amount of confusion is not always sneered at in our day, and that, for example, the absence of punctuation—that old novelty—gives pieces of writing a guarantee of modernity. But this fashion will pass, as does everything that is based on artifice.

It is in the nature of every beginner to be tempted—as I was myself—by startling effects of editing. That is a facile proceeding of which you soon tire, and, when you have thought about it for a while, you come to wish that every filmed sequence, no matter how intercut it is with different shots, looked as if it had been cast in a single piece. The best editing job is the one that is so right, you do not notice it.

¶ "Would you have wanted the film to remain silent?" you will ask, to finish off the list of regrets.

Permit me to extract the answer to this question from an article already quoted: "It is not the invention of the talking picture that frightens us, it is the deplorable use that our industrialists will not fail to make of it," and from another article that will be found later in the book: "No one is sorry that sound has been added to the image. No one thinks of condemning this admirable invention per se. All that is lamented is the arbitrary use that has been made of it. . . ."

If I may be permitted a retroactive wish, let me say that it might have been desirable for the entire realm of the *visual* to have been explored before the "talkie" arrived on the scene with its facile effects, and for the technical progress of the cinema to have occurred in the following order: first, three-dimensionality; then, color; finally, sound and speech. Too bad! But as Armand Salacrou wrote at the same time and on the same subject: "You can imagine how much sweeter the earth would have been for some people if electricity and water power had been thought of before coal and mines, but things are invented in a much more disorderly sequence than is generally believed—and this is very disconcerting."

The most gripping evocation of that transitory and troubled era is still the one written by Alexandre Arnoux: "For weeks I refused to believe in the talkies, in spite of that American, who had said something very profound to me: 'Once you have given a child a doll that says "papa" and "mama," even badly, it doesn't want any other. People are children. I am staking everything I have on the sound film.'"

To which Arnoux replies, in the name of those who thought as he did: "As for me, I have no capital, but I hesitated to stake my faith, which is all I possess."

In Self-Defense

1950. No one thinks of denying that the cinematic machine can be used for various purposes, just as a theater can receive jugglers as well as political orators on its stage.* But is everything that goes on under the proscenium arch related to dramatic art, and is everything that is printed considered literature? Many arguments would have been avoided if the word "cinema" had not been used to designate a means of reproduction and a medium of expression at one and the same time. It is the latter, constantly threatened by the former, that this book intends to "defend and illustrate."[1]

If I had to define that "film sense" that is so often mentioned, I would no doubt say that it is nothing but common sense placed in the service of the cinema. A wooden wheelbarrow can float on water, but to cross a river it is wiser to use a rowboat. To have film sense is to use the cinema for purposes that suit its nature. The fisherman and the gardener know that every tool has its particular use, and the carpenter does not drive in nails with his plane.

¶ "The King is dead. Long live the King!" After that cry had proclaimed a change of reign at court, there were only disinterested servants to be found among those who sought the favor of the new sovereign. When the silent cinema disappeared, the advent of its successor was greeted by songs of gladness and offers of service that were not solely inspired by the love of art and progress. In a dash that resembled a gold rush or a rush for the spoils, people raced toward the screen, which seemed to promise a fortune to anyone dealing in adjectives and noise: authors of stage dramas and farces, manufacturers of topical skits, composers of puns, writers of song lyrics and librettos, baritones, ventriloquists, tragedians and imitators of animal calls.

---

*Foreword to *Réflexion faite*.

[1]Clair refers to a Renaissance treatise on the French language written by Joachim du Bellay, called the *Defense and Illustration of the French Language*. The treatise, written to promote the use of French instead of Latin for poetry, contained two major sections. The Defense set out to prove that French was as flexible and expressive as Latin, and the Illustration pointed the way toward enriching the language.—ED.

This situation, which naturally alarmed lovers of the cinema, should have caused some worry to theater people.

> But (André Lang wrote) the heedless and frivolous playwright did not then think that either his dignity or his purse was threatened. The stormy and difficult birth of the talking picture —the first reels were hissed in every theater and articles appeared everywhere calling it an experiment as ridiculous as it was ephemeral—did not worry him for a moment. Rather, he was glad of it! He saw in it only a new source of profits.

Nevertheless some playwrights took a different stand. Thus, Armand Salacrou wrote:

> I give you a few years of high dosages of *talking pictures,* and after that, successful sound films will have no more than ten spoken titles, as simple as they are overpowering. And something that many efforts would never have managed to obtain in the world—a cinema that is not filmed theater—will be obtained by the sound film through a reaction against the overly talky picture.

Meanwhile, at the Le Havre high school, a young teacher named Jean-Paul Sartre, in the course of a speech he gave at a presentation of scholastic awards, claimed that too much attention should not be paid to the talking picture:

> Pirandello said, not without sadness, that the cinema is like the peacock in the fable. It spread its wonderful plumage in silence and everybody admired it. The jealous fox persuaded it to sing. It opened its mouth, projected its voice and uttered that notorious cry. But what neither Aesop nor Pirandello says is that, no doubt, after this experiment the peacock was glad to go back to its taciturnity. I think that the cinema is now busy acquiring the right to keep quiet.

1970. When the above quotation was published in *Réflexion faite,* one of the staff of *Les Temps Modernes* displayed some pique because I had taken the liberty of recalling this old text by his director.[1] His point of view was that if Jean-Paul Sartre still remembered it, he must surely smile at his mistake.

Forgive me! There are mistakes for which there is no reason to smile or blush, and which are preferable to banal truisms. Moreover, the entire speech of the young teacher deserves to be quoted. For instance:

---

[1] *Les Temps Modernes* is a journal founded by and still directed by Sartre. —ED.

I claim that the cinema is a new art which has its own laws and its individual methods, that it cannot be reduced to the theater, that it should be as useful to your education as Greek or philosophy.

¶ I asked for nothing better than to share these noble illusions, and when I myself wrote: "If the future of the sound film is practically assured, that of the talking film still remains uncertain," I was expressing not so much a conviction as a wish. I was wishing that the new cinema would not call into question the achievements of the old, that the resources of sound and speech would be prudently and gradually annexed to the language of images, now free of the intertitles which were its chief blemish, so that we might see the creation of "that art peculiar to the talking picture," which could find its form only if it were preserved from the contagion of theatrical routine.

At that time an incident occurred which André Lang summarizes as follows:

> Beginning in 1930, after the dazzling twin success of *Topaze* and *Marius,* Marcel Pagnol moved, bag and baggage, into the talking-picture camp, launching a sort of manifesto that disseminated laughter and disbelief. As he saw it, the theater was not threatened, but sentenced to death! "The art of the theater is coming back to life in another shape, and will enjoy an unprecedented prosperity," he wrote. "A new field is opening for the playwright, and we will be able to produce works which neither Sophocles, Racine nor Molière had the means to attempt" (*Le Journal*). And, a year later: "The talking picture must reinvent the theater" (*Les Cahiers du film*).
>
> Forgetting at the time how much of the air and sunshine of La Canebière[1] went into these remarks, we felt wounded in our respect and love for the theater by these sacrilegious declarations.

We were wounded, too, you can imagine, in our respect and love for the cinema. For a man like Marcel Pagnol to take such a definite stand was much more dangerous for the future than the occupation of the studios by a few people fishing in troubled waters, whose reign we were sure would be of short duration.

I was in disagreement with Marcel Pagnol on every point: his

---

[1] La Canebière is one of Marseilles' main streets, and Pagnol is a Marseillais whose best-known plays are set in that city. The expression connotes the volatility and ebullience traditionally associated with the people of Marseilles. —ED.

conceptions appeared to me as "a horrible confusion," in which both the theater and the cinema were bruised and dragged through the mud, and if his talent as a writer of comedies had not led me to be considerate through regretting it, I would have liked to compare him to those devouring dogs mentioned by Athalie.[1] Thus, I seized on the first available pretext—some humorous statements made at the banquet of a Society of Poets, for which the author of *Marius* was in no way responsible— to reply to him:

> Not every man may call himself a poet, and there is no law forbidding those who call themselves poets to form a club.* And yet I confess that the existence of a society of poets, duly organized with statutes that have been registered with a lawyer, is a thing that passes my understanding. (Have these gentlemen determined in their statutes what references would be demanded of Rimbaud, Lautréamont, Baudelaire or Corbière, one of those savages for whom the word "poetry" must still have a live meaning? On the contrary, I think that this assembly took every possible precaution to avoid having poetry—which is dynamite —served up by mistake at their annual banquet. I dare not imagine the dreadful consequences of this absentmindedness on the part of the cook.) . . .

¶ An aside: It is not by chance that the name of Corbière is mentioned above. In a period when Rimbaud and Lautréamont were reigning over French poetry, Corbière was once again forgotten. "Rimbaud's elder brother but not his big brother," as Verlaine put it, Corbière cannot be loved in moderation. You detest him or you put yourself under his spell. I took every opportunity—and I still do today—to mention the name of the author of *Les Amours jaunes,* the ever-accursed poet. End of

---

[1]Athalie, one of Racine's tragic heroines, had a prophetic dream about her mother:

> I held out my hands to embrace her
> And found nothing but a horrible confusion
> Of bones and flesh, bruised and dragged through the mud,
> Of rags full of blood and frightful limbs
> That devouring dogs were fighting over.   —ED.

Pour Vous, July 1930.

the aside, with my excuses to those readers who are not interested in such matters.

. . . So, then, a society of poets exists, and *Comœdia* informs us that at the last banquet of this society, the cinema was discussed.[1] A speaker said to the members: "The cinema must belong to us. Here it is. Take it." And someone replied: "We don't want it. It isn't pure enough for us."

This incident is not very serious in itself, and I would scarcely dwell on it if it were not one among several recent incidents. For some time now, people in various places have been selling the skin of the cinema before they have killed it. One after another, playwrights, men of letters, and finally members of the Society of Poets announce to us that their kingdom has come and that thanks to the talking picture, fiction and the dramatic art will consent to collaborate with the celluloid merchants and their inferior accomplices called directors.

A particularly shocking article appeared recently over Mr. Marcel Pagnol's signature. This author, surprised to learn that the box office receipts of a film were greater in two months than those of one of his plays in a year, suddenly became attracted to the screen and proclaimed that henceforth the cinema would be the property of playwrights or would not exist at all. Certain declarations by Mr. José Germain, Mr. Kistemaekers and a few others were added to those of Mr. Pagnol, and we thus learned that the cinema had been nothing up to today, but would become something when its "intellectual" control belonged to the authors of plays, novels or alexandrines[2]—to every imaginable author except film authors.

We know that this term "film author" is open to much discussion. People do not know "film authors"; they know—when they are willing to—only directors, or *metteurs en scène,* a title which came from the theater, as has everything harmful to the

---

[1] *Théâtre et Comœdia Illustrés* was an arts magazine to which Clair contributed regularly in the twenties. He also edited the cinema section for two years during that time.—ED.

[2] The alexandrine is the traditional French verse line, composed of twelve syllables. Its complete prevalence over all other systems of versification makes the word virtually interchangeable with poetry in French parlance.—ED.

cinema.[1] For some time now, people have been playing on words and the sleight-of-hand trick has been successful. As incredible as it may seem, the writer who merely supplies a film-maker with the plot of a film is an author, but if that writer directs his own screenplay, he becomes only a *metteur en scène*. On the pretext that the cinema—like the theater and fiction—harbors a good number of incompetents, people pretend not to know that there are film authors who are much more properly authors of their own works than many playwrights and novelists are of theirs. Now, it happens that all the films it pleases us to remember were made without the assistance of novelists or stage writers.

From the films of Méliès to *The End of Saint Petersburg*—including the works of Chaplin, Sennett, Stroheim and many others—all the things that justify the existence of the cinema in our eyes are the work of men "in the trade," true *film authors*. And when, by chance, a worthwhile film is adapted from a piece of fiction or a play (for example, Feyder's *Thérèse Raquin*), it takes only a little insight and justice to discern the contribution of the true film author, who has been able to dominate the author of the original anecdote and, making the most difficult gamble, has been able to recreate, for a new form of expression, a subject that was not intended for it. . . .

¶ This sentence elicited some cries from the ignorant. And yet it is only a truism that M. de la Palice wouldn't dispute,[2] and which there is no need to recall to anyone who has any degree of familiarity with the French classic writers. It is well known that those writers were concerned very little with the

[1] French has long had trouble with the term *metteur en scène*, which, as Clair observes, comes from the theater, and means literally "putter on the stage." Although words comparable to the English "director," devoid of generic associations, exist in French, they have never become widely accepted. For reasons that remain questionable, American "auteurist" critics have recently adopted the French term along with its correlative, *mise en scène* (putting on the stage) , to designate "director" and "direction," rather than use the more satisfactory English terms already in existence.—ED.

[2] M. de la Palice was a Renaissance gentleman who was killed in battle. Through an accident of faulty transmission, a song describing his adventures came to be popularly interpreted to mean that he was extraordinarily naïve, and his name is now commonly used to connote a purveyor of blatant, obvious truisms. We might describe him in English as a man who has just been out for a nocturnal walk and has discovered the moon.—ED.

authorship of a subject. In this second preface to *Britannicus,*
Racine wrote: "I copied my characters from the greatest painter
of the ancient world—that is, Tacitus. And I was so immersed
at the time in that excellent historian that there is hardly a note-
worthy feature in my tragedy for which he did not give me the
idea."

If Zola is the author of the *film* named *Thérèse Raquin,* then
by the very avowal of Racine, Tacitus is the author of a tragedy
in French verse wrongly attributed to Racine, while Gounod and
his librettists must give Goethe the credit for a famous opera.

To the eternal question "Who is the real author of a film?" no
definitive answer can be given. In this area there are only individual cases. Certain film producers (especially in the United
States) take advantage of the confusion prevailing in this regard
to claim for themselves the prerogatives of an author. Following
this theory, Chaplin would not have been the author of his own
works until he began financing them himself. Before that time
the *author* of Charlie Chaplin's films would have been a joint-
stock company or a bank!

In reply to an opinion poll on this subject very long ago, I
wrote as follows:

> If people were to agree that the man who supplies the *idea* for
> a work is the author of that work, we would have to revise the
> entire history of the novel and the play. For example, none of
> Racine's tragedies would have had Racine as their author, but
> rather Seneca, Segrais or even Henriette of England. In fact, in
> each of his tragedies Racine is merely the author of the plot de-
> velopment (shooting script) and the ultimate form of the play
> (direction).
>
> If people were to agree that the man who supplies the *money*
> necessary to execute a work is the author of that work, we would
> have to revise the entire history of architecture and part of the
> history of painting and sculpture. Thus, the author of *Moses*
> and the Sistine frescoes would be Julius II, and not Michelangelo,
> his hired workman.

. . . Because of the birth of the talking picture, it seems that
the adventure of the early days of the silent cinema is beginning
again. About 1907, when the first film authors revealed the un-
suspected riches of the screen in works that were often admirable, some producers thought that everything would be better

if "artists" deigned to concern themselves with this magic lantern: the Académie and the Comédie—both Française—entered the studio.[1] The sickly screen was forced to swallow so many medicines that disagreed with it that it is a miracle it did not die of the cure.

The situation today is still more serious. The talking picture will survive only if the formula suitable to it is found, only if it can break loose from the influence of the theater and fiction, only if people make of it something other than an *art of imitation*. It is self-evident that playwrights and fiction writers are in a very bad position to accomplish this task, which would require them to fight hard against the habits their craft has given them. This new form of expression needs new men. We will not find such men, except by chance, among those who have devoted their lives to the theater or to fiction. They are already deformed, lost to the cinema, from which they can no doubt derive some material profit, but to which they cannot contribute any spiritual profit. We will find the right men among ourselves, among those young people whose passion for the film compels them to accept the most thankless chores in the studios and who, after an exhausting day's work, still take the time to compose some screenplay no producer will ever consent to read. We will find them among those—I know such people—who devote a year's salary to making a small film, of which they have the pleasure of being the sole guiding spirit. We will find them among those with a passion for the cinema, who love it for itself and not merely as a providential source of profits. We could find some such men immediately if the producers agreed to treat the film as something other than an illustration of stage successes and best sellers.

The remarkable thing in the statements recently exchanged on this subject is the tone adopted by fiction writers and dramatists when speaking of the cinema. They seem to be saying to us: "Be patient, my good people. You haven't been able to make anything out of your little contraption. But here we are—the brains. You shall see what you shall see. We are doing you the favor of coming among you. . . ." Thanks a lot. You do us too much honor. . . . But might we point out to these gentlemen—who, nine times out of ten, are familiar with hardly any films

---

[1]That is, the official establishment organizations.—ED.

besides *Cabiria* and *Ben-Hur*—that the cinema requires specialists and not amateurs? The profession of film author demands at least a technical apprenticeship, for which the putting together of one-act or three-act plays demands no equivalent. It is a thankless and difficult task, in which love for new things and a certain taste for adventure are indispensable to anyone who wants to bear the disappointments every film brings to an honest author. No one but those who practice this profession wholeheartedly can know how many struggles, calculations, ruses and concessions are necessary in order to succeed in putting into a film a tenth of what you wanted to. All this for a work which will be disfigured in a few years by time, if it is not disfigured at birth by undesirable intervention. . . .

¶ "The profession of film author demands at least an apprenticeship . . . ." That is true, but should have been explained better. I meant that an unknown man buried in the country can write an excellent play without practical knowledge of stagecraft, whereas it is difficult to conceive and write the complete screenplay of a film without some notion of cinematic technique.

Let us note in passing that the film writer is always a professional writer. Screenplay contests and numerous surveys carried out in various countries have not led to the discovery of the unknown screenplay writer. The case of Emily Brontë composing one of the greatest novels of world literature far from cities and all literary circles has no equivalent in the cinema. This phenomenon, which is rather strange in view of the enormous publicity given to movie matters, has not yet been explained satisfactorily.

. . . Far be it from me to discourage those fiction writers and dramatists who would like to learn this profession. But in that case, let them learn it seriously, let them direct their own works! Then they will be able to call themselves authors, then they will be able—one never knows—to *be of use to the cinema,* and not merely make use of it.

In the discussion that arose after the incident at the "Poet's Banquet," Mr. Ricou pronounced the following words, which express perfectly the thought of many writers: "If the poets, fiction writers and playwrights do not attempt to tap that prodigious power source . . . the talking cinema will become a scourge."

The case could not be better stated, and now we have been warned. It is quite obvious that if Mr. Pagnol gives no advice to Charlie Chaplin, if Mr. José Germain does not come to the aid of Pudovkin, if Mr. Kistemaekers does not help King Vidor, these film authors, left to their inspiration alone, will be lost. They will have only one other recourse: to make films in which there is no trace of theater or literary fiction. That is the good fortune I wish them.

¶ The end of this article touched off a little squabble. Some authors flew to the defense of Marcel Pagnol, no doubt hoping that by placing themselves at the side of the great man they would pick up a few crumbs of his fame. The author of *Topaze,* who had no need of allies, continued imperturbably to issue paradoxical theories, to which we will return later.

There was no need, however, to defend a cause which seemed won at that time. *Jean de la Lune* was hailed as a revelation because this tender comedy by Marcel Achard was filmed practically as if the camera had been set up in front of the stage of the Comédie des Champs-Elysées. After we had seen other less agreeable productions, it seemed that the French cinema was even outdoing Marcel Pagnol's predictions, and was about to become not only filmed theater but also something without a name in any language, a phonograph record prettied up with a few illustrations.

Even today, how many films are just that! In every film-producing nation, how many authors working for the screen would hardly have to change their style if they worked for the radio!

1970. The same fault can be found with television. When the writers are unable to make us *see* an event, they *tell* us about it. In that case, what difference is there between radio and television? The sight of an announcer chatting is not enough. But it is easier—and cheaper—to record sound than to photograph visuals. That explains the abundance of words on both the big and the small screen.

Theater and Cinema

It has been said that nothing essential had been added to the technique of the "silent art" by Griffith's successors. In the same way, it may be claimed that nothing *essential* has been added to the technique of the sound film since 1932.

By that date it was already possible to take stock of the new cinema and examine the conditions of its existence. The opportunity to undertake this examination was given to me by the newspaper *Le Temps,* which published the following article in July 1932:

The theater is not yet dead. It was said that the cinema would destroy it; now, it may be the thing that will save it. The cinema will probably rid the theater of the most mediocre part of its audience and its artisans. No doubt the theater business as it exists today is threatened. No doubt, instead of fifty theaters in a major city there will soon be room for only twenty or even ten. No doubt businessmen will abandon the theater and move on to another trade more suitable for speculation. (And by businessmen we mean not only certain administrators, but also certain authors who are old hands at deals of all sorts.) Perhaps the theater industry will disappear, but the true theater will enjoy a new life if it no longer has to satisfy the taste of the least demanding audience and the appetite of the most demanding businessmen. . . .

1950. Would I have made a good prophet? It seems—but one swallow doesn't make a summer—that this prediction has been more or less fulfilled. The "theatrical industry" has not disappeared and what was called in Paris the "Boulevard theater" still has an audience, but the quality theater has made considerable progress. Today, Copeau would not be compelled to close the Vieux-Colombier.[1] The emergence, in Paris and even in the

---

[1]Jacques Copeau founded the Théâtre du Vieux-Colombier in 1913 to promote the production of good drama, especially unknown or neglected work, regardless of its date or origin. The theater was known for its inventiveness, its absolute integrity, and its refusal to capitulate to successful commercial formulas. Although it enjoyed strong critical support, it closed its doors in 1924 for financial reasons.—ED.

provinces, of troupes which would once have been called "avant-garde," the success of plays which would formerly have been considered "daring" or "difficult"—all this testifies to a renewal of the theater in our day.

1970. This emergence has done nothing but increase during the last few years: national and municipal theaters, provincial companies, "houses of culture," festivals, etc. In spite of numerous difficulties, the theater has widened its audience as well as its repertoire.

Whereas nowadays not only the cinema but also television, magazines of all sorts and the obsessive images of advertising populate our minds with fictitious creatures, it seems that the public, saturated with the intangible, is feeling the need to find once more on the stage *real* beings who live and breathe like them. A phenomenon which should interest the mass-media specialist.

. . . Those who claim that the theater will be killed by the cinema seem to be unaware of the nature of these two arts (let us use the word "art" for lack of anything better). Whoever thinks they are alike is mistaken about both of them. Everything the stage borrows from the film, everything the cinema borrows from the theater, threatens to divert each of them from its proper course. The talking picture has thoroughly exasperated this confusion, which dates from the earliest days of the cinema. The film, even talking, must create means of expression very different from those used by the stage. In the theater, action is carried on by the dialogue; what you see is secondary to what you hear. In the cinema, the primary means of expression is the image, and the speech or sound element should not be preponderant. It might almost be said that a blind man attending a true dramatic work and a deaf man attending a real film, *even though they are both losing an important part of the work being presented,* would not lose the essential part. . . .

1950. This sentence had the good fortune to be noticed—that is, to annoy people. Those whom it annoyed never fail to quote it incompletely, omitting the clause italicized above, so that they can comment, with good faith equal to their cleverness: "So the cinema is meant only for the deaf?"

. . . I hope I will be excused for giving this somewhat simplistic example and for repeating these basic truths. But for several years everybody, or almost everybody, has pretended to be in agreement on these principles, while nobody, or almost nobody, can bring himself to put them into practice. Everywhere in the circles where films are prepared, you hear: "Not too much dialogue, a lot of visuals; the cinema must remain cinema. . . ." But despite this, ninety films out of a hundred today are still more or less well filmed theater.

Filmed theater . . . . More than one person acts up at hearing this. Film authors rarely like to see their work given this name, even if they have made it deserve the designation. Such delicate feelings are surprising. The filmed theater exists and will continue to exist for some time to come, even if the real cinema succeeds in taking shape. It is a type of show that has found its audience, its theaters and its authors, and that cannot be denied its right to exist. Filmed theater will replace road productions of plays in neighborhood and provincial theaters, just as mass popular editions have made literary titles more widely available than the original editions alone could have done. . . .

1970. Unfulfilled prophecy. Real filmed theater has not replaced the provincial and neighborhood theater, as we have seen above. Even American film producers who have bought the rights to a successful Broadway play do not simply photograph the play on the stage of the theater. They try, if only feebly, to adapt it to the cinema, but preserving the stage script, each line of which cost them its weight in gold. A system which seldom gives good artistic results.

A remark apropos of this: it is a shame that the cinema, taken separately as a simple recording method, is not used to set down and preserve an exceptional stage production or performance: nothing remains of *The School for Wives* put on by Jouvet, the *Amphitryon* staged by Barrault, the acting of Gérard Philipe in *The Cid* or *The Prince of Homburg*. When you think of all the money and celluloid wasted on pictures devoid of interest!

But, it will be said, such an undertaking would hardly be profitable. No doubt. Therefore, a government agency should take charge of this type of picture—which is not so expensive, anyway —and establish that real Conservatory whose archives would acquire inestimable value as time went by. What lover of the theater would not like to see today Talma, Marie Dorval, Mounet-Sully or Sarah Bernhardt in their best roles?[1]

. . . The cinema is threatened today as it always was. An original sin weighs on it: money. Money was necessary to create and expand the film industry. The laws of money continue to control the cinema and stifle it. It may be said that its development, except in Soviet Russia, has been completely controlled by financiers. Despite everything said to the contrary, the theater is not entirely in this situation, and thus has an advantage over the cinema. In the theater, it takes only an auditorium, a few yards of cloth and a few actors to present a worthwhile play to the public and give it a chance. The cinema is altogether different: money has given the film industry powerful technical facilities, has endowed it with enormous publicity and has brought millions of viewers into its thousands of houses, but these overwhelming benefits have permanently enslaved the film to the power of finance. . . .

1970. "Permanently" was one word too many. Nothing is ever permanent in these matters. In one whole section of the world today, the cinema is controlled not by financiers but by government agencies, with the well-known advantages and disadvantages.

Besides, in the nations with a liberal economy, the situation has changed considerably. The break-up of the film market, the lightening of equipment, and the interest of part of the public in new formulas have permitted the production of less costly films which can be made with greater independence.

1Marie Dorval played ingenue roles in melodrama, then moved into Romantic drama at its inception, since it provided the perfect showcase for the particular talents she had developed while working in the emotion-charged genre of melodrama. Mounet-Sully, an equally famous tragedian, flourished later in the nineteenth century and into the twentieth. Their talent, along with that of Talma and Bernhardt, remains legendary in France.—ED.

. . . It is easy to imagine the consequences of this situation. What is less well known is the extent to which money is able to subject to its domination the film craftsmen themselves: if an author, director or actor has had some success, he is usually approached with tempting propositions. If he accepts unreservedly, he may get rich, but he is soon lost to the cause of cinema. Accustomed to the pleasures of life made possible by easily earned money, he will no longer have the strength to react. He will be paid for every concession he makes; the praise of the publicity department will stand him in stead of glory; material satisfactions will lull his scruples to sleep. How many examples we see of the cinema's best craftsmen betraying it in this way! What individual could resist the power of an organization like that of the whole film industry? Whoever tries to do it, if he does not enjoy unusual luck, will soon be put back in his place. Each of his attempts threatens him with the loss of the little credit and freedom his earlier successes won him.

Success, good contracts, the glare of publicity; failure, financial ruin, sudden obscurity—these are the brutal ways of the cinema. The man who is familiar with them understands why the film, despite the collaboration of so many excellent minds, progresses so slowly and gives so little satisfaction to a clearheaded spectator.

What is a "good film"? A movie house manager declared recently: "A good film is a film that makes money." The condemnation of present-day cinema is contained in this answer. With the exception of a few visionaries, everyone making his living from the cinema thinks like this manager. Making money is not an activity in which you can be particular in your choice of means: they are all proper if you want to have a commercial success, even if this success is obtained at the cost of the public.

But, it will be asked, cannot this public exercise its control? Is it happy to accept the merchandise it is offered? If it is, everybody is satisfied and all argument is pointless.

Not yet. The effects of the cinema are not the same as those of the theater, and the government has made this difference clear by subjecting the former to a censorship it does not dare to impose on the latter. To justify this arbitrary measure, the government points to the considerable effect the cinema has on the masses. But if the cinema has such a hold on its millions of viewers, *can we allow this force to be handed over to a few financial groups that have the right to stupefy the mind of the public if that operation brings them a material profit?* The public is a child that is perpetually ready to accept whatever amuses it: sometimes an excellent work of art, sometimes a piece of nonsense. How can this great docile crowd, whose critical sense no one has done anything to awaken or shape, defend itself against the degrading entertainment handed out to it in the shape of so many mass-produced items manufactured according to the most vulgar recipes? When we hear: "What else do you want us to do? We are giving the public what it likes . . . ," we think that this excuse impugns the role of those who invoke it. We are not asking for the reign of a moralizing or intellectual cinema, but for the coming of a cinema worthy of the responsibilities its power confers on it. . . .

1970. A moralizing or intellectual cinema? We have them today! And it is not always a cause for self-congratulation. Never in the past have morality and amorality so served the reputation of a film and inspired its publicity. The lovers of theses and collectors of messages can be satisfied. As for the "intellectual" cinema, it exists with a vengeance, and we will discuss it later. (See the chapter "A Retroactive Revolution.")

. . . Why is there no censorship against stupidity in the way that there are measures prohibiting traffic in absinthe and dope? Is the mind of a nation, then, less important than the health of its body? That is not what we are told in those ministerial harangues which are so steeped in an innocuous but traditional idealism. . . .

1950. Whatever the reason for the existence of censorship may be, we are so well aware what use can be made of it, under any regime whatsoever, by bureaucrats who are always ready to prove themselves more State-ist than the State,[1] that we cannot be

---

[1] The expression is based on the popular French formula "more royalist than the king" or "more Catholic than the Pope," used to designate an extreme zealot.—ED.

sincere partisans of that institution.   Nevertheless, since censorship exists (in different forms, but in every country), it may be held that a censorship against vulgarity of mind is at least as defensible as political or moral censorship.

The most pernicious censorship is *the fear of censorship,* whether official or commercial: the inner censorship that smothers every bold or original idea, at the moment of its conception, in the mind of the man who knows its rules so well that they impose themselves upon him without his knowledge.

. . . The question raised here does not concern the cinema alone.   Radio, television and all the forms of expression that technology gives us will be faced by the same problems.   *Will these enormous forces be left in the hands of anyone who possesses enough capital to get hold of them?   Freedom granted to private initiative in these matters is a caricature of freedom; its effect is to impose the absolute dictatorship of a few industrial or financial groups upon a domain which is not solely material. It is possible that the economic and political system governing us at present does not permit us to envisage other solutions: this would mean that this system no longer corresponds to the needs of our time and will have to be changed.*

1970.   *Le Temps* was not a particularly amusing paper, and by a regrettable mimicry this article adopted its tone.   And yet the management, no doubt fearing that the lines italicized above might shake up the columns of the quasi-official organ of the Third Republic,[1] deleted them.   I had been quite naïve to think that my reference to the dictatorship of industrial and financial groups would be accepted in a daily which was one of their spokesmen.

But since I had been invited to fill the famous column at the foot of the paper's front page, in the absence of Pierre Brisson, who wrote that column regularly, and since I had not been given notice of that deletion, I felt that the proceedings showed a lack of courtesy.   Not to be deficient in cheekiness, I sent the incrim-

---

[1]That is, the form of French government under various leaders from 1870 to 1940.—ED.

inated passage to *L'Humanité*, where it was published with the commentary that was to be expected.[1]

. . . To stick to the present and to humbler considerations, let us examine the current state of world cinema. Except for Soviet production, whose organization and aims are not the same as in the capitalist countries, it may be said that the entire cinema is paralyzed by the concentration of facilities in the hands of a few big companies, and by the industrial structure which these companies have given to a production that needed creative freedom, above all else, to renew itself. . . .

1950. That has no longer been true in France for a good number of years, but it should be noted that most of the works that count in the history of French cinema since the beginnings of the sound film were produced outside of the big companies mentioned above, which have more or less disappeared today.

The system of production called "independent," despite its serious economic disadvantages, is the one that seems best suited to "individualistic" countries like France and Italy, countries that are relatively unamenable to the type of organization found in the United States or Germany.

. . . The businessmen placed at the head of these groups delegate their powers, when it comes to making films, to directors of production. It may be generally said that the latter are seldom chosen for their competence and experience in the cinema. Most often, they owe their job to some financial, family or friendly connection with the managers of the enterprise. An extraordinary situation like this could not exist in an industry in which the quality of the product is easily controlled. This system, applied to the manufacture of automobiles or to steel construction, would soon be severely criticized: the cars would not go and the bridges would collapse. Here we touch upon one of the anomalies of the cinema: anyone at all would hesitate to give advice to an engineer; the engineer would quickly point to calculations that would compel the ignoramus' respect if not his silence. But anyone at all, when it comes to the cinema, can

[1] *L'Humanité* is France's leading Communist newspaper.—ED.

give his opinion to, or impose it on, the finest craftsmen; he can evaluate a screenplay, the work of a director, the performance of an actor. It is true that there are not many unanswerable authorities in the cinema, but it must be said that it is rarely to them that the managers have recourse.

The result: a timid, routine production; rules and standards that may be applicable elsewhere but are disastrous here. Things have not always been the same: in the past a creator like Charlie Chaplin was able to express himself and to benefit the entire cinema with his own successes. Today, a new Chaplin just starting to work in the studios would be unable to prove his worth. He would have to submit to the established rules or disappear: in either case, it would be impossible for him to become Chaplin. . . .

1950. When he started, Charlie Chaplin had several pieces of luck: he had genius, which was his most important piece of luck, and he was coming into the cinema at a time when this genius could reveal itself with a minimum of restraints. Lastly, his popularity as an actor helped the creator in him to maintain an independence just about unequaled in the United States.

1970. I had the opportunity to bring up this subject with Chaplin shortly before he left the United States. In that period, the early successes of television were causing panic in the studios. It meant the fall of the empire whose might was symbolized by the roaring M-G-M lion. We both thought that the confusion produced in the film industry by that decline, as well as the gropings of a still unorganized television industry, would recreate the conditions of fertile anarchy in which the genius of the young American cinema had once been able to explode.

What we did not foresee in our optimism was that television, placed under the authority of the big bosses of advertising, would soon be more rationally administered and more closely controlled than Hollywood had been at the peak of its power.

. . . In the name of the principles of finance and in fears of endangering their capital, the businessmen who rule the cinema refuse the immense riches they could gain by giving credit to, and putting to use, young talent. Naturally we do not care if these industrialists neglect a chance to make additional profits, but since these profits are the only interest attaching them to the cinema, this negligence on their part appears to us as the sign of an unusual lack of capability. After all, they should not forget that it was thanks to the new methods contributed by new men—Sennett, Ince, Griffith, Chaplin and a few others—that the American cinema, between 1913 and 1917, was able to achieve the supremacy that it has held for so long.

Today, the system established by the businessmen and their subordinates makes any revelation of genius or budding talent all but impossible. This system represents the most perfect organization of defense against the unknown forces that might revive the lagging cinema.

Can the present setup be changed? Is there any hope of seeing the cinema rediscover its youthful inspiration and the fertile genius that enlivened its heroic age? This is not impossible. The world crisis is hitting the big firms hard. Tomorrow they may no longer have sufficient credit to keep the monopoly on a production that requires enormous capital. In that case, the system of mass production divided among a few consortiums will make way for the independent labor of numerous groups. Even today, cooperative production has begun in several countries. Under this arrangement, a film is made by an association of the different craftsmen whose skills are needed; in these undertakings, the "supervisors" and other agents of the industrial cinema are no longer allowed to exercise absolute power. This allows films to be conceived and executed with more freedom than those produced under the blind discipline of the big firms. Naturally, these will not all be worthwhile films; no system by itself can create talent. But by this means, men of talent will have an opportunity to show what they can do and to reveal to the cinema works worthy of it and of its vast audience.

1950. It seems that, for France at least, this apparent prediction was partially fulfilled about 1935, as Georges Sadoul observes in his *Histoire d'un art:*

> The French monopolies and the international combines were succeeded by artisans without honesty or imagination, whose

checks were issued with insufficient funds, whose fictitious companies were established in furnished rooms,[1] who were involved in productions without capital or guarantors, in bankruptcies and even swindles.

In fact, however, the reign of the hucksters had fewer disadvantages than that of those living corpses, the putrefying big companies. The film market once again enjoyed free, or at least relatively free, competition.

1970. The "film market of the United States" is now also enjoying the relative freedom that has been made possible by the decline of the big firms. The imperatives of business, morality and politics have lost some of the hold they exerted. Temporarily, no doubt.

At the time when Senator McCarthy was terrorizing Hollywood, a woman journalist who shared his convictions attacked a number of writers and artists. When she was asked: "Doesn't an artist have the right to express political opinions?" she replied: "Of course he has. Providing they are the correct opinions."

Today that answer can be heard all over, from the East to the West. Tolerance was a luxury of the eras of tight control.

---

[1] In France, a furnished room specifically denotes a rented room with rented furnishings, which connotes insolvency on the part of the person who occupies it, whether it be as a home or an office. In any case, it suggests either poverty or a fly-by-night operation.—ED.

Beginning to Take Stock

The arguments raised from 1928 on by the coming of the talking picture were still continuing five years later, at least in France, a country where people like ideas.

"Cinema 1933" was the title of the following article, in which I impartially took stock of the foregoing years and tried once again to make clear the difference between the theater and the cinema, for the benefit of those who "have eyes yet see not."

"Before the war—no, I mean: before talking pictures . . . ."
How often have we heard those words? When we want to discuss the cinema that still existed five years ago, the expression "before the war" comes naturally to our mind. The confusion created in our mind on such occasions is food for thought to those interested in the fate of the cinema.

It must be admitted. Most of the apprehensions aroused by the coming of talking pictures were justified. The prophets of doom were right this time. The others, those who always play on the word "progress," uttered cries of enthusiasm when they heard an image making a speech for the first time. Let these people now take stock honestly: how many cinematic works today deserve a place in our memory alongside those the cinema of yesterday gave us?

Useless regrets, no doubt. But let us be precise: no one is sorry that sound has been added to the image. No one thinks of condemning this admirable invention per se. All that is lamented is the arbitrary use that has been made of it. No doubt the silent cinema was not always up to the highest standards, but on the whole it seldom descended to the level of intellectual vulgarity characteristic of most talking pictures.

Let us chalk up one improvement to the credit of the new cinema: it has freed us from those unbearable intertitles. But their text, usually pretentious and trashy, still exists. We no longer read it, we hear it from one end of the film to another, howled out by a loudspeaker.

Sometimes the dialogue of a film is written by a dramatist; that does not always make it better. Often the very structure of the film is created by a dramatist, but the cinema does not always gain anything by this contribution.

Please do not think me full of hostile intentions toward everything in the cinema that comes from the theater. Good stage authors and actors can be good cinema authors and actors. But that is not the rule. A painter may also be a sculptor. Not every good painter is a good sculptor. Painting and sculpture set themselves different goals and obey techniques peculiar to themselves. Why is it that this observation, which is banal, sounds to some people like a presumptuous proposition when it is applied to the relationship between the theater and the cinema?

A stage actor speaks and moves in an abnormal way before spectators who are far away from him. This actor must therefore speak loudly and enunciate very clearly; he must gesticulate and mime with sufficient expression for a spectator who may be twenty or thirty yards away from him to be aware of what he is doing.

The cinema actor moves and speaks in front of a camera and a microphone, which are often placed as close to him as a person would be to whom he was telling a secret. The least exaggeration of gesture or speech is picked up by the merciless machines and amplified when the film is projected. . . .

1970. While on this subject, let us speak out today against the lack of reflection, if not the childishness, of numerous television directors who use the close-up without moderation, in the belief, no doubt, that they are emulating Gance or Eisenstein by placing their lens on a character's nose.

Nothing is more artificial than those enormous faces that seem to be viewed through a magnifying glass, clearly revealing every trace of makeup. There are not many beauties this microscopic examination does not spoil. The use of the close-up should be limited in order to preserve its effectiveness when it is needed. It is never necessary to look right into a singer's mouth. Unless you are a dentist.

. . . In the theater, an actor has several weeks of rehearsals in which to learn his lines and perfect his role; he will have to perform long scenes in their entirety with no possibility of interrupting them in front of the audience. From the first rehearsal to the last, he works at creating the character he is playing, at feeling or feigning an emotion that he will have to express without variation every night.

In the cinema, the actor has several minutes in which to give the expression of a feeling its definitive form. His talent owes more to spontaneity than to experience. Furthermore, the actor almost never has the opportunity to play out an entire scene. He can express only fractions of emotions, which, connected to one another later on, will form a succession the quality of which cannot be completely evaluated before this operation of assemblage.

As you see, although the talent of the stage actor can be of use to him when he comes to the cinema, the technique of his first profession can only be a hindrance to him. An antinomy that is seldom reconcilable exists between the laws of these two professions. Certain exceptional people can practice both. This does not mean that anyone who excels in one can adapt his talent to the conditions of the other.

The same holds for authors. *If, by a quirk of fate, the cinema had been invented before the earliest forms of theatrical expression had been conceived, it is a certainty that the authors of a film would not have thought of summarizing the most important phases of the film's plot in scenes of dialogue.* The existence of these scenes, which are contrary to the nature of the cinema, is due to the intrusion of stage conventions into a medium of expression that deserves to enjoy an independent life. . . .

¶ I take the liberty of asking the readers who are not put off by these questions (which are raised here in very theoretical fashion, forgive me!) to reflect on the above supposition.

To make clear, without wandering off into abstractions, what the truly cinematic drama can be, the simplest thing is to resort to a comparison between the classic theater and the novel.

Take *Le Cid* or *Andromaque*: most of their scenes are given over to comments on past or future actions; the other scenes contain, if I may use this expression, "action capsules" presented in the form of dialogue. *The theater recomposes the separate elements of an action to form a synthesis of it.* It is in this adjustment of events to fit verbal expression exclusively that the difficulty of dramatic art and the loftiness of its conventions reside.

In the novel, which can both describe a gesture and express a secret thought, it is permissible to *analyze an action* as our memory does. The same goes for the film. If you recall an episode in your life, the salient events of that episode do not return to your mind in the form of conversations alone. Leaf through *Manon Lescaut, The Red and the Black* or *Lost Illusions:*[1] the most action-packed moments are not often those when people are *speaking.* If you were Julien Sorel locked up in the prison of Besançon, what would you remember most vividly? Such and such a *phrase* of Mme. de Rênal, or the moment when you hesitated to take her hand while the clock began to strike twelve midnight? Such and such a *verbal* skirmish with Mlle. de la Môle, or that lock of blonde hair which she dropped from her window into the night?

Let me repeat: if the theater had not existed and had not offered a model easy to copy, it is not very likely that the cinema would be using the long, stationary scenes of dialogue to be found in most films of yesterday and today.

This comparison between theater, novel and cinema led to many other reflections. Thus:

If it were necessary to give yet another example of the difference between the stage performance and the film, it would suffice to recall that plays have always been printed, whereas the works conceived for the screen are rarely offered to be read.*

The reason for this anomaly is, no doubt, that the form in which the film work is written makes it hard to read. The film, though it may talk, remains a medium of expression that affects the eye more strongly than the ear. Now, if a reader's imagination can be stirred by dialogue, to which it lends the sound of the human voice, it refuses to be stirred by the description of

---

[1] In addition to Prévost's *Manon Lescaut* and Stendhal's *Le Rouge et le noir,* both well known outside France, Clair mentions Balzac's long novel, *Les Illusions perdues.* The characters and incidents mentioned in the following lines figure in *The Red and the Black.*—ED.

*Excerpt from the preface to *Le Silence est d'or* (Masques, 1947).

movements, facial expressions, sets and all the visual details of the action which are often its most dramatic elements.

When you read a play, you learn within a few lines when and where the story is taking place. For instance: "A villa on the coast of Normandy. It is summer. In the background, a veranda facing the sea. Etc." That being understood, the reader need no longer worry about the setting or the season, and can concentrate his interest on the characters who will surely appear promptly in the place that has been described, in order to discuss their small or great affairs there.

But how many traps there are for the absentminded in the text of a work written for the film! The action moves flexibly through time and space. No set holds it prisoner, no unit of measure prescribes its duration. My readers may remember a silent film of the golden age in which Buster Keaton played the part of a film projectionist; he fell asleep on the job, then in his dreams entered the screen and joined the characters of the drama that was being shown. From that moment, the unfortunate dreamer was lost in a world whose images succeeded one another around him in an unforeseeable order. When he dived off a rock to save a blonde heroine who was struggling in the waves, he landed on the desert sand face to face with an astonished lion. Thus, if the reader of a film work does not pay attention to the changes of time and place, he is in danger of getting lost in the course of a story which will seem incoherent to him, whereas the film narrating it on the screen would appear well arranged to him.

The freedom of the film author to avail himself of time and space is also used by the novelist. In the novel as in the film, one evening may occupy the entire work, but several years may pass by, in a few lines here, in a few seconds there. Transitions are accomplished with the same ease. When, for example, we read at the end of one chapter of *Sentimental Education*:[1] "His face appeared to him in the mirror. He found it handsome and stopped for a minute to look at himself," then, at the beginning of the next chapter: "The next day, before noon, he had bought a paintbox, brushes, an easel . . . ," we see that

---

[1] Flaubert's novel *L'Education sentimentale.*—ED.

the passage from one scene to another takes place as it does in a film, in disregard of the unities of time and space.

Nevertheless, the novel, which is intended for a reader who can shut the book whenever he wants or whenever his ability to concentrate is diminishing, is not subject to the rules of the performing arts, in which the author must hold the audience's interest uninterruptedly from the exposition to the dénouement. In his obedience to these rules, the film author is not different from the playwright, however different the techniques they employ may be. That is why we may say, if we want to define the nature of the film narrative by comparisons, that it is related to the stage play in structure and to the novel in form.

¶ In 1947, when the above lines were written, the talking picture was no longer a subject of contention, and it was possible to discuss it serenely. But in 1933 our tone was not yet free of passion:

. . . It is the difference in technique that, there again, prevents most stage authors from becoming the authors of real films. When a man has been accustomed for years to condense an action into scenes of dialogue, meant to be acted on an immobile stage, it is understandably difficult for him to subject his inspiration to a rule diametrically opposed to the one he is used to. If an author succeeds in placing his talent in the service of the two different techniques of the theater and the cinema and becomes equally adept in both, this can only be an exceptional case, and one on which experience teaches us not to count too much.

If it is not the influence of the theater alone that can be blamed for the sad state of the cinema in 1933, it is nonetheless true that this influence is lamentable. From its earliest days, the cinema has been rocked by movements similar to the political upheavals that occur in new nations. The coming of sound and talking pictures hit it like a new revolution in a country beset by a permanent crisis. It was possible to hope that in the resultant anarchy the cinema would find an organization suitable to its nature and would shape itself on its own. But the theater came along, like those neighbors who are always eager to establish order in other people's houses. Relying on its long experience, it dictated its old laws and old conventions to its young rival, which is now wasting away under the constraint of foreign rule.

If it is still possible to speak of cinema today, it is only from time to time, because of a few outstanding films that awaken our hopes and recall the period when we looked to the screen as to a new world. Anyone who did not live through that period of discovery will never understand what a film can be for us.

The cinema we loved is as far away from us now as the prewar era. In a few years, young people will no longer understand what the word "cinema" meant to an entire generation. No doubt this word will acquire another meaning. But what? Our uncertainty as to the future of the cinema is the only consolation we can find when we think of its present state.

1970. What pessimism! What gloom! Viewed in retrospect, the cinema of 1933 does not seem to have been in such sad state that consolation was necessary. The drawing power of the novelty of sound technique was not yet exhausted; the public was flocking to the movie houses; the best films were free from the influence of the theater, and this era saw the birth of many remarkable pictures.

But passion is demanding. If you expect too much of the beloved object, you are in danger of being disappointed. Hence, no doubt, those melancholy remarks which seem somewhat excessive today.

Other considerations on the same subject will be found in the following article. Around 1934, Marcel Pagnol issued a new manifesto, which I thought it necessary to answer anew:

"I would like to think that we will have good films. But they will be exceptions to the rule. For the cinema isn't in our blood. Not all nations like all the arts, do they? Well, France, which likes poetry, the novel, the dance, painting, has no feeling for music, doesn't like music, doesn't understand music.

"I tell you—we'll see if the future says the same—that France has as little feeling for cinema as it has for music."

The preceding lines date from 1918. The man who wrote them died ten years ago, in March 1924. If he were alive today,

Louis Delluc might well be proud of his clearsightedness. An opinion which sixteen years have not managed to date is fairly close to having permanent value. . . .

1950. It would be unfair not to admit today that Louis Delluc was not altogether right on this point. The good French films produced from the early period of the sound film up to today are no doubt exceptions (in what country are good films not the exception?), but there are enough of them to make it impossible to deny the existence of a French school.

. . . In the land of the Lumière Brothers, a discovery has just been made which is causing a bit of a stir. To summarize it in two words: up to today, the cinema has only been imperfect theater; from now on, it will be just plain theater or, to put it more precisely, the cinema will become only a method of disseminating plays.

In a great number of countries, such a proposition would hardly seem new. It could be pointed out that precisely the worst films fit that definition. In France, it is possible to discuss this theme almost seriously. Decidedly, Louis Delluc was not wrong.

Certain minds are confused by novelty and can only understand a new conception if it is rigged out in the old clothes of the past. Thus, many playwrights cannot admit that the cinema exists. They grant it the right to exist only if it resembles the theater and follows the old routine of the stage.

It is useless to tell them that the immobility and narrowness of the theater stage have given the stage performance its necessary form and outlines, that the cinema, which is not subject to the same restraints, does not need to obey the laws to which they gave rise. It is useless to tell them that of all the aspects of life that the cinema can reflect thanks to its wonderful mobility, there are more stirring ones than that of a few characters busy chatting. They will not understand. Their professional deformation is such that life appears to them only as a series of conversations. The shock of the most expressive images and the newest sounds is nothing to them in comparison to an exchange of solid tirades larded with witticisms and epigrams.

And yet it takes only a little common sense to grasp that the cinema, radio and television—which we will be using tomorrow —are media of expression whose particular technique requires them to be used for ends that are suited to them. . . .

1950. Sixteen years have passed, but we are still not using television "for ends that are suited to it." The period of groping in the dark is far from over for television, which it would be wise to consider, *while waiting for something better,* as a medium of dissemination rather than as a medium of expression.

1970. And twenty years have passed since that last remark. . . . And yet we must still "wait for something better" before declaring that television is a completely original medium of *expression.* This question calls for further discussion. (See the chapter "On Television.")

. . . The most striking thing in the writings of Marcel Pagnol and most of his colleagues who have joined this debate is their cockiness and their astonishing ignorance of the cinema. He seems to know nothing of its past, its present facilities or its very essence. Pagnol says, and I am quoting: "The silent film was the art of printing, preserving and disseminating pantomime. The talking picture is the art of printing, preserving and disseminating theater."

To gauge the worth of the first proposition, it is only necessary to go back to see any silent film of quality made from 1920 on. Except for a few exceptional moments in Chaplin, there is not one scene which borrows the methods of the pantomime.

In formulating his second proposition, Pagnol puts himself in the place of an old painter who, discovering the existence of a camera, declares that photography offers no interest in itself but is only good for reproducing pictures painted by himself or his colleagues. If this painter said that photography can *also* be used for reproducing works of art, we would agree. But if he claims that the lens is unable to reflect the images of the world directly, we can only lament the weakness of his judgment or smile at his paradoxical fancy.

One of Marcel Pagnol's co-workers—who I think is not in disagreement with his superior—writes: "What is the cinema-cinema? It is a mystique."

The author of this sentence no doubt meant that he does not know what the cinema means. Joking aside, this admission has its importance. It throws light on the debate and reduces it to its proper proportions.

Where I am in complete agreement with Pagnol is in his defense of the rights of the author. I have good reasons for that, and I go even further than he does. To put an end to many current arguments, my wish is that the author and the film-maker will be one and the same person—in short, that authors will do without *metteurs en scène* and will themselves practice that profession which they consider so easy. I myself practice this twin profession, and I think the method would not be bad for others.

And since Pagnol has written: "A new field is opening for the playwright, and we will be able to produce works which neither Sophocles, Racine nor Molière had the means to attempt," I cannot encourage him too strongly to lose no time in putting into effect such a fine project, which, it must be admitted, is not well exemplified in his first film achievements.

I think that the time for manifestos and theories has now passed for Pagnol. He must make a film, a real film. He has told us that, having found no master in the cinema, there was nothing for him to do but become one himself. He must keep his word. When he has "reinvented the theater," as he puts it, when he has really worked for the screen, he will be able to speak about the cinema however he wishes, and then we will listen to him without smiling.

Meanwhile, I hope he will permit me to give him a piece of advice: he should go to the movies once in a while. If he knows how to choose the show, he will not always kill the evening. Let him learn this profession, which is new to him, and in which his talent can work wonders if he is not satisfied with ready-made answers.

I have been striving to learn it for over ten years, and I am far from being familiar with every difficulty: its constant development merely allows me to gauge my mistakes better every season. Every time I start work on a film, I feel like a beginner. It is in all friendship that I hope Pagnol will experience this feeling in the face of the unknown that the cinema still is for us.

1950. Friendship is not mentioned here as a mere polite formula. I have never been able to have a serious argument with Marcel Pagnol except far away from him—that is, in writing. Face to face with him, no one can withstand the charm of this extraordinary character who, after enjoying the greatest theatrical successes of our time, threw himself into the cinema with the youthful enthusiasm he brings to all his undertakings, became a film producer, built a movie studio, set up a laboratory and opened movie houses—all this while attempting to revolutionize the automobile industry by the invention of a new motor and while becoming in his spare time a farmer, an architect, French consul in Portugal and a member of the Académie Française. . . .

1970. One should never speak too lightly of the Académie Française. One never knows what can happen.[1]

1950. This character out of Balzac's nineteenth century, who landed in ours by mistake and moves about here with the ease his talents and his taste for life give him, would make the subject of a biography that could be as entertaining for our descendants as Alexandre Dumas' memoirs are for us. . . .

1970. A wish partially fulfilled. *La Gloire de mon père, Le Château de ma mère* and *Le temps des secrets,* these recollections of childhood whose poetic quality is equal to their delightful humor, are part of an autobiography which we hope will continue for a long time.[2]

1950. . . . Marcel Pagnol was certainly one of the first to forget that, according to his own formula, "the talking picture is the art of printing, preserving and disseminating theater," or,

---

[1] In 1950, Clair had no idea that ten years later he would become the first member of the Académie Française to be elected primarily on the basis of work in film.—ED.

[2] The three volumes of Pagnol's reminiscences have been translated into English by Rita Barisse, the first two in one volume with the title *The Days Were Too Short* (Doubleday, 1960), the third as *The Time of Secrets* (H. Hamilton, 1962).—ED.

if he did not forget it, he displayed extremely felicitous absent-mindedness when he created films like *Angèle*, *The Baker's Wife* and *Manon des sources*. Although our dispute has no foreseeable ending, he arranged to have the last word in advance when, around 1945, he published an article that recalled its principal terms and closed as follows:

> Without admitting it, we have convinced each other.
> He started to make talking pictures that talk. I tried, because of him, to produce images. If our battle continues, and I think it will continue as long as our friendship, which is absolutely indestructible, I will end up making silent films and he will become a charmer on the radio.

In fact, the great battle of the "talkies" never ended. Neither of the two extreme opposing factions won the victory. The film did not become merely a means of disseminating theater, but the formula which prevailed by force was surely not that of total cinema.

Men like Raphael or Rimbaud can revolutionize painting or poetry by their genius alone. But the development of the performing arts does not depend solely on creators. It needs the collaboration of the public. It may be said without paradox that when, at the end of the sixteenth century, the English theater shone so outstandingly, the Elizabethan public was as brilliant as a crowd can be. If things had been otherwise, men like Shakespeare, Marlowe and Ben Jonson would have been discouraged by failure and would have given up writing for the stage.

It is contact with the public that has given the cinema its present form, just as the waves shape the pebbles on a beach. The public is not creative, but it chooses among the creations of the performing arts in such a way as to make its will felt. Those theater managers and film producers who are in despair because they cannot guess what the public wants, can be given the consoling reply that the public does not know what it wants, either, *in advance*. The public knows what it wants *after* it has been shown it; by selection it finally imposes its tastes, which appear to be permanent until the day it chooses, from among the various formulas proposed to it, a new one that there was no particular reason to think would catch its fancy.

Some time ago, in the United States, I attended the screening of a new film, the first scene of which, lasting two or three minutes, was completely silent. The humorous details of the scene elicited laughter, then smiles, but as soon as the action stopped being comic, a feeling of annoyance and oppression seemed to come over the viewers. Although the music coming from the screen continued to be heard, it was as if the sound apparatus had gone out of kilter and the spectators were waiting with a sort of anguish until it was repaired. And when the first line of dialogue was spoken by one of the actors, there was practically a sigh of relief and joy to be heard in the auditorium.

The audience in that auditorium, as in most American movie houses, was made up chiefly of children and adolescents—that is, spectators who had never known any films but talking pictures. They were not capable, as viewers of silent films used to be, of following the thread of a story through the succession of images unfolding on the screen, and, in obedience to habit and the law of least effort, they were waiting for the words to define the meaning of the scene they were watching, although it was very clear.

It is no doubt the same phenomenon of habit that has forced the animated cartoon, the last refuge of visual expression, to make its unreal characters talk. The effects of this phenomenon will be felt until the time that the public has acquired other habits—in a manner which cannot be foreseen—as the result of a new formal or technological development of the cinema.

This constraint which makes the creators collaborate so closely with the public should no doubt be discussed in a light tone rather than with bitterness. If Chatterton's vocation had taken him to the studios, he would have acquired sufficient philosophical irony not to be tempted to die, as the English put it, "by his own hand."[1]

1936. Although he [the author] does not regret the interest he has taken in things of the cinema, he cannot help comparing

---

[1]Thomas Chatterton, eighteenth-century English poet, is better known in France than in English-speaking countries because Alfred de Vigny centered one of French Romanticism's most famous plays on him. In Vigny's drama, Chatterton committed suicide when the government refused to recognize the value of his work and when, on top of that, he was accused of plagiarism.—ED.

the lot of the writer with that of the maker of films.*

How fortunate is the literary artist, whose task of creation calls only for a pen and plenty of paper! The film director, on the other hand, is no more than a gear in the cinematographic machine. What complications are involved in bringing the slightest of his ideas to fruition! How many obstacles, both moral and material, must he not overcome if he wishes to impart a personal or original note, however faint, to the result of his labours!

People who are difficult to please, or who have a certain taste, are sometimes astonished by the mediocrity of motion-pictures. But to anyone who knows how films are produced what seems fairly inexplicable is that works of value do appear from time to time on the screen. Such accidents are no doubt due to a momentary distraction on the part of the producers, and we may be sure that a better organization of the film industry will one day effectively guard against the occurrence of any such unpredictable phenomena.

Journalists are apt to ask the film director: "What would you do if you were at liberty to make a picture exactly as you liked?" Poor man, he cannot say. Once, long ago, he might perhaps have answered that question, when he was not yet bowed down in the service of his job; but now—you might as well ask a fish what it would do if it had legs and could stroll down Piccadilly.

From the young men who suppose that the film may be a means of self-expression for the artist—as a book is for the writer —it would be charitable to remove this dangerous illusion. Experience will teach them that the cinema's reason for existing is to seat a given number of persons of both sexes in so many rows of stalls. Truth requires us to add that the said persons, before occupying their seats, will have disbursed a certain sum at the entrance to the picture-theatre. The significance of this part of the ritual cannot have escaped the reader; it is by this means that the value of films is assessed and their ethic and aesthetic determined. . . .

1970. A certain critic, reading these last lines long after they

---

*Excerpts from the preface of *Star Turn*, the English translation of *Adams* (Chatto & Windus, 1936; quotations are from this 1936 translation by John Marks) .

first appeared, took them literally and accused me of the vilest commercial ambitions. This made me regret that the "irony mark" once proposed has not found its place among the typographic signs used for the benefit of hasty readers and sluggish minds.

. . . It would therefore not be unreasonable to claim that, if films acted exclusively by trained frogs induced a greater number of spectators to enter the portals of cinemas than do the pictures at present shown, producers would set about training frogs and would furiously outbid each other to acquire the brightest specimens of batrachian talent. As you might suppose, the freedom of a director of films is somewhat limited by such conditions.

Because the cinema borrows from the theatre, literature, and the visual arts, we tend to class it among the arts. In actual fact the motion-picture is a means of expression which may at times serve artistic ends—like broadcasting, television, and the other forms of expression, as yet unknown, which science will duly create for us—but it can only prove a disappointment to those who look upon it as an art and who attribute to that word the meaning it was given in the last century.

There is not an author, a director, or an actor in the film world who is not subject absolutely to the verdict of the box-office, which is the voice of the great majority. One wonders how the genius of Shakespeare, of Wagner, or of Cézanne could have developed if their work had depended on the inappellable judgment which *several millions* of their contemporaries would have passed on it *at the very moment of creation.*

1970. These last lines, if I remember correctly, were written in England. No doubt it was raining that day, which would explain the morose mood they reflect.

The characteristic of the above-mentioned media of expression, the thing which differentiates them from the traditonal arts, is, indeed, the fact that they are intended for, and depend upon, a wide audience. But to aim at the approval of a work of quality by the greatest number is no mean ambition. Technology will, in one way or another, force some form of socialism upon us. This seems inevitable. That is why those who dream of a cinema reserved for privileged groups seem to be manifesting a backward-looking spirit.

In what century do they think they are living?* The units of measure they use for their opinions are as out of date as the cubit or the ell when applied to a medium of expression that reaches the entire world. The card tricks suitable for the living room are out of place in the circus ring.

For our part, if a cruel fate compelled us to choose between an outworn estheticism and the doctrine according to which the public is never wrong, we would be forced, though heartsick, to join the ranks of those who see in popular success the only sanction that counts. It is not definite that the public is always right, but it is definite that the authors who hold it in contempt are always wrong.

Does this mean that we must stick to tried-and-true formulas, distrust all innovations and work in the shadow of a prudent academic spirit? Quite the contrary!

¶ Quite the contrary. To go forward with artistic experiment while keeping in touch with the general public is a difficult undertaking, but it may be the essential problem that all the arts will face tomorrow. (See the later chapter "A Retroactive Revolution.")

---

*Preface to *Comédies et commentaires* (Gallimard, 1959).

Speed and Shape

By 1930 the first chapter in the history of the cinema is finished. The silent film belongs permanently to the past. But the split between the old system and the new causes a technical schism, the effects of which will continue to make themselves felt long after this passage "from the Middle Ages to modern times."

1963. Although the kingdom of speed has now come, on earth as it has in heaven, young people, and youthful people, have every reason to believe that they have invented slowness. When a few scenes shot in the silent film period appear on the screen, they think that the men of that remote era walked and stirred as if there were not a minute to lose before the end of the world.

I do not advise the sociologists to draw any conclusions from this prevailing haste. The explanation of it is very simple: from the time of the Lumière Brothers to the last days of the silent cinema, images were recorded and projected at the average rate of sixteen frames per second. At the coming of sound film, this rate was raised to twenty-four. As a result, all projectors were modified, but the old films remained as they were. And when one of them is entrusted to the new-style machines, the movements it contains seem exaggeratedly speeded up.

To exhibit old documents in this manner, without giving notice of the change, is to treat the public somewhat offhandedly and to show very little respect for the past. Film comedies are not all equally harmed by this artificial frenzy. But when it comes to the dramas that are sometimes presented to us as masterpieces and are made ridiculous by a rhythm for which they were not conceived—what opinion can be formed of them by someone who has not seen them in their prime?

In the case of old newsreels, the situation is even worse. The soldiers of the First World War move as jerkily as robots, Joffre and Foch join in a fast-walking contest, the last tsar of Russia gambols toward his sad fate, Lenin is epileptic, and Clemenceau flings himself into the arms of Poincaré with the impetuosity that seizes on Punch when he wants to wallop Judy. If the cinema had been invented earlier, how many historic events would suffer the same fate and would look on the screen like the episodes of a burlesque comedy! Napoleon would make his farewell at Fontainebleau swinging to and fro, Danton would dance on the deadly tumbril, and Joan of Arc would hop and skip across the main square of Rouen.

It would be desirable to have a law protecting cinematic documents against these degrading slurs. Various procedures exist that permit films of the old style to recover the pace that suits them. It would be honest to use them. The panes of glass that protect some paintings in museums are not distorting mirrors.

¶ The universal nature of the cinema, already jeopardized by the use of words, was to be threatened again with what can be called a question of form. About 1950, various processes that altered the classic shape of the screen began to be used, with varying success. The one that has been most generally adopted is Cinemascope.

To change the shape of the image, which had remained practically the same since Lumière and Edison, was an interesting possibility. But people should have determined what they would gain by substituting one arbitrary convention for another.

The new ratio is perfectly suited to all views that glorify the horizontal: big gatherings, parades, races, battles, etc. But for scenes in which interest centers on a few characters, it is a problem to contain easily within a strictly horizontal framework creatures whose biped nature most often imposes verticality upon them. Is the reclining position that so many heroes and heroines of recent films adopt for intimate ends a result of Cinemascope? Let us leave the problem of throwing light on this question to future Doctors of Filmic Sciences, and let us merely observe that painters seldom use for a portrait the format suited to seascapes.

I admit that I was somewhat annoyed when the new process was sent abroad into the world with all the publicity the American industry is capable of giving to its undertakings, and this annoyance, which now seems less justifiable, was reflected in an article I published on my return from a trip to the Soviet Union.*

1955. The universality of the cinema—which has been pre-

---

*Les Lettres françaises, October 1955.

served after a fashion by the artifices of "subtitles" and "dubbing" —is now once again in danger. A few days after our arrival in Moscow, when we were visiting the Mosfilm studios, we were shown some Soviet films on a wide screen of the Cinemascope ratio. I could not resist the temptation to tease my hosts: "Why are you imitating the Americans, since you aren't forced to for commercial reasons?" They exclaimed:

"What, you don't believe in progress?"

"A novelty doesn't necessarily spell progress."

This argument was soon interrupted, but I would like to resume it here. One of the great difficulties presented to us by a period rich in upheavals is to distinguish progress from novelty. Progress is beneficial. A novelty may not be.

A little history, if you don't mind. A few years after the first public showings of moving images, an international conference met in Paris, I believe, under the chairmanship of Méliès. This conference reached a major decision: a single ratio for all films, a single system for projecting them. The universal cinema was born. From the Lumière Brothers until recently, the shape of the screen was practically unchanged. However, the possible modification of that shape had often been discussed by the technicians. During a convention held about 1950, at a time when there was not yet any talk of Cinemascope or similar processes, this question was discussed by various film-makers, among whom was Pudovkin. The wish expressed by our colleagues was that the screen should be enlarged, but—contrary to the style today— *upward*. This may seem surprising now, but will not surprise either painters or set designers. What is a landscape without treetops, sky and clouds, or a palace without its ceilings?

To defend a tradition is not a comfortable position in these times. It takes a little courage to write, for example, that meter and rhyme in poetry are as good as free verse. It would not take too much pressure to make me say that, perhaps by chance, the classic screen shape was very judiciously chosen. It is the one which best permits us to isolate a character without leaving too much empty space around him, to group several characters without squeezing them together too much, and to follow a moving object without imposing too great a surface of moving background on the eye of the spectator.

However, if it is unreasonable to claim that the "normal" screen should under no circumstances be changed, it nevertheless would have been reasonable not to adopt these changes without serious examination and an international exchange of views beforehand. That is not at all what happened.

A chance occurrence. A financial necessity. A lucky poker hand. That is what is today endangering the universality of the film. Isn't that laughable? Everyone knows what gave rise to Cinemascope. An extraordinary lens, designed nearly forty years ago for tank drivers. An American firm whose stocks were doing very badly on the market gets hold of this forgotten instrument, organizes a vast publicity campaign around this old novelty and—with the aid of all those who always jump onto a new bandwagon—the trick has come off.

And yet most technicians recognize the imperfections of the process. Most film-makers who have used it admit through their very work that it is not easy to fill the absolutely inhuman frame imposed on them. Even in the United States the critics have the most serious misgivings in regard to this. But so what? The cinema still bears the mark of its midway origins. "Step right up, ladies and gentlemen; on the inside you will see . . . ." What is seen inside is not the mountebanks' chief concern.

Once again, let us say that we do not mean to oppose research, invention and progress, the value of which is incontestable. But you need only see the films projected onto the excessively widened screen to realize that *for the moment* this novelty is bringing us back to the conventions of theatrical staging, or at least is restricting the use of the essential resources of the cinema: editing, the changing proportions of shots, and camera movement.

And that is not the most serious danger. Now that the classic screen has burst, every caprice is permissible. Attempts are being made to remedy the defects of Cinemascope—imprecision, transparency of bodies, lack of that "depth" indispensable to the illusion of reality—by inventing other systems. If Vistavision and Todd-AO offer solutions to the problem of the wide screen that are more correct technically, it is still true that these systems differ from one another. A film shot according to one of them cannot be shown on a projector equipped for another. From the confusion that seems to be coming, we may fear the worst.

No matter what shape the screen is, talent will always be able to find room on it, and mediocrity will not appear less mediocre on it. But when the multiplicity of systems threatens the universal nature given to the cinema fifty years ago, progress is illusory and retrogression is a fact.

If I am thought to be pursuing too strenuously the friendly discussion begun a few days ago in Moscow, please permit me to quote this remark by Benjamin Constant: "We in France like only those things that can be of universal application."[1]

1970. In the above article I forgot to mention another objection—not really very serious—to the use of the wide screen. With the classic ratio, it was always possible to enlarge the field of vision *horizontally* by following a character with a pan or tracking shot. In the wide ratio, it would be desirable for this to be possible in the *vertical* direction. But the law of gravity opposes the upward movement of characters with regrettable persistence. The Assumption of the Virgin is not a subject that is filmed every day.

However this may be, I was wrong to fear the worst. The defects of the process have been corrected, film-makers have learned to use it and—partly by force of habit—fewer and fewer films will probably be made in the old ratio. But, to close this discussion with the example of two films by the same creator, let us say that the wide screen—and even color—would not have added much to Fellini's touching film *La Strada;* on the other hand, the vast tableaus presented in his *Satyricon* could not be imagined without color and wide screen. And the wide screen itself will be replaced some day by other technological innovations, as has been suggested in our Foreword.

The only regret that we may retain is that people have abandoned the *single* ratio, of whatever dimensions. The disparity of ratios offers various disadvantages. On television, for instance, where with the present-day screen shape, the characters in a wide-screen film at times hide modestly behind the sides of the set or at other times seem to hit up against the top of the screen like visitors bumping their head on a beam in a low ceiling.

---

[1]Benjamin Constant was a Romantic novelist and a liberal statesman.—ED.

But how little these "questions of ratio" matter in our memory! A short time after seeing a film, you no longer know what boundaries its images had. If the film reached you, these boundaries disappeared! You were *inside* the screen. And for the spectator nothing else should count. Here as in painting, it is not the frame that is important, but what it surrounds.

On Hollywood

1944. An enormous library would be needed if someone wanted to gather together everything that has already been written about Hollywood.* And among the dwellers in these more or less gilded cages that the studios reserve for writers, there are few who have not been tempted to paint the true face of this movie Mecca. Nothing is more difficult than such an undertaking. Between the dream Hollywood whose duly retouched image is disseminated in innumerable magazines, and the monstrous Hollywood that is the subject of so many satirical stories and so many farces written for Broadway theaters, there is enacted the truth, as impalpable and fluttering as the beam of light issuing from a projector.

Everything that is said about Hollywood—even the worst extravagances—is true or could be. But anyone who would trust these anecdotes alone would not know Hollywood better than the Parisian knows Provence if he does not go beyond the dialogue of Marius and Olive.[1] The ignorant, tyrannical Producer and the self-centered, capricious Star are characters whose names change but whose nature has remained the same since the time Robert Florey first arrived in Los Angeles after a seven-day train ride. What has changed is the rules of the movie game, a fundamental truth that is less well known to the public than the legend that hides this truth from it.

The age of exploration of unknown lands has given way to that of industrial organization. The pioneers in high boots have made way for the financiers with eyeglasses. Hollywood, which used to be a sort of flea market of the moving image, full of the unexpected, the ridiculous and the charming, has become like a big well-polished shop in which mass-produced merchandise is sold from one end of the year to the other.

The cinema machine is very well regulated today. Too well, no doubt. As paradoxical as this may seem, it should be allowed to go out of order a little to make it work better. Don't take too seriously this reflection of a malicious wit. We are entering an era in which machines are no joking matter.

*Excerpts from the preface to Robert Florey's book *Hollywood d'hier et d'aujourd'hui* [Hollywood yesterday and today] (Editions Prisma, 1948).

[1] Legendary heroes of traditional Marseilles yarns.—ED.

To the young people in Europe who dream of Hollywood as if it were the magical place where they could make a personal film; to those who continue to consider the cinema as an art just like poetry or music; to the naïve people who think it is an accident that for twenty years neither a new Griffith nor a new Chaplin has been revealed, Florey, who has directed American films for a quarter of a century, could give some lessons that would destroy their illusions.

Among the four or five hundred films produced each year in California, how many bear the stamp of a particular style, how many seem to be the work of an original artist or craftsman? It is through a sort of superstition that people continue to name the director and writers of an American film. With very few exceptions, their signature means little more than those appearing on bank notes, where the name of one treasurer can be substituted for another without changing the value of the note by that operation. Therefore, despite the majestic typography and fanfare accompanying the appearance of these titles on the screen, the names read there are generally only those of the employees of an administration controlled by an all-powerful corporation. . . .

When I too was brought to California by the chance events of an era rich in surprises of a dubious taste, Florey, as soon as I arrived, insisted on showing me around—in his fashion, which is not everybody's. He didn't take me to the big modern studios, solid and white as New York banks, vast and well-organized as Detroit factories. He didn't introduce me to the powers of the day, the fashionable stars, the private swimming pools or the nightclubs in which the customers are seated according to their weekly paycheck. No, as sentimental at the wheel of his car as Olympio in the valley of the Bièvre,[1] he led me along nameless roads onto empty lots where a few sheds are all that remain of the Hollywood of the past, which the Hollywood of today is no more eager to remember than a rich courtesan is to talk about her adolescent years of love in a garret.

You may smile at my friend's attachment to these old planks, these artificial streets that no longer need the art of the set de-

---

[1]In Victor Hugo's sweeping poem, "The Sadness of Olympio," the hero sadly and passionately reflects on the passage of time, the impermanence of man's efforts, and the mutability of his surroundings.—ED.

signer to give them the patina of time. I did not smile any more than he did at those worm-eaten sets that used to imitate the past and today seem a caricature of it. Doesn't this world of illusion of which only the skeleton remains become confused in our reminiscences with the real world we thought we lived in but of which only pallid images now remain, projected onto our memory?

For the young people of today, the cinema no longer seems to possess that magical value it took on during the years following the end of the First World War. To those who lived through its heroic age, it would seem to have lost the enchantment that the spirit of adventure and joy of discovery lent it. But perhaps we should beware of comparisons between two states of something time has changed as much as it has changed us. The cinema was younger then, but—useless to dodge the fact—we were less old at the time.

Later on, the cinema of today will no doubt seem as surprising as Mack Sennett's bathing beauties are to our era. Will the same charm emanate from these films when they have grown old? Probably, but I am a bad judge. To each man his own past. Every generation possesses a few years and later returns to them to find the image of its youth in them.

1970. I was not acquainted with the Hollywood of the pioneers, but at the time the preceding pages were written, the capital of the cinema was still at the peak of its activity. Each big production company occupied an actual city: M-G-M, Fox, Paramount, Warner's, R.K.O., Universal. . . . All these fortresses have been more or less dismantled, and enormous buildings are being constructed where entire districts of homes and phantom palaces once stood.

At that time there still reigned over Hollywood the last great monster of the prehistoric age: Cecil B. DeMille, director of *The Cheat* in his early days in the cinema, and later producer of enormous machines contrived with such a keen knowledge of the American public and such a flair for publicity that all, or almost all, his films were box-office successes.

But this Barnum with the face of a shrewd lawyer also possessed on occasion an unquestionable visual sense. This struck me particularly when I attended an unusual screening in a studio. In preparation for a project that was quickly forgotten, we were being shown different segments of films whose titles we did not know, all taking place at the time of Christ. These excerpts, inspired by the tritest religious imagery, were all alike, except one that stood out for the sureness of its movement and the grand scale of its composition. I asked the name of the author. It was C. B. DeMille, who without his knowledge easily won this anonymous contest between different displays of togas, robes, camels and palm trees.

I saw C. B. (as every one called him with deferential familiarity) every day in the Paramount commissary, where a large table was reserved for him, at the center of which he held sway, surrounded by his chiefs of staff. I even think that, like Victor Hugo, he sat in an armchair higher than the other seats. Among his customary table companions, who were sometimes joined by some visiting dignitary, was a woman secretary who noted down —for the sake of posterity?—everything the Master said. This potentate was so accustomed to marks of respect that on the day that Salvador Dalí, who is not afraid of spectacular gestures, met him and prostrated himself before him, he is said not to have appeared especially surprised. If this scene took place as it was reported to me, I am very sorry that I was not an eye witness.

Around 1942, during the darkest months of the war, which the United States had entered, President Roosevelt one evening made famous the name of a modest hero. During one of his "fireside chats," as his occasional radio speeches were called, he told the story of Dr. Wassell. This brave doctor (a navy doctor, I think) had saved a number of women and children, leading them through some jungle, in the face of various perils, to a place of safety.

No sooner had the President ended his talk than C. B. had found the subject for his next production. And in the days that followed, perhaps the very next day, the newspapers announced that *The Story of Doctor Wassell* was going to be reenacted on the screen. A contract was signed with the doctor, who soon arrived in California. He was welcomed to the studio with all possible ceremony, then at lunch was seated on C. B.'s right.

On that occasion, no doubt, he met the male star who was to portray him in the studio jungle beneath the sun of the spotlights. Hollywood was not afraid to reconstitute war scenes at home and, since a number of actors were in the service, it was precisely those men whose health or age or some other reason kept them far from combat, who were fought over to take the role of heroes.

The good doctor surely had many opportunities to savor the irony of this parallel between fiction and reality. While the screenplay was being worked out—a long process in which he took part—I think he was surprised more than once by the addition of sentimental or dramatic incidents with which the professionals saw fit to enliven the simple narrative of his adventure that he had given. I can picture the scene: "But that never happened!" "Leave it to us. We know what the public wants." Probably after a few sessions not much attention was paid to his opinions.

It seems that not much more attention was paid to him personally. In the commissary he did not remain for long on the right hand of the Master. As the weeks went by, his table setting became gradually more distant from this place of honor. And one day when C. B. was entertaining important guests, I saw Dr. Wassell lunching at a small table along with a secretary.

The last time I caught sight of him was during the shooting of the film which was to glorify his exploits on countless screens. The working day had just ended. Actors, bit players, technicians and assistants were leaving the studios, getting into their cars and departing in all directions to the cheerful hum of their motors, while, all alone at the corner of the street, the glorious doctor was waiting for the bus.

This sight gave me the idea for a film which would tell the true adventure of Dr. Wassell—his mishaps among the artificial flora and made-up fauna of the cinema. I submitted the project to the high authorities of Paramount, but I was given to understand that war in Hollywood was not a laughing matter.

1944. If the Frenchmen who admire American films want to see everything Hollywood produced between 1940 and 1944, they will have to spend every evening at the movies, Sundays and holidays included, for nearly two years. However, those among them who want to attack the job more expeditiously may attain the same result in some six months, providing they remain in front of the screen eight hours a day.

Since the time American films stopped arriving in France, Hollywood has made more than a thousand feature films (those over an hour in length). The government of the United States classified film production as an essential industry, thereby preventing Hollywood from suffering appreciably from wartime conditions and, despite a few restrictions, permitting the films to continue being made with a technical luxury superior to that of any other country.

Among all these films the French public has not seen, many of which are interesting in more than one respect, it does not seem possible to discern any sign of a revolution in the art or technique of the moving picture. That at least is what the serious American critics think—those who do not automatically give the name of masterpiece to every production costing over two million dollars. Walt Disney is the only American producer who has continued to seek new means of expression in the tradition of the pioneers of the film who, a quarter of a century ago now, made Hollywood the capital of the world of pictures. With the exception of a few of his productions, the admirers of American cinema in France will find again in the recent films most of the formulas that they liked in 1939. But nothing leads us to believe that the years that have just passed will mark an epoch in the history of the cinema like the era of the first sound films or the heroic times of D. W. Griffith and Charlie Chaplin. . . .

1970. I still think so, but I should at least have added that it was during those years that the name of Orson Welles appeared on the screen with its well-known blaze of glory, and that the American comedy was rejuvenated by the handful of films made by the fascinating Preston Sturges.

It is not by chance that I mention these two together. About 1933 Preston Sturges, then a screenplay writer, wrote the script of a film which, under the direction of William K. Howard, became *The Power and the Glory*. For the first time, to my knowledge, Preston had used for dramatic purposes the decomposition of time, the mixture of the present and the past, and what might be called the "future perfect tense" of cinematic grammar.

This innovation (which historians of cinema have barely noticed) did not upset the orthodoxy of Hollywood screenplay writers, and several years had to pass before Sturges' invention was again used in *Citizen Kane*. But since Welles' masterpiece, how many imitations there have been! That which is originality in the work of a master quickly becomes a routine procedure in that of his followers. Even today, many beginners would consider themselves dishonored if they respected chronology and if the spectator were not plunged into a timeless fog in which before, during and after are confused.

Orson's spectacular personality could not brook Hollywood discipline for long. He had to leave. Preston, less intransigent and of lesser stature, though endowed with a real personality, was forced to depart also. The big picture factory, with its perfect mechanism, could not keep within its fold individuals with too strong a feeling for independence. How sad it is to think of the films that should have been made there, but which we will never see!

. . . Although the war did not renew Hollywood's style, it should not be thought that during the war Hollywood was locked up in its celluloid tower. Fifty or sixty per cent of the films recently produced are "war pictures"—that is, films in which the events of the war are the basis of the plot or at least the backdrop. If you are aware that after all Hollywood is only a show-business center where box-office receipts are the supreme law, you will understand that the American producers found some difficulty in reconciling their desire to amuse the paying public with their desire to describe the not very amusing realities of our age. This led to a few misunderstandings. Frenchmen who remember the touches of "local color" sometimes added to the depiction of French life in some Hollywood films, will understand that American fighting men do not always take kindly to the combat scenes which allegedly portray the present war, filmed as they were in California studios. In an article that

pressed the following opinion on this subject:
has aroused some polemics here, the novelist Elliot Paul ex-

> If an American moviegoer is to find out what is happening in
> countries occupied by the Nazis and the Japanese, if he is to see
> the effects of an invasion and feel what other nations feel when
> the sacrifice of their children, their homes and their farms is the
> price of a victory, we must call upon new film producers who will
> be able to choose themes that have some relationship to reality.

It is not very likely that these new producers will be called
upon as long as this prosperity lasts—prosperity created by an
era in which a ticket to a film show is one of the rare objects
that are not rationed; a prosperity that insures the financial
success of the least well-made productions, and which caused a
disenchanted author to say one day: "To lose money on a picture
today, you really have to produce a masterpiece." . . .

1970. This prosperity did not last long. After the war, the
big American firms started to notice the first cracks appearing
in their foundations. It was soon to be learned that this superb
edifice was no more solid than a set shaken by the wind. People
like to say that it was television that brought about the decline
of the cinema. It would be more correct to attribute this decline
to what might be called "the democratic comforts," of which
television sets, like automobiles, are a principal element. In
this regard it has not been sufficiently noticed that the number
of admissions to movie houses has decreased in exact proportion
to the increase in sales of gasoline.

. . . If Hollywood has not yet produced a picture which is to
the present war what *The Big Parade* and *All Quiet on the
Western Front* were to the preceding, there is no need to be
surprised. Important reminiscences of contemporary events will
probably not appear on the screen until 1955, when these events
have been sifted by memory, and when people will be able to
believe in the fictions of the novel-like films that pale today
beside the documents that cameras are recording on the very
sites where the war is being fought. These documents, of which
the public sees only tiny excerpts in the weekly newsreels, will
later form a unique collection, which will testify to the most im-

portant contribution Hollywood made to the war effort. In fact, all these "documentaries" and "photo reports," all these films made for propaganda, instruction or history, whether made by the film services of the Administration or by those of the armed forces, are due for the most part to Hollywood technicians and the pupils they have trained.

At the beginning of the war, the government of the United States had a very simple idea, so simple that it seems extraordinary: it entrusted the job of organizing its film services to those whose profession was precisely the making of films, and, more extraordinary yet, it chose these people without taking anything into account but their preeminence in their profession. In this way the American war cinema has been guided by some of the best craftsmen of the Hollywood cinema. At the Office of War Information is to be found the writer Robert Riskin; in the army, the director Frank Capra, promoted to the rank of colonel; in the air force, the lieutenant colonels William Wyler and George Stevens; in the navy, Commander John Ford—to mention only a few of those whose names appear most often in the honor roll of the American film, and who today, provided with the material means and the requisite authority, are directing the execution of the enormous filmed fresco in which in the years to come the world at peace will be able to rediscover the overpowering images of the world at war.

It is well known that the government of the United States has long understood the importance of the film industry. In peacetime it aided the spread of Hollywood films throughout the world, and in wartime it asked Hollywood for the assistance of its technicians and its incomparable technical facilities. Now that Hollywood is suggesting that the problems of international cinema be discussed at the peace conferences, the government will probably not reject this suggestion, which once might have seemed outlandish. In every large country from now on, the cinema, like the radio, is no longer simply the object of an industry and a business, it is also a government matter.

1950. If I had thought that the last sentence of this article would elicit the variety of comments that it did inspire, I would have explained myself more clearly.

It was not my purpose, in these few words, to set up the formula "Politics first" in opposition to the American formula "Profits first," source of such well-known misdeeds.

The state does not have the right to consider a film as a piece of merchandise subject only to the rules of business. On the other hand, a national film industry cannot solve the problems on which its very existence depends, without some assistance from the state. But this does not mean that it is desirable for the state to *control* inspiration and *supervise* the production of films. Civil servants are no more creative than bankers, and in art, conformity is the most sterile and, all in all, the most "reactionary" state of mind there is.

In our day, unfortunately, there are intellectuals in different countries whose minds work in such a way that if they had lived under Louis XIV, they would have approved of *Tartuffe* only because of the speech in which the officer proclaims the greatness of the Prince and the beauties of the regime.[1]

1970. A discreet reference, perhaps too discreet, to those who demand that a work of art serve to promote political (or moral, or religious) ideas first and foremost—that is, to the orthodox of all causes and faiths. In the preface that Louis Daquin asked me to write for his book *Le Cinéma notre métier* (The cinema, our profession),* I said:

Naturally, not all readers will agree with the opinions expressed in the following pages, and I would be adorning the truth if I claimed to share them without reservation. (For example, I would have more than one thing to say about realism and escape and about the social role of the cinema, especially this: the charming or amusing film is *useful,* even if it does no more than give our contemporaries a few moments of happiness.)

What a daring thing to say in this age, in which "involvement"

---

[1] *Tartuffe* concludes with a patriotic speech by a *deus ex machina* officer that has virtually nothing to do with the central conflicts or comedy of the play. Molière inserted it there to assure himself of the king's protection, since he knew that the play itself would be rather offensive to a number of powerful people at the court.—ED.

*Editeurs français réunis, 1960.

has not yet gone out of fashion! Would not readers of this statement scent some frivolousness in it, or even some reactionary dilettantism? " 'A few moments of happiness!' Did I hear right? In what age do you think you're living?"

Today, the theory of utilitarian art seems to have been abandoned, sometimes even by those who would have most reason to defend it. For example, listen to Roland Leroy, Secretary of the Central Committee of the French Communist Party:*

> Some people find blameworthy, or at least not recommendable, any public performance which is not directly intended to make the working class politically conscious.
> Thereby they completely obliterate the borders between art and politics. They deny the specificity of art and, in regard to the performing arts, they deny a notion which is linked to this specificity: the notion of pleasure. There are some people for whom the idea of pleasure for the workers has something impious in it, so long as they have not accomplished the revolution. . . . According to some present-day theorists, the theater, the popular song and the cinema should be nothing but a political speech; otherwise they would only be class—middle-class—culture. This confusion mutilates the arts and impoverishes politics.

For some people, that goes without saying. For others, it is much better to have it stated as precisely as it is here.

---

*Speech at the inauguration of the Gérard Philipe Theater in Saint-Denis, February 1969.

A TRIBUTE TO RENÉ CLAIR: The following twenty-two pages contain stills from nineteen of his finest films, 1923–1957. (For stills from two other Clair films, *Entr'acte* and *Silence Is Golden,* see the illustrations following pages 12 and 222, respectively.)

Paris qui dort (title in America *The Crazy Ray*; 1923). The watchman of the Eiffel Tower, who has escaped the ray that put Paris to sleep, wanders through the streets observing the "frozen" citizens. (The Museum of Modern Art Film Stills Archive)

Le Voyage imaginaire (The Imaginary Journey; 1925). The entrance to fairyland. (Herman G. Weinberg Collection)

La Proie du vent (Prey of the Wind; 1926). A scene with Charles Vanel and Sandra Milovanov. (Herman G. Weinberg Collection)

Un Chapeau de paille d'Italie (The Italian Straw Hat; 1927). The bridegroom (Albert Préjean) finds that his horse has chewed up the straw hat of a married lady (Olga Tschekhowa) while she was entertaining an officer (Vital Geymond) behind the shrubbery. (The Museum of Modern Art Film Stills Archive)

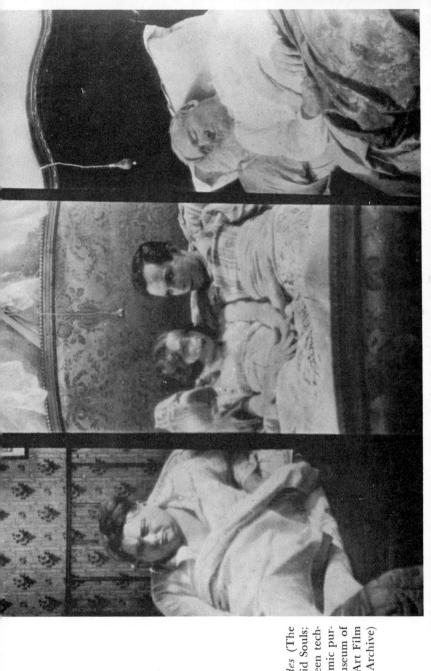

Les deux Timides (The Two Timid Souls; 1928). Split-screen technique for comic purposes. (The Museum of Modern Art Film Stills Archive)

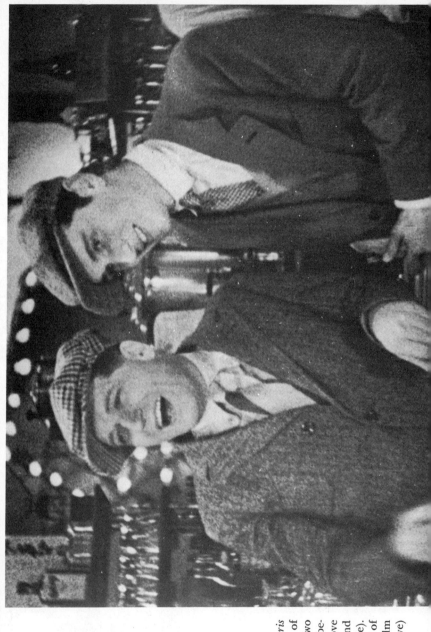

Sous les Toits de Paris (Under the Roofs of Paris; 1930). The two companions who become rivals in love (Albert Préjean and Edmond Gréville). (The Museum of Modern Art Film Stills Archive)

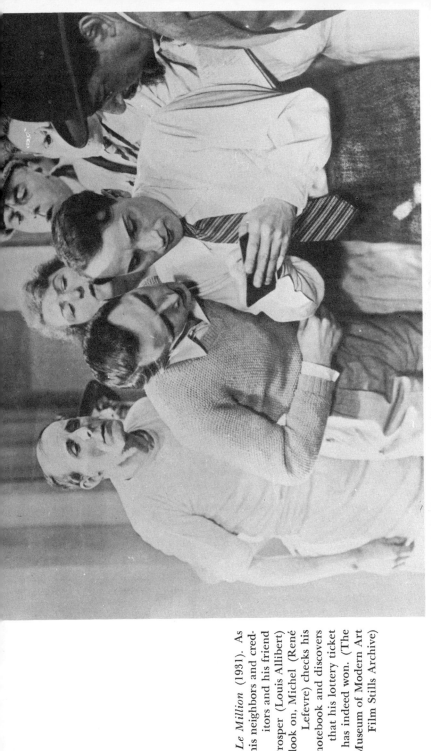

Le Million (1931). As his neighbors and creditors and his friend Prosper (Louis Allibert) look on, Michel (René Lefevre) checks his notebook and discovers that his lottery ticket has indeed won. (The Museum of Modern Art Film Stills Archive)

A Nous la Liberté (1931). Two former prison companions: the wealthy industrialist who made a successful jailbreak (Raymond Cordy) and his artless new employee (Henri Marchand). (Herman G. Weinberg Collection)

A Nous la liberté.
With blackmail in
mind, some old cronies
make an unexpected
call on the industrialist.
(The Museum of
Modern Art Film
Stills Archive)

Quatorze Juillet
(The Fourteenth of
July; 1932). This
frame enlargement
shows Georges Rigaud
as the taxi driver
and Pola Illery as his
former mistress.
(R C Dale Collection)

Le dernier Milliardaire (The Last Billionaire; 1934). High jinks in the palace of Casinario, with Marthe Mellot as the Queen and Max Dearly (at the phone) as Banco. (The Museum of Modern Art Film Stills Archive)

The Ghost Goes West (1935). The house-warming party thrown by the American millionaire (Eugene Pallette) who has had a Scottish castle re-erected in Florida. (The Museum of Modern Art Film Stills Archive)

The Flame of
New Orleans (1940).
Marlene Dietrich as
the adventuress and
Bruce Cabot as the
sailor she loves.
(R C Dale Collection)

I Married a Witch (1942). A scene with Cecil Kellaway, Veronica Lake, Fredric March and Robert Benchley. (The Museum of Modern Art Film Stills Archive)

It Happened Tomorrow (1943). A scene with Jack Oakie and Linda Darnell. (The Museum of Modern Art Film Stills Archive)

And Then There Were None (1945). Walter Huston, Louis Hayward and Roland Young discover one of the many murder victims. (The Museum of Modern Art Film Stills Archive)

La Beauté du Diable (Beauty and the Devil; 1949). Mephistopheles (Michel Simon) leers at a pretty servant girl. (The Museum of Modern Art Film Stills Archive)

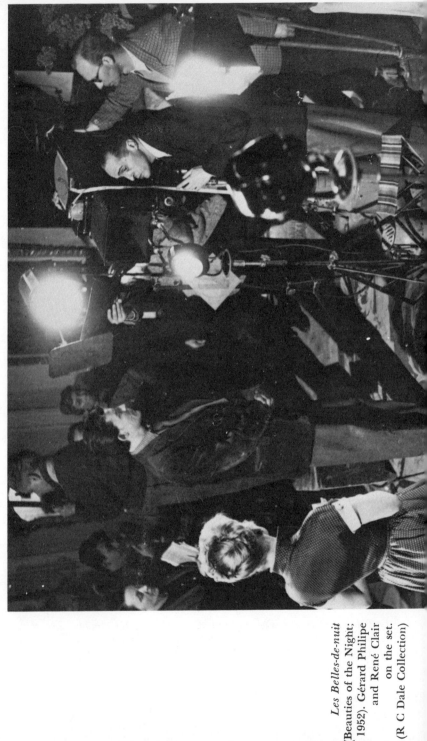

Les Belles-de-nuit
(Beauties of the Night;
1952). Gérard Philipe
and René Clair
on the set.
(R C Dale Collection)

Les Belles-de-nuit. A scene with Gérard Philipe and Martine Carol; the young composer dreams he is a great success in the nineteenth century. (Herman G. Weinberg Collection)

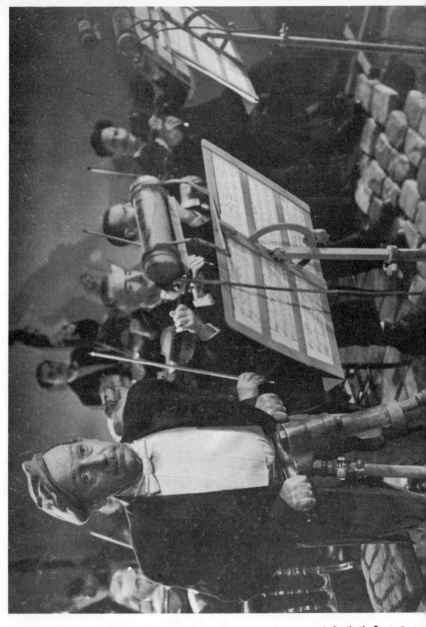

Les Belles-de-nuit.
A nightmare symphony
in which all the noises
of the composer's
waking life combine to
destroy his music.
(R C Dale Collection)

Les grandes Manœuvres (The Grand Maneuver; 1956). The lovely Marie-Louise and her admirer Duverger (Michèle Morgan and Jean Desailly). (The Museum of Modern Art Film Stills Archive)

Porte des Lilas
(Gates of Paris; 1957)
Juju (Pierre Brasseur)
attempting to filch a
bottle from his
neighborhood bar.
(R C Dale Collection)

On International Cinema

1945. The situation of the international cinema can be summed up as follows: while the number of films that can be produced in the world is unlimited, the number of film theaters in which these films can be shown is limited in practice. If all the films produced by the different studios in the world were to be projected in all the movie houses of a country like France, French film production would be buried beneath them. That is why every country must make a choice—whether it wants to or not—among the foreign films that are offered to it. Up to now this choice has been made in a more or less arbitrary manner; it has been subject to temporary commercial agreements, to mutual understandings between industrial groups or, more often, to the laws of supply and demand, bronze laws of the economy of the past which modern trusts have been able to give the flexibility of brass. And yet it seems that this choice—which is important because it involves the exchange of influences between different civilizations—should be determined by other rules than those of an outmoded spirit of barter. That is why it seems that the time has come to draw up an international charter of the cinema.

And right away, if you don't mind. Before the European war was over, people were already talking about the battle to win film markets. Some film producers are thinking only of invading the markets that seem most vulnerable to them, and are no more concerned over the national production of those countries than the Nazis were over the independence of Czechoslovakia or Greece. Naturally, the countries threatened are talking about defensive measures, which of course would be met by opposing measures. To hear the two sides speak, one advantage of the peace will be that of placing the various film industries in a state of permanent conflict. Unfortunately, the outcome of this conflict might very well be that one day or another, every country will lock itself up within its own borders and will no longer see any films but those of its national industry, in accordance with the best Fascist principles. Is that the result being aimed for?

It is not easy to define here what an international charter of the cinema would contain. But if you are willing to admit that it is every country's duty to insure the existence of its own film production, and that international film exchange has an intellectual value that is greater than its commercial value, it will not be impossible to find a solution to the problems that concern us.

As I say these words, I already hear stirring the numerous survivors of an age in which, under the banner of economic freedom, a system of industrial and financial imperialism had been organized which, let us hope, will be a source of amusement to our grandnephews. Let those people understand us: we do not advocate a return, in this area, to strictly protectionist measures taken to defend private interests. Instead, we want to ensure a sound basis for the exchange of films between countries and the preservation of the international nature of the cinema.

It is to be hoped that France will take the initiative toward a world conference in which these problems will be discussed. If I think that this role is proper to France, it is first of all because Paris is the natural junction point between the Anglo-Saxon production centers and those of continental Europe and the Soviet Union; and also because the French cinema, impoverished by the war and its aftermath, cannot be suspected of any ambitions of unlawful conquests.

Meanwhile, if France is to play this part with the requisite authority, she must first of all set her own house in order— that is, she must have a program of national production, new ideas supplied by its management personnel, and especially government agencies that will finally take the cinema seriously. If we do not cure the French cinema of its prewar ills, it is pointless to seek its salvation in artificial protectionist measures. Yes or no? Is the French cinema to be seriously reorganized, or are the men and the methods that kept it in a state of permanent semi-bankruptcy to be allowed gradually to take over again? Action must be taken today.

1950. Naturally, the suggestion presented in this article was received with the polite smiles that people reserve for chasers of rainbows. Nothing is more rational, however, or—to speak the language of the day—more "realistic."

In fact, most of the regulations that apply to the export or import of films will be valid only so long as a cinematic work is represented by a few reels of film that can be physically examined at borders by customs officials.

If the progress being made in television permits us tomorrow to telecast films from one country to another, what will these regulations be worth? Radio, which had less important problems to deal with, had to submit to an international convention, at least for the assignment of wavelengths.

1970. If it is true that radio was able to solve this problem, it may be the only international convention that has been established and more or less observed since 1945. The relative optimism prevalent at that date makes us sigh today. But at the end of the Second World War, it was possible to dream of a better organization of our planet, just as it was permissible in 1918 to imagine that the war just ended would be the last. . . .

Even now, there is no international regulation insuring a rational dissemination of films. And tomorrow, when hundreds of satellites will be able to pour onto any country a gigantic rain of images coming from any source? If our politicians thought about this, they would no doubt murmur in secret: "After us, the deluge of pictures and sound!"[1]

---

[1] A play on the statement made by Louis XV's mistress, Mme. de Pompadour, who said: "After us, the deluge." She was referring to the political ramifications of Louis' reign, which did indeed contribute to the Revolution.—ED.

A Retroactive Revolution

1961. We hear all too often: "My film this, my film that, my film the other thing."* After this come commentaries on what the intentions of the said film are, what people ought to think about it, what should be understood between the lines of dialogue or behind the images. And the problems! So many complex problems encumber the cameras that you wonder how those machines can still operate! "This problem, that problem, the other problem." You cannot keep count of the problems that must be solved on the blackboard of the screen. Dear Mack Sennett, how many professors there are among your descendants!

And the worlds! There are worlds, too. That is the latest find of our filmologists. From his very first film, a director who has a way with people brings us "his own view of the world" or more simply "his world" or "his universe," in all modesty. And when A's world meets B's universe, this shock does not produce, as you might think, a cosmic cataclysm, but just simply one more film. There is the world of C, which is "strictly subjective," that of D, which is "a world divested of all interiority," and that of E, which is "a world without finality." I will stop here. The alphabet would be too short to catalogue this plurality of worlds if these different worlds did not tend to form a single one: the world in which we are bored.[1]

Nowadays boredom has its titles of nobility. It is the sign of the serious, of the distinguished—in a word, of the "intellectual" —and for some people, a public performance cannot be altogether delectable if it is not seasoned to some extent with some such condiment. Dare I admit that in the long run this kind of food kills the appetite? It is necessary to face the fact that in the short history of the cinema and in the long history of the theater, the works that have made a mark and have survived are not boring works. Sophocles, Shakespeare, Molière and Chekhov knew how to hold their audience's interest and are no worse for it today.

---

*R.C., preface to *Tout l'Or du monde* (Gallimard, 1961).

[1]Clair refers to the title of a well-known nineteenth-century comedy by Pailleron, *Le Monde où l'on s'ennuie.*—ED.

Don't you feel that it would be polite to think a little bit about the audience when you invite them to sit down in a theater and they put an hour or two of their existence at your disposal? A spectator is not a reader. The reader can close the book whenever he likes. The spectator is unable to slacken in his attention for a moment. A minute of boredom during a show does not seem to be a serious fault, but if a million people are watching that show, that minute will create a million minutes of boredom, and that weighs heavily in the balance of time.

Now that antimatter has just been discovered, it is not surprising that the concept of "anti" is prevalent in artistic creation: anti-novel, anti-painting, and tomorrow, no doubt, anti-music and anti-poetry. The cinema owed it to itself not to be left out. We do not yet have the anti-film, but we are on the right path, because some people are already sketching out the theory of the film without an audience. Let us make this clear. These people do not intend to do without the audience altogether, and they would even welcome graciously those stubborn viewers who absolutely insisted on sitting down in front of a screen. It seems, however, that the most important thing for them is to "express themselves" with a camera, just as people used to "express themselves" in essays, poems and novels.

Let us recall in passing that the great novelists do not seem to have conceived such a purpose. It may even be assumed that it never entered their mind and that they would not have understood the meaning of this jargon. Did Balzac, Stendhal and Dostoyevski want to "express themselves"? They were more interested in the characters they were creating than in their own person, although this does not prevent them from being reflected in their works more clearly than many writers of memoirs or intimate diaries. A writer who accidentally reveals himself often tells us more than a writer who is making a conscious confession.

In the cinema, this desire to "express oneself" bears the stamp of a very outspoken vanity. It is indecent to attach so much importance to oneself. And to admit to this desire is to display a lack of humor that would be odd, had not humor become one of the scarcest commodities. Where is humor hiding at a time when everyone is so serious about taking himself seriously? Aldous Huxley recently asked: "Where is Rabelais? Where is Swift?" I do not know how to answer this question, but I can give him the address of Vadius and Trissotin.[1] They are still alive and well, the lucky dogs! Their influence is great in the arts and letters. They must like this century, in which they have found the right people for their ideas. They are not the ones to shout, as Huxley does: "Long live satire!" They are not the ones to be stirred when the author of *Brave New World* states: "Humor is extremely important. It is the modern manifestation of humility."

One of the forms of humility for a dramatic author—here, stage and screen are alike—is to think about his audience. A cinema cut off from its roots among the people would soon be desiccated by academicism. An "artistic" cinema would in reality be an old-fashioned cinema inasmuch as it would only be renewing in another form the error of the *film d'art* of the heroic days. To create a "literary" cinema is an ambition befitting men of letters who do not feel much like writing, or cinema people who have not retained much from their reading if they have read at all. To dream of films for a limited audience, like the slim volumes of poetry that were published at the time of Adoré Floupette,[2] is to display a strange misunderstanding of our era. It is equivalent to wanting to cross the Place de la Concorde in a sedan chair.[3]

It can never be repeated too often: painting or poetry can wait until "communication" is established between the work of art and the public, but the performing arts do not share this privilege. Immediate "communication" is the primary condition of their existence. For the film creator that is the only problem, the most difficult one too, the problem of style. A novelist can do away with most of the rules of fiction, but only

---

[1] Characters from Molière's *Les Femmes savantes*. Vadius was a comical pedant, Trissotin a pretentious precious poet.—ED.

[2] Adoré Floupette was the imaginary author of a book of poetry that parodied symbolism toward the end of the nineteenth century.—ED.

[3] The Place de la Concorde is Paris' busiest intersection, at which about fifteen lanes of traffic swirl in a mad circle about a central island. Pedestrians wishing to cross it must plunge right into the traffic and hope for the best.—ED.

providing the result is something like *Journey to the End of the Night*.[1] Oddness or obscurity of style too often does nothing but disguise the weakness of the thought. People with nothing to say attempt to make their commonplace remarks look original, whereas the sign of a good author is that his originality sounds commonplace. Nothing becomes conventional more quickly than the unconventional. Condillac was correct in thinking that "the mania for appearing out of the ordinary denatures the best minds."

More than one newcomer to the cinema ought to meditate on that sentence. I quote it with newcomers in mind. Some of them, by their talent, their knowledge of the craft and the enthusiasm they feel for this craft, can bring to the cinema the new blood that its huge organism needs more than ever. It would be too bad if, in the quest for genius, they were to follow the blind alley into which they are called by the professors of fashion, the admirers of the ineffable and the people who jump onto the newest bandwagons. Genius is like Jean de Nivelle's dog.[2] To acquire talent, you need a little knowledge and a great deal of patience. But to ascribe genius to yourself, you need only be ignorant. When talk turns to genius, it should be remembered that Griffith, Chaplin and Eisenstein were working neither for themselves nor for the filmologists, but for the public of the whole world. . . .

I do not think that a moral must necessarily be found in every tale. This one possesses none of the glamour of allegory. You know what I mean: the light of a street lamp represents loneliness, a garbage can is civilization, the chase after a gangster is the quest for God. . . . No, you will find in our story none of those profound things, and if by chance a character gets kicked in the behind, I can assure you that this kick has no symbolic meaning and aims at no other goal than the one it reaches.

Ideas are suitable in literature, but a show, though it may

---

[1] Céline's *Voyage au bout de la nuit* (1932) breaks most of the rules for polite fiction to create a highly colloquial journey through a land of corruption and despair—contemporary life.—ED.

[2] Jean de Nivelle, like M. de la Palice, is a victim of faulty cultural transmission. Through that distortion, a popular French locution formulizes certain sorts of perversity by saying that Jean de Nivelle's dog always runs away when it is called.—ED.

offer the suggestion of ideas, is not the right place to express them explicitly. If it presents them, all right, but it should not demonstrate them. If there was ever a man guided by his ideas, that was Voltaire. And yet it was he who said: "The aim of the theater is not to win an argument, but to stir the emotions."

In this respect the history of the theater gives us lessons that the cinema would be wrong to disregard. Just look what has become of the works of Dumas *fils* and so many other preachers![1] To contemporary eyes, the ideas of the day shine brightly in the glow of the footlights, but later nothing remains of a play but the characters, the sentiments and the style. Of all the ideas that can be expressed on a stage, there are very few which do not remain rolled up like old backdrops in the dust of their time.

1970. This innocuous pamphlet raised a storm of protests. And yet it contained only very simple truths. To assert that the performing arts are intended for their audience is a truism worthy of M. de la Palice. But that legendary marshal would cut a sorry figure compared with our modern dialecticians.

An art critic communicated a very interesting thought to us the other day: "If you like a painting at first glance, that means it is completely uninteresting. A work of art demands an effort on the part of the viewer or the listener. More than that. It must DISPLEASE them at first."

This inversion of roles takes some getting used to. In the past, the artist had to try to *please* or to be understood. In our century, the art lover must do the work. Let the poor fool sweat it out, it was high time! Besides, he is fully inclined to do so today. His middle-class ancestors failed to buy at the right time the Cézannes, Van Goghs and Monets which they did not like. Now there is weeping and gnashing of teeth among the heirs. Just think what those pictures are worth now! The descendants promptly set themselves a rule of conduct. They still rely on their taste, but take the opposite action. They consider good

---

[1]Along with his novels, Alexandre Dumas *fils* wrote a number of *pièces à thèse*, or problem plays, of which the best-known is *La Dame aux camélias* (*Camille*), in which he criticized bourgeois attitudes toward prostitution. In later plays, he became increasingly polemical and decreasingly dramatic, so that despite their vogue in the middle of the nineteenth century, the plays are completely neglected today.—ED.

the things which displease them "at first glance": constructions of matchstick splinters, burlap, poster scraps or empty frames. Fifty years after Dada created such things and Marcel Duchamp produced his "ready-mades"! You must keep up with the times, damn it! For my part, I see nothing wrong with that. But what are people talking about?

"There is anti-art and there are non-artists," says Hélène Parmelin. "There is a bazaar of ideas. There is kinetic art. There is anything you want.

"Then, in another area, there are painting and sculpture, with or without easel."*

The same goes for the cinema. A film-maker recently declared that a film can and should express "the denial of the idea of a performance"; what it should express in a positive manner is "the idea of an ordeal, if not imposed on, then at least proposed to, the spectator." That at least has the merit of being clear. As soon as the idea of a performance is denied, no more discussion is possible. If we continue to believe that the cinema is a performing art and, what is more, one intended for the people, all we can do is blush with shame. But we will be blushing in good company.

What did Apollinaire say? "The real epic was the one recited to the assembled people, and nothing is closer to the people than the cinema."

What does André Malraux hope? ". . . that art and literature will finally assume the dimensions of that mass world which is ours."

What does Raymond Queneau say? "There is no doubt that the cinema is an art, but it is as unrelated to literature as sculpture is to music. Outside intellectual circles, the cinema was born on the fairground, lived in working-class neighborhoods and flourished without the aid of the cultivated."

What did Jean Epstein assert over forty years ago? "It is wrong to speak of cinema for the elite. . . . For that is no longer cinema, but literature." About the same time, Léon Moussinac added: "The cinema will exist for the people or will not exist at all."

But just wanting to be a folk artist does not make you one.

*L'Anti-art et les anartistes (Christian Bourgois, 1969).

"Art is not born of the masses," Mayakovsky said, "it is made theirs only after a large number of efforts."

There we have it! "A large number of efforts" requires perseverance and humility, not to mention talent. It is less difficult to play the part of the "accursed" artist.

Ingmar Bergman has this to say:

> The film creator is dealing with a medium of expression that interests not only him but also millions of other persons.* . . . As for the public, it asks only one thing of a film: "I paid and I want to be amused, caught up, involved; I want to forget my troubles, my relatives, my job; I want to be taken out of myself." . . . The director who recognizes these demands and who lives off the public's money is placed in a difficult position, one which gives him obligations. While making his film, he must constantly take into account the reaction of the viewers. I, personally, keep asking myself: "Can I express this more simply, more purely, more briefly? Will everyone understand what I mean here? Will the simplest mind be able to follow the course of these events?"

A statement that honest can only come from a true film author. Only nostalgic dilettantes still believe that two cinemas should exist: one for the public and one for an alleged elite. I thought so myself at the time when it was necessary to try to protect a "quality" cinema from catastrophe. But the distance between this position and that of championing an unusual cinema *first and foremost* is one that is too great to expect to bridge.

In France, certain movie houses are officially called "art and experimental" houses. "Experimental," all right, but "art"— what do you mean? What ordinance, what civil servants, can determine legally (as wines are given their *appellation contrôlée*) [1] what is art and what is not? Has anyone thought of drawing up the statutes of the *official* avant-garde?

A few showy successes in poetry or painting make the naïve think that the admiration of the future is assured to everything

---

Les Lettres françaises, April 1959.

[1] In France, wines are assigned specific names, somewhat in parallel to American brand names, which cannot be used by any producer other than those registered to make any given wine.—ED.

that repels the public at first.* An illusion like that is characteristic of an era among whose weaknesses is that of confusing the notion of progress with the notion of novelty. Lack of comprehension of an author's work is not a firm promise of his future glory. The mystique of the "avant-garde" is a very recent creation, and most of our contemporaries would be astonished to learn that neither Lautréamont nor Alfred Jarry ever claimed to be in the vanguard of anything whatsoever.[1]

But since every thesis invokes an antithesis, let us give the floor to Eugène Ionesco. Speaking of the avant-garde in the theater, the author of *The Chairs* writes: ". . . there is a language of the theater, a theatrical gait, a path to be cleared in order to reach objectively existing realities: and this path to be cleared (or rediscovered) is none other than that which is suited to the theater when it deals with realities that can only be revealed in theatrical terms. It is what is generally called experimental work."†

All right. There are also realities which can only be revealed in cinematic terms. And no one is trying to deny the usefulness for the cinema of experimental work. But only if things are called by their right name. And if it is remembered that conformity is quick to change masks. Furthermore, let us not forget this: when, in London, theaters reserved for a select audience replaced the popular enclosures within which the Elizabethan genius had fluorished, the most glorious era of the English theater came to an end.

Jean-François Revel has written:

> No work of art can now be introduced to the public without the idea of novelty.‡ That is, novelty plays exactly the same role that academic conceptions did a century ago. To be admitted to the Salon in 1860, an artist had to follow Ingres's canons of draftsmanship, and had first to meet certain demands which were con-

---

*R. C., *Discours de réception à l'Académie française.*

1Lautréamont and Jarry, late nineteenth-century authors respectively of *The Songs of Maldoror* and *King Ubu,* were among the most extraordinary innovators of French literature.—ED.

†Eugène Ionesco, *Notes et contre-notes* (Gallimard, 1966) .

‡*Arts,* 1959.

sidered as the basic platform of all painting.[1] Any attempt at renewal in regard to that platform was taken not as a renewal, but as a mistake. The result was that the creator of every really new approach practically tried to deny its novelty (Manet, for example) and to justify himself in the light of the established values. Today it is just the opposite; every one with a worn-out and exhausted idea must burst forth saying: "I destroy all previous ideas; no one will understand me, etc." That is because everyone who counted in literature, painting or music between 1860 and 1960 corresponded more or less to the pattern of the "misunderstood creator." This pattern must now in turn constitute the basic platform, and we end up with the prototype of present-day academicism: the misunderstood creator who is immediately understood.

Thus, the concept of avant-garde no longer includes the unexpected and unpredictable, but has a predetermined subject matter, in which the hunters of new esthetics are sure to find, in a well-guarded preserve, a wealth of game officially labeled as "wild."* . . .

Someone for whom music is automatically good if it is twelve-tone, a painting automatically good if it is abstract, a novel automatically good if it is written in the *nouveau roman* style[2]—that man is the victim of a new academicism; he is relying on criteria exterior to the work of art, on outward descriptions, on mechanically applied rules. To be sure that you are dealing with someone who really believes what he says, you must be able to ascertain whether, when looking at paintings (for example), he makes a distinction between good and bad both in abstract and in figurative works. The area in which the retroactive revolution has most spectacularly succeeded *is the cinema.*

The idea that every artist must create his own little revolution is not new. Fernand Gregh showed its origin in his *Victor Hugo:*

The fault that could perhaps be found with the Preface to *Cromwell* is not so much that it buried a part—the part least to

---

[1]Revel refers to the yearly exhibitions of French painting that were sanctioned by the government and administered by the School of Beaux-Arts. Ingres was the leading neo-classical painter. In 1863, Manet and other young impressionists were refused the right to hang their canvasses at the official salon for the reasons Revel mentions. Responding to public outcry, Napoléon III allowed them to display their works in a separate part of the exhibition hall, in what became known as the famous Salon des Refusés.—ED.

*Let us recall the epigram attributed to Louis Jouvet: "In the performing arts, everything is evolving, everything is in ferment. There is only one thing that never changes: the avant-garde."

[2]The French "new novel" style involves an objective, dispassionate and intensive examination of the exterior aspects presented by various subjects.—ED.

be missed—of what came before it, as that it had some unfortunate consequences.[1] In fact, the Preface is inspired by the memory of the French Revolution, applied to drama and poetry; naïvely imitating politics, it introduced political behavior and vocabulary into literature; it made popular the concept of literary and artistic revolution; it replaced the idea of normal continuity, which was the idea of properly understood tradition, with the idea of progress achieved by sharp and catastrophic breaks with the past.

This idea was eminently successful. It prevails today in the area of artistic production, or at least the part of that production that is most discussed. In his brilliant essay, "Finie la comédie" (The comedy is over),[*] Bertrand Poirot-Delpech took stock of this new academicism:

> And also for the idea that every work of art must be decidedly new or must not exist at all. What? They dare disturb us for something that does not turn its back on the past? That is the latest reproach spread abroad by the arbiters of intellectual and artistic elegance. A dreadful reproach for the impressionable creator, because, failing to reach an agreement on what modernity should be, the augurs pronounce in chorus that everything has been said in every way. All that remains to be done it to hide old merchandise, that disgraceful thing, under a smokescreen in so far as possible, just as other manufacturers, in the furniture department, put a patina on new merchandise to make it look old. The last few seasons, just as women's dresses have had to be short, so art has had to be obscure, and that is all there is to it.
>
> This is apt to discourage the public. But it has become a sign of quality to be understood only by the specialists, the writer only by writers, the film-maker only by film-makers, if at all! The use of artifice makes real inventiveness unnecessary. Take your love story that is dumber than a gossip columnist's novel, or your B-picture detective story screenplay, and start telling them from the end backwards, with blackouts of memory; splice in tracts and newsreel footage; throw in technical conversations about visual and audial experience—and it will be hailed as a revelation, no! a revolution, provided the general public, that fathead, screams for mercy.

¶ The above-mentioned formula of Mayakovsky concerns all

[1]Victor Hugo's preface to his play *Cromwell* forms one of the two great manifestoes of French Romantic theater. Although Hugo's ideas were mainly borrowed from Schlegel and Stendhal, his ringing, militant language gave the preface a great deal more notoriety than the earlier works ever gained.—ED.

[*]Gallimard, 1969.

forms of artistic activity, as far as I know, but is particularly applicable to the performing arts. It is well known that Mayakovsky wrote for the stage, and he even sketched out a screenplay for the cinema: *The Ideal and the Blanket.*

"Am following negotiations screenplay René Clair." This sentence from a telegram he sent from Paris to his friend Lily Brik* in 1928 finds no echo in my memory. This screenplay never came to my notice, and I don't think I ever saw Mayakovsky. No doubt some go-between told him that I might be able to use his screenplay, but neglected to inform me of this. I don't know. Perhaps he wanted to meet me; I would have liked to make his acquaintance. . . . Mayakovsky killed himself in 1930, when the era of "revolutionary romanticism" was coming to an end.

How many meetings have failed to take place, through the years, and how sorry I am about them! But there are also some that were arranged to perfection by some practical-joker Fate, and these are amusing.

When I saw the Marx Brothers' first films, I dreamed of working with these funny characters. But how could I let them know I wanted to? I was in Paris, and they were in Hollywood, where they were bound by impressive contracts. Furthermore, it was not very likely that they had the slightest need of my services or even knew my name. I soon filed away that dream among the dead letters.

Some ten years later, in Hollywood, I became friendly with Groucho and Harpo. One day, while we were talking about Paris, one of them said to me: "We looked for you in Paris; we wanted to see you. But it was the summertime and you weren't there." What did they want of me? "To ask you to work with us." And when? Exactly at the time I dreamt of working with them.

---

*Letters from Mayakovsky to Lily Brik (Gallimard, 1969) .

On the Morals of Our Day

At the time when France still possessed those "houses" which hypocrisy closed down in 1945, thus benefiting the sidewalk industry, some of these establishments had a movie auditorium in which they showed films that were not erotic—the term has been sullied now—but honestly pornographic. In these modest films, everything was open and aboveboard, and no matter what the plot was, it was easy to foresee how it would come out.

I particularly recall one evening on which a festival of these films was given by Mme. Aline, the owner of the most famous house in Marseilles, where some friends and I happened to be. The five or six films we saw differed very little from those I had seen in similar places, and their naïveté was not without its charm. But in the long run that sort of stuff produces a rather unhappy effect of monotony. My companions were Surrealists of the deepest dye, but even though nothing concerning love was alien to them, they finally seemed to become as bored as I was.

This feeling of boredom still comes over me occasionally, and for the same reasons—no longer in a brothel, but in normal commercial movie houses. There are fashions in the profession of the performing arts: they say that around 1900, an alert playwright would always make sure that in at least one act the leading man appeared on stage in full evening dress. Around 1925, many producers required every film to include at least one society reception, if not a vaudeville or nightclub scene. From 1960 on, their successors insisted on at least one bedroom scene in every production, and wanted the public to get their money's worth on that item.

And so, how many heroes have we seen without their shirt, how many panting ladies whose lascivious delirium does not affect the perfection of their makeup! There is absolutely no call for big expenses or for genius to manufacture plot situations of this type. It takes only a camera and actors willing to strip. The recipe is easy enough for any beginner who wants to gain a reputation for boldness, and even renowned film-makers do not disdain to resort to it. When their inventiveness wears thin, so do their actresses' costumes, and it is a rare spectator who would dare to complain about this easy way out and not be afraid of being called a prude.

Such liberties would be justified if the subject or the action of a film made them necessary. But, to be serious about it, this would be an unusual case, and in these matters what is involved is not so much artistic necessity as submission to business demands. The story went around a few years ago that in some South American country close-ups of anonymous genitals were spliced into love scenes made in Hollywood. It is no longer necessary to make these charming additions. The merchandise is delivered with nothing missing, and professors, both men and women, preferably Nordic and wearing glasses, look at it with a gravity devoid of any trace of humor.

In his review of film production in 1968, Mr. Jean-Louis Curtis wrote:

> Eroticism seems to have become something like the law of the three unities, an esthetic imperative which no conformist film-maker would think of infringing. . . . But, of course, it is out of the question to demand a law forbidding non-geniuses to photograph breasts and rumps. It is impossible to imagine a censor whose duty would be to eliminate mediocrity. Everyone has the inalienable right to express himself, even idiots.

To make the gratuitous nature of these practices clear, it is only necessary to recall that in most films of the past it would have been easy to insert such scenes without changing anything in the story. Just think of Greta Garbo, Marlene Dietrich and all the former screen goddesses. If, at the moment when the object of their affections embraced them, the scene had not been interrupted by a fade-out for modesty's sake, we would have been permitted to become familiar with all the charms of their persons in detail and in action. Some people may be sorry that the censorship of that era deprived us of that pleasure.

Others, however, will be rash enough to claim that if American comedies used to exhibit a refined eroticism, they owed it to the restraints imposed on them by the then all-powerful surveillance of the Hays organization and jointly interested parties. These restraints led film-makers to practice a wide gamut of allusion, ellipsis and litotes, with which the public had become familiar, and which afforded it the pleasant role of a smirking accomplice. I will refrain from dwelling on this point of view for fear of being supposed hostile to "freedom of expression."

Nevertheless the examples of this sort of reticence to be found in literature should make us stop and think. The realist Flaubert describes a country fair or a clubfoot operation in precise detail, but when he shuts Emma Bovary and her lover into that well-known hansom cab, a hand lowers the window curtain. Does not that lowered curtain, that cab traversing the streets of Rouen, offer the imagination a more voluptuous allurement than any description of what is going on in the semi-darkness of the vehicle? Eroticism with the virtue of secrecy has nothing in common with exhibitionism, which is as disheartening as morose delectation. The Catholic Office of the Cinema would do very well to encourage the current fashion: there is nothing more calculated to make people disgusted with what was considered a sin.

¶ "Sooner or later," says André Malraux, "the dream factory falls back on its most effective means: sex and blood."*
"A girl and a gun," D. W. Griffith used to say, even back then. But for a long time, violence was the substitute for eroticism, which was proscribed. Now these two "effective means" are used with full freedom, with very few exceptions. Nevertheless, the attraction of eroticism is not inexhaustible, and it is already passing out of fashion. "It's always the same!" sighs the disenchanted voyeur. Whereas violence does not loosen its hold.

One might have thought that the war crimes, crematory ovens, genocides and various tortures would have caused a salutary dread of violence. That was to mistake human nature, and just the opposite has come about. The dear public became used to it, then began to enjoy it. A sign of the times: "cruel" is an adjective used as a term of praise by publicity writers and film reviewers. Since we always have folly with us, gentle souls accumulate stacks of signatures denouncing violence when it is practiced by politicians they do not favor, but they are not afraid to exalt it when it appears in a stage or screen work. Ubu was more logical and frank.[1]

It is difficult to refer to this subject without conjuring up the

---

*Speech on the use of the French language, 1969.
[1]Alfred Jarry's King Ubu was the antithesis of a logical and frank man. See note on p. 247.—ED.

hateful shade of censorship. For a psychiatrist or a sociologist gauging the number of weak brains and defenseless nervous systems in relation to the power of modern mass media, "freedom of expression" entails other consequences than it did in the nineteenth century. . . . Fine. That is not my business.* Let us merely observe that if the carrying of weapons were forbidden on the screen, many film-makers would have to sign up for unemployment.

"An author who does not censor himself," writes Claude Mauriac, "who is unable to evaluate his own responsibility, sanctions by this thoughtlessness the intervention of those who theoretically have the young under their care.† It is not a question of good and evil. But of the public good. Of the good of the public. Of the young public especially. . . . Am I then in favor of censorship? I am against the vindication of murder.

Do not speak to us about art or boldness in regard to those submachinegun concertos and bloody carnivals! There, too, what is involved most of the time is merely easy work and high profits. Do not bring in the names of Sade or Artaud![1] Neither of them trafficked in his obsessions. As for the public's desire to be frightened, Alfred Hitchcock explains it as follows:

> There is nothing more pleasurable than the sentiment of fear caused by a book or a performance, when you yourself are comfortably settled in a good armchair and are running no risks.

That is very well said, and this delicate epicureanism is liable to encourage other pleasures. Thus the gourmand is able to increase the enjoyment he obtains from a luxurious meal: he need only recall that half the people in the world do not have enough to eat. And in wintertime, in front of the fireplace, I would advise you to think about the sufferings of the destitute who are dying of cold. That should not fail to heighten your sense of well-being.

---

*It is the traditional mission of authors to protest against all censorship. "But," Jean Rostand says, "if I protest against the prohibition of a work, that by no means indicates that this work does not disgust me."

†*Le Figaro littéraire,* January 1970.

[1]Antonin Artaud was a twentieth-century essayist, poet, and dramatic theoretician who advocated a theater of total involvement between audience and performance, largely promoted through "cruel" situations both in staging and in incidents portrayed, since he felt that audiences cannot intellectualize and remain detached from cruel situations.—ED.

Since we are discussing the morals of the day, is it not high time to dust off our vocabulary in order to "give a purer meaning to the words of the tribe?"[1]

Our tribe, despite its eagerness to be modern, young, new, liberated and abreast of the times, still expresses itself as if we were living in the nineteenth century, when Baudelaire, Flaubert and Maupassant were tried for criminal writings. All I show as evidence is the adjective "courageous" used on all occasions by contemporary critics.

Courage was needed to proclaim oneself a freethinker in the reign of Louis XIV, an Encyclopedist under Louis XV, a liberal during the First Empire, etc. One's freedom or life was at stake. But what do people risk today in modern nations by tilting at windmills which ceased turning long ago, by dealing in ideas which, though explosive a hundred years ago, have become as harmless as the paints given to children?

When nonconformist plays are applauded by the middle class, when "protest" songs make record dealers rich, and "forbidden" films make their producers' fortune. Bravo! But do not go on speaking about courage, my good reviewers, as if Empress Eugénie were still ruling in the palace of the Tuileries.[2] That would be an insult to those who have tried throughout history, and are still trying, to express sentiments opposed to the dogmas of oppressive regimes and police states.

In this area, to show courage would be to go against the current, to be chaste and tender in this era in which every sort of violence is triumphant. As, for example, in that film we saw a few years ago. You be the judge:

The hero of the story is an old man—but not one of those smiling old fellows who give an optimistic idea of the end of existence—an old man living, or rather subsisting, on a pension, a "wild ass's skin" which shrinks daily.[3] In his life there is a girl,

---

[1] A line from Stéphane Mallarmé's "Le Tombeau d'Edgar Poe" relating to his wish to purify language of its everyday usage so that it would reflect pure concepts.—ED.

[2] Eugénie was the wife of Napoléon III. Their reign, the Second Empire, was a period of material prosperity and intellectual repression.—ED.

[3] The skin, from the novel *La Peau de chagrin* by Balzac, granted its possessor's wishes, but with each wish, the skin grew smaller and the man aged. One day, he made a final wish, which brought about his demise as well as that of the skin.—ED.

young of course, but she is a servant and is expecting a baby. Just think! A gloomy old man and a pregnant maid: two tabus, two characters who, according to the customary practice of the film market, should not exist, in fact do not exist.

This masterpiece—*Umberto D.* by Vittorio De Sica—was not even a "dark" film! It did not tend to take advantage of the vogue of the "unpleasant" film, it contained none of the effects of spectacular realism in which contemporary conformity delights. It was not without moments of comedy or satire, and it is the height of art to have been able to paint so gloomy a picture with such a light touch.

I do not think *Umberto D.* won a prize at any festival, and it was barely mentioned in the press. No doubt, in the opinion of the specialists it was not a "courageous" film.

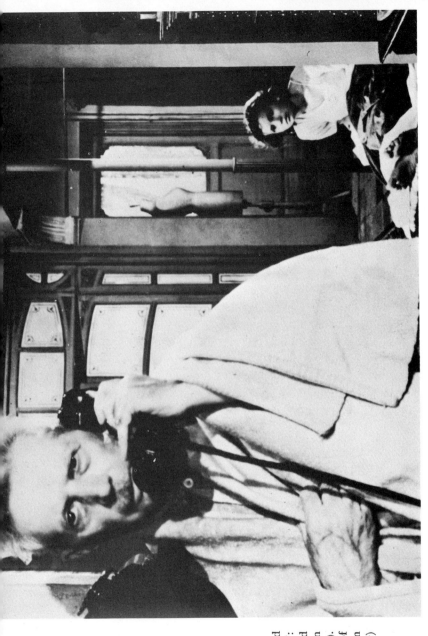

"A gloomy old man and a pregnant maid": Carlo Battisti and Maria Pia Casilio in *Umberto D.* (1952). (The Museum of Modern Art Film Stills Archive)

From *Silence Is Golden* (1947): on a rainy day in the year 1906 or so, an aging but still gallant film director (Maurice Chevalier), armed with an umbrella, comes to the aid of a lady outside the movie show. (The Museum of Modern Art Film Stills Archive)

On Comedy

1947. It may be thought that the list of best films drawn up at a festival like the one held at Brussels has only a quite relative value, but it is more comfortable to say so if you have had the honor to be placed at the head of this list, and the freedom thus granted to an author to discuss this subject is not the least of his rewards.*

A jury whose task is to choose from among numerous films is led by its choice to give a tacit definition of what it considers a good film. Now, it is understood that this definition, however it is framed, cannot satisfy everyone's taste. For some people a good film is one that conforms to certain moral or political ideas; for other people—less often found nowadays when art for art's sake has very few professed partisans—it is one that exemplifies certain esthetic principles; for others, finally—and they are the most numerous—a good film is quite simply a film that makes a lot of money. The difficulty encountered in defining a good film shows that it is impossible for a jury to declare without fear of contradiction that one of several good films is the best.

Besides, that is not the real object of a film festival. Here, it is less important to prefer than to compare. This comparison between works varying in inspiration and coming from different countries offers lessons profitable to cinema everywhere. The lessons given this year by a few English and Italian films, for example, can bring new vigor, like a plant graft, to the American cinema, which seems to have become strangely etiolated during recent years in its splendid isolation. In an area when planes cross physical frontiers in a few moments, while invisible Great Walls of China seems to be rising all over the world, we must not neglect any opportunity which would allow the cinema to re-assume the international nature it had from its inception and without which it wastes away. (When it is said that the cinema should be *international,* what is meant is that films should carry to the greatest possible number of countries the image of the *national* genius that inspired them.)

However, a film festival that did not undertake a classification

---

*Prize list of the world film festival at Brussels (1947).

and give out awards would be fulfilling only a part of its task. Since the film industry classifies pictures according to the amount of money they make, it is not unnecessary from time to time to remind those who control this industry that films can also be classified according to quality, and that, if all classification has some arbitrary element in it, the latter type is not less justified than the former.

But even quality is a rather imprecise criterion when the works offered for judgment to a jury like the one in Brussels belong to various genres, the qualities of which cannot be compared equitably. To take lofty examples from the history of the theater, what common yardstick would permit the judges to decide between the respective merits of *Le Bourgeois Gentilhomme* and *Polyeucte*,[1] or even, to stick to works by a single author, those of *A Midsummer Night's Dream* and *Hamlet?*

The reader will surely smile if I take the liberty here of complimenting the Brussels jury on the audacity it showed in giving its highest award to a comedy. If the author of this comedy did not expect such an honor, it is not because modesty leads his judgment astray, but because he doubted that a jury would manage to overcome the prejudice against comic works, a prejudice that Molière pointed to ironically when he made Lysidas say "that there is a great difference between all these trifles and the beauty of serious plays."[2]

To tell the truth, many people share Lysidas' opinion more or less consciously. It has been said that *Silence Is Golden* belongs to a minor genre, and some people have blamed this film for lacking *power*.[3] "Light," "slender" and "tenuous" are in fact the words most frequently used by those who review a comedy even when they praise its good features. What then do they want a

---

[1]Clair contrasts Molière's comedy to Corneille's tragedy.—ED.

[2]Responding to various criticisms of his comedy *L'Ecole des femmes*, Molière wrote two playlets, *L'Impromptu de Versailles* and *La Critique de l'école des femmes*. In the latter, Lysidas, a writer of "serious" plays, complains that people are scrambling to see "bagatelles" such as those Molière composes, while the theaters in which tragedies are staged remain empty.—ED.

[3]*Le Silence est d'or*, one of Clair's most endearing semi-comic films, was made in 1947. Although it was originally released in America in an unfortunate voice-over translated version, even that version has been out of circulation here for years, so American audiences remain unfamiliar with the picture.—ED.

comedy to be? If the critic who uses these adjectives is thereby exhibiting some thoughtlessness, he has the excuse that he is faithfully expressing the opinion of the common spectator, in whom the feeling of "beauty" is aroused only by tragic emotions. Tears, even when elicited by vulgar artifices, seem to have more nobility than laughter caused by subtle means. That spectator who would never think of calling out "How beautiful that was!" at the end of the best Charlie Chaplin film, will do so without effort after seeing a filmed melodrama. Does not the public seem to be proud of the tears it sheds and somewhat embarrassed by the laughter coaxed out of it? You might say that, like the nations that forget the peaceful kings thanks to whom they lived happy days, but respectfully erect statues to the conquerors who have led them to the slaughter, the public, by the effect of the same masochism, is ungrateful to those who make it laugh and grateful to those who make it cry.*

Nevertheless, without going so far as to subscribe to Paul Léautaud's epigram that the only good play is a comedy, one may still think that those who believe in the preeminence of the tragic mode are sometimes the victims of an illusion. The "serious plays" are considered the best during their authors' lifetime, but comedy sometimes comes back into its own under the test of time. Molière is closer to us today than Corneille, or even Racine. Voltaire's tragedies, so highly acclaimed in their day, have crumbled into noble dust, whereas Marivaux's work has retained its freshness.[1] And the admirers of Hugo or Dumas *fils* would have been mightily surprised to learn that of all the playwrights of the nineteenth century, it was those two "minor" authors of the time, Musset and Labiche, whose genius would show fewest signs of age.

Having said this, I would not want anyone to misunderstand the meaning of the profession of faith just presented. No one

---

*When it is said of a king that he is a good man, there you have an unsuccessful reign": Napoleon.

[1] In the eighteenth century, Voltaire's regulation tragedies were received with great respect, while Marivaux's strange, delicate little comedies were regarded as amusing pastimes. Allowing for the differences in traditions, the same can be said for the celebrated nineteenth-century dramas of Hugo and Dumas *fils*, as opposed to the light comedies and vaudevilles of Labiche, and the haunting bittersweet closet comedies of Musset.—ED.

admires a fine dramatic film more than I do, and some of those shown at Brussels had every right to claim first place. In these few lines, I merely wished to spell out the reasons that make it desirable for future festivals to award one prize for drama and another for comedy. In fact, it may be feared that there will not always be a jury like the one assembled at Brussels in 1947, which was sufficiently enlightened to judge that there is not so much difference between "serious plays" and "trifles."

On this subject, let us quote Ingmar Bergman again:

> There is nothing easier than to frighten a spectator. You can literally drive him mad with fear, since most people have somewhere within them a fear that is all ready to burst forth. It is much more difficult to make them laugh, and to make them laugh wholesomely and heartily. It is easy to put a spectator in a worse state than he was in when he entered, but hard to put him in a better state.*

No doubt it is difficult: just compare the great number of talented authors who cultivate the time-tested virtues of the drama with the small number who venture into humor or comedy and try to make people laugh "wholesomely and heartily."

"That's perfectly natural in our day and age. Do you think our times make for laughter?"

Do you think Rabelais was living in the golden age? The gloomier an era is, the more we find that humor, satire and laughter are the best witness we can bear to our liberty.

---

*Les Lettres françaises, April 1959.

On Television

1948. It would be rash to speak about the distant future of television, since this will be fashioned by technological progress as well as by economic and social factors, but it is perhaps not pointless to speak about its immediate future—that is, what will later be considered as its early years.

It is to be feared that television will suffer from the same childhood diseases that the sound and talking picture had. Let us recall the period of *The Jazz Singer* and the enthusiasm of certain good people who are always ready to be dazzled and taken in by any novelty. It seemed then that everything the cinema had achieved in thirty years so fertile in inventions and discoveries might be thrown overboard because a sound came out of a loudspeaker exactly when Al Jolson's mouth opened. The rest of the story is well known, and it is only necessary to see *Intolerance, The Pilgrim* and *Greed* over again to realize that the *essential elements* of the cinema had appeared before 1927 and that, if attention is paid to substance rather than form, the progress made since that time seems secondary.

It is well known that television can present on the screen both directly photographed scenes (that is, scenes occurring at the moment you see them) and previously filmed images. "Live" television is far superior to ordinary cinema *when it comes to presenting events that are in the nature of news items,* and television's success with sporting events proves that in the purely documentary area, television has won the match.

But when it comes to a "composed" show—that is, a work written by an author and performed by actors—the use of "live" television arouses some misgivings. Here the news element does not enter the picture. If *Hamlet* is given on television, for instance, it does not matter much if you know that the gravedigger's scene is being performed ten miles way from the viewer (live television) or if it was performed twenty days earlier (televised film).

At any rate, what I see is never more than a shadow projected onto a screen, what I hear is only a sound reproduced by a loudspeaker, and the whole thing is only a timeless fiction. If I am told that there is a considerable difference between an image transmitted live and the same image first filmed and then televised, I reply that this is a purely technical imperfection that will no doubt be corrected later on. The example of radio shows us that it is very difficult to distinguish between a live broadcast and a recorded broadcast, and the television technicians who are ready to construct a system on the basis of this difference between the two types of telecast seem to me to be the victims of an illusion that is as childish as it is dangerous.

The danger comes from that same desire to throw everything overboard that imperiled the very existence of cinematic art at the start of talking pictures. But this danger would not exist if live television had attained the same degree of technical flexibility and had the same possibilities as real cinema. That is not the case and possibly never will be. To assert the opposite is to ignore the vital importance of cinematic editing. A dramatic film of normal length includes several hundred different shots, the assemblage of which gives the work its movement and its style. Now, the technical conditions of live television, which do not permit this photographic luxury, tend to make the show fall into a semi-theatrical pattern from which it will be hard for it to escape. We hope that television does not follow the wrong path and that its technicians do not forget the lessons of the cinema.

1950. At this date, television seems to be an extraordinary medium of *dissemination,* but nothing yet permits us to discover in it any facilities for *expression* with which we were not already familiar.

If there are fundamental differences between the theater and the cinema, there do not seem to be any between the cinema and television. A show made up of *live* actors moving on a *motionless* stage is subject to other laws than those of a show consisting of moving *shadows,* in which the *mobility* and *multiplicity* of the settings are unlimited. In the things which the television screen has presented to us up to today, we have seen *nothing which could not technically be shown on the movie screen.*

Let us ask those who persist in believing in the virtues of "live" television to exercise their imagination just a little. Let us suppose that television exists but the cinema does not (in view of the chaos presiding over the chronological order of inventions, this could have happened) . Here is what you would read in the paper one morning:

> A new invention is going to revolutionize television. From now on it will be possible for a television show to include innumerable sets and an infinite variety of photographic shots. The action will be able to move in an instant from a drawing room to a street, from the sea to the mountains, from Europe to America. Furthermore, it will be possible to correct televised scenes in every possible way after they have been recorded, to lengthen some, shorten others, change the order of their appearance and give them a permanent form. Finally—and this is not the least remarkable thing—it will be possible to reproduce the televised show as often as desired, like a simple photograph.
>
> This invention takes the form of a roll of celluloid, called "film," which moves through a photographic device to which its inventors, two young men named Auguste and Louis Lumière, have given the name of "Cinematograph." Within a few years all television shows will be cinematographed before they are telecast.
>
> The invention of the Cinematograph represents the most important progress made since the earliest television experiments.

1970. This dispute between the partisans of "live" television and those of "filmed" television is a thing of the past, and it is surprising that it caused so many arguments. The facts are accepted today, and there is now hardly any "composed," or fictional, show for which television does not use film—that is, the traditional methods of the cinema. Even the remarkable technical feats of men like Jean-Christophe Averty[1] are set down on celluloid and could be projected in any auditorium.

1962. There are fashionable words.* "Specificity" is one. Since our era is not unmoved by the charms of pedantry, it uses this word frequently. Thus all sorts of theories have been constructed on the "specificity" of television.

Let us get things straight. When it comes to showing scenes that are in the nature of news items, of course television differs from the cinema. But though it may transmit things *more*

---

[1]Averty is one of French television's leading directors and experimenters. French television, run by the State rather than by advertisers, tends to be much more inventive than its American counterpart.—ED.

*Cahiers de la télévision, December 1962.

quickly, it does not show them *in a different way.* And when it comes to a fictional show in which timeliness is irrelevant, television, though a new mode of dissemination, is not yet a new medium of expression.

What is this "small screen" that we hear about all too often? A screen appears big or small depending on its distance from the spectator. The largest cinema screen would seem tiny if it were possible to look at it from a great distance. Before long, the television screen will be as big as desired, and all the considerations inspired by its smallness will suffer the fate of dead leaves.

Another fable invented by the theorists: the difference between a scene transmitted directly and the same scene first filmed and then retransmitted. Viewers are unable to perceive this difference when the second of these modes of reproduction (which is nothing other than cinema) has the benefit of suitable technical conditions.

Yet another fairy tale: it is allegedly hard for television to show many long shots, and the close-up is one of its essential attributes. That is tantamount to saying that television can only show us a game of dominoes, but not a soccer match. We see proof of just the opposite every week.

It is futile to contrast television and cinema. The former is the extension of the latter. But an extension the limits of which we are very far from knowing.

1970. Which does not mean that television is merely an annex of the cinema. In fact, this new mode of dissemination, which we hope will become a thoroughly new medium of creativity, enjoys two privileges: *instantaneousness*—that is, the possibility of transmitting an event immediately—and *intimacy*—that is, the possibility of offering a viewer, seemingly for himself alone, a show that is actually seen at the same time by millions of viewers separated from one another. If television has a specific characteristic, that is it; it is from this that a new dramaturgy can arise.

From this moment, it must be admitted that Volume One of the "General History of the Kinetic Arts" ends at 1950. The age of television began precisely at the midpoint of the twentieth century.

On Credits

The French term *générique* is a strange one. Littré's dictionary lists it only as an adjective meaning "pertaining to a genre" ["generic"]. The cinema has made a noun out of it, and we can wonder why this designation has been given to the listing of the collaborators which appears at the beginning or end of a film. In English this is more correctly called the "credits."

We may also wonder why the thing itself has become what it is today. The Programming Council of French Radio and Television, upset by the proliferation of these texts, took up the matter one day. Since I was then a member of this council, I was assigned to present a report on the question. Some excerpts from this report are given below for those who are interested in the sidelines of history:

1958. What do these titles mean and of what use are they? In the early years of cinema, there were no credits. Actors' names began to be given prominence when it was noticed that such publicity could stimulate public interest. It was for the same reason that, later on, the author or the director, or both, were named. D. W. Griffith was the first author-director whose name attracted spectators as much as that of a star, and since the era of his successes, directors and authors have been named on the screen, even though in most cases their names did not mean much to the public.

Following on the heels of the authors and directors, the most important technicians asked to be named. From that moment on, credits lost their original meaning and took on another function, that of satisfying not the public, but those whose names are mentioned on the screen. That was the beginning of a mistake and of the abuses derived from it. Once the door was ajar, it was hard to shut it again. The abuses have become so numerous that it is possible to make the following observation: the vitality or importance of a film industry is in inverse proportion to the length of the credits this industry presents. When Hollywood was at the peak of its fortunes, the credits of the powerful American firms were extremely short (in professional terminology, nine or ten cards). Films coming from countries that are cinematically poor, or whose film production is not highly developed, present excessive credits (from twenty to thirty cards). The inflation in credits, like all inflation, is a sign of weakness or ill health. In the cinema, it is a mark of amateurishness, if it is not the avowal of a lack of money or authority, these factors often being concomitant.

If you take the trouble to reflect on the expansion of this odd custom, you can find three reasons for the existence of credits:

The first, the original reason, is to give the public information which can arouse or satisfy its curiosity. No objection to that.

The second justifying reason, more arguable, is that credits can technical collaborator. I repeat, "professionals," and I limit it to draw the attention of professionals to the name of an artistic or them, because the public is very little concerned with these names. Let us be frank: whatever the merits of a set designer or a sound engineer—and I am purposely naming those film workers who play a major role—it does not appear that a spectator ever entered a movie house because the sets of a film were by Mr. X or the sound recording by Mr. Y. In this case, their mention in the credits is only a trade matter; its benefit is restricted to a few people, but for millions of viewers it causes only boredom or, at best, indifference.

Finally, it is completely without justification when the credits present the names of collaborators *whose individual contribution to the common effort cannot be discerned,* and when this mention cannot give these collaborators any other benefit than the satisfaction of a decidedly childish vanity. Is a producer or director going to hire a continuity girl, an assistant editor or an assistant costumer because he has noticed the quality of their work? It is not likely. In that case, why is the technician mentioned? What interest can this mention have for the public, for the film or for the technician himself? It would be desirable for the professional organizations to come up with their own answers to these questions.

Here we come to the bottom of a matter that is seemingly trivial, but that, moving on from one weakness and concession to another, has assumed the shape of a disease of the film show, a disease that has spread by contagion to radio and television.

To speak only of television, let us take at random one list of credits from among those that were offered to us for examination. . . . Please note that here, the name of the director has been mentioned four times between the opening credits and the closing credits; to this must be added the spoken mention of his name by the lady announcer. The same name given five times! Here, even the cinema is outdone.

Now, to be sure, in this case we were dealing with a dramatic telecast of some importance. But, to take another example at random, let us look at the closing credits of a news program only a few minutes long, which was telecast recently. . . . I remind you, this was a brief news program—that is, the equivalent of a newspaper article. Why must the presentation of this simple news program imitate that of the biggest film productions? If our dailies followed the same practice, we might read in their columns, every day and on the same subject, bylines something like this:

THE . . . FESTIVAL

An article by:	A. B.
Telephoned to Paris by:	C. D.
Typewritten by:	E. F.
Set in type by:	G. H.
Proofs corrected by:	I. J.
Headlines by:	K. L.
Page layout by:	M. N.
Edited by:	O. P.

And we would get to X, Y and Z just as easily.

In the two telecasts we have just mentioned, I defy anyone who is not a television staff member to evaluate in any way whatsoever the merits of the four or five cameramen who are named, or at least to single out the individual contribution each one made. In this case, how can this mention serve their interests?

As for the assistant set designer, the art director, the assistant sound engineer, the background music supervisor, the video engineer, the two assistant directors, etc., it must be admitted that even the people in the business, let alone the laymen, are unable to pay homage to their talents. So then, if these talents can only be gauged by those who work in the TV studios, what is the purpose of pointing them out to the public?

We know the answer: "What does it matter to you? A few seconds go right by, and if it gives them pleasure. . . ." But they forget that it is only the public we have to please, and that in show business everything counts, everything is important. Besides—and I shall merely indicate this, because a discussion of it would take too long—the unlimited extension of the "right to be credited" endangers the rights of the author himself, rights that our predecessors instituted and defended with such great difficulty. When everybody is named, then in actuality nobody is named any more. *To regulate strictly the right to be credited is to take up the defense of the true creators.*

Having said that, what is to be done? No doubt the best method would be not to name anybody on the screen, and to leave to the newspapers and trade journals the job of naming the authors and co-workers of a telecast, if they wished to do so, just as in the theater this is done in the program, which no one is forced to look at.

If, however, it is impossible to do away with credits, precise rules should be applied to their composition, rules that would allow no one to be arbitrary or obliging. The first rule would be to name only those collaborators on a program whose contribution is easily discernible and without whose contribution the program would be noticeably *different.* . . .

1970. In short, this note was meant as a reminder that radio and television are not at the service of their craftsmen but at the service of the public. This audacious viewpoint was unanimously approved by the Programming Council and submitted to the administrators. After which, nothing was ever said of it again, and, naturally, everything continued as before.

Time That Does Not Go By

1962. When the first moving images appeared on a white canvas, man had every reason to believe that those views of living things and objects in motion would be preserved forever and that he could justly cry out: "The past, the past belongs to me!"* But the past does not belong to anyone, to judge by these images which, deprived of the retouching our memory imperceptibly performs on the things it summons up, seem all the more dated for not having been aged by the years. Ancient poems live again on young lips. Certain novels have left to posterity the task of recognizing their value. Plays, as perishable as they are, can on occasion outlive the actors who first created them. But the film work, attached to its era like a shellfish to its rock, undergoes in reverse the law of time, which it attempted to defy, and, changeless in a changing world, seems to move further away from us at the same rate that the tide of years carries us further away from it.

1947. While we are led to fear the consequences of scientific progress more every day, it is comforting to think that, among the great inventions made during the last hundred years, the cinema is one of the most innocent, one of those that have lent themselves least to dangerous ends.†

Once again, let us be grateful to those scientists and craftsmen, whether they are called Plateau, Reynaud, Marey, Edison, Muybridge or Demeny, or whether they bear the beautiful name of Lumière, to all those who, incited by love of experiment, contributed to the invention of something they thought was only a scientific toy, and who created a new medium of expression, a dream-making machine, an arsenal of poetry.[1]

A new poetry has been born of the screen, a poetry that its authors created unconsciously, a poetry whose nature would be difficult to define had it not already been defined well before

---

*R. C., *Discours de réception à l'Académie française.*
†Méliès Exhibition, Brussels, 1947.
[1]These men, with the exception of Edison and Lumière, were all pre-cinematic pioneers. Clair calls Lumière's name beautiful because it is also the French noun for "light."—ED.

the birth of the cinema, in the following lines, where the screen seems to be speaking in the first person:

> For a long time I had gloried in the possession of all possible landscapes . . . I had dreamt of crusades, voyages of exploration of which no account had been written, . . . social revolutions, wanderings of peoples and continents; I had believed in every enchantment . . .

Does not this famous passage from *A Season in Hell* sound like a poetic manifesto of the cinema written a quarter of a century before Méliès first saw the Lumière Brothers' machine in the basement of the Grand Café?[1] It is because the cinema of the early years "believed in every enchantment," it is because it had been born with the blessings of prestidigitators and magicians, because, like Rimbaud, it loved "painted sets, backdrops of street acrobats, shop signs, brightly colored popular prints, . . . our old wives' stories, fairy tales" that it found its poetic vein right from the start and awakened in our hearts that love of the miraculous which brightens our childhood years.

And yet, it would not have taken much to leave us in complete ignorance of these first years of the moving image. Now that we turn toward that era with so much affectionate curiosity, it is difficult to believe that our interest in it took so long to manifest itself.

Among the important dates in film history, writers often neglect to mention one that cannot be forgotten by those who were young at the time: 1925, the year in which the Studio des Ursulines opened in Paris. On the screen of the small theater whose name conjured up the "gentle shadow and peace" of linen coifs,[2] there appeared one evening films that had grown pale and were marked with those streaks that are the wrinkles of celluloid—a program of "prewar films." In illusionistic settings, heroines of Paul Bourget or Marcel Prévost, with dresses by Worth or Doucet,[3] expressed with numerous gestures and

---

[1]The Grand Café is France's equivalent of America's Koster and Bial's Music Hall; it was there, in 1895, that the Lumières first displayed their marvelous invention—and there that they told the enchanted passerby Méliès to forget about it, advising him that it was an invention without a future.—ED.

[2]The Ursulines, named after an order of nuns, conjured up the image of their habits.—ED.

[3]Bourget and Prévost were novelists popular in the early years of the century; Worth and Doucet were the couturiers then most in fashion.—ED.

much mime the sentiments inspired in them by their thin-mustachioed swains. And the audience laughed.

In 1925, when the cinema turned back toward its past for the first time, the very modern spectators, who were accompanied by ladies wearing Chanel or Lanvin dresses—short, with low waistline—and who had left the Art Deco exhibition and come to the Ursulines in their five-horsepower cars, roared with laughter at the sight of those scenes photographed fifteen years earlier, which seemed to have been taken out of a family album created by a relentless caricaturist.

Now that 1925 is buried beneath a layer of memories scarcely less thick than the one covering 1910, the recollection of that laughter makes us stop and think. The films being shown this season will also look like parodies in a few years. They will be said to have grown old because they will be less young, and because we suffer the illusion that the things outside us pass by while we stand still, just as a child amuses himself in a train by watching the telegraph poles whiz by.

Anyone who compares the art of the film to those arts that have enduring products misunderstands its nature. What remains of a film creator's efforts is not so much a body of work as the inspiration this work can give to those who follow him. The shadows regain the kingdom of shadows more quickly than the human being who created them. They dance like moths in the flame of the magic lamp, and disappear.

No doubt it is this rapid recession into time which, in the eyes of some viewers, gives old films a part of their poetic character, but this phenomenon produces less pleasant effects as well. The laughter heard years ago in the Ursulines auditorium may be heard again on any occasion. A film that is growing old confuses the greater part of the public, who consider the cinema an amusement that exists only in the present, and it soon ceases to interest the industry that produced it and the businessmen who deal with it. It is because the film is a medium of expression that is more seriously menaced by the passage of time than any other that we must try to preserve the works it has produced. Today we lament the loss of a great part of the work of Méliès and his contemporaries. But what are we doing to prevent a similar fate from befalling the works of their successors? Despite the dedication of those members of film libraries and clubs who are trying to save the documents most useful to the history of the cinema, there is reason to fear that our descendants will not be much more familiar with the films being made now than we are with those made thirty years ago.

¶ The above text, written for the inauguration of a Méliès exhibition held in Brussels, treats of a problem that should have been solved long ago in one way or another. On the occasion of a conference of film societies and cinema academies held in Venice, I had the opportunity to return to this subject:

1950. When the cinema was invented, its first craftsmen employed commercially something that then seemed to be only a scientific toy with no great future. They did not take the trouble to insure the preservation of their works, only a tiny part of which have come down to us. These first craftsmen should not be blamed. Who could foresee in their time that the cinema would win the place it has today in our society?

But, fifty years later, now that the cinema has become one of the world's great industries and an art form particularly indicative of our civilization, it seems incredible that no law, no ordinance, no measure protects cinematic works against the destruction to which the fragility of their physical form exposes them. If we do not take action, there is reason to fear that the films we are making today will soon be as completely forgotten as those made fifty years ago. And we will not have the excuse of ignorance that our predecessors had.

Everyone knows the difficulties which the heads of film libraries encounter in the accomplishment of their task. Everyone knows the deplorable conditions in which those old films that have escaped annihilation are presented. From an old discarded copy, which is stained, streaked and often incomplete, and whose defects are beyond repair, other copies are printed that show up these defects even more clearly. The film museums whose mission it is to show their audience the most important works in the history of the cinema, present only a caricature of these works. We wonder sometimes whether it would not be better if the films we loved most were completely destroyed, so that our memories of them will not be degraded.

A half century has gone by and we have still not made a choice between these two extreme solutions, total destruction or careful preservation. We continue to let chance decide the fate of films for us. In an era in which the cinema is definitely considered a major art, we treat the works it gives us with the same neglect as at the time when they were exhibited in carnival booths.

It would be pointless to ask the industry to remedy this situation. Producing and releasing firms are perishable, as men are. Their activity is carried out in the present, and history is not their business. The problem before us cannot be solved without the participation of the government. Film producers jealous of their independence should not be frightened by this proposal, which does not attack their temporal interests. The proprietor or tenant of a building that is a historical monument enjoys its use, but the decision to keep it up or to demolish it is not up to him.

In what way could the government assume this task without unnecessary complications? By an extremely simple measure, for which precedents exist; in fact, it is surprising that it was not applied to the cinema long ago. This measure is called *dépôt légal.* . . .[1]

Film creators must not continue to write their works on the sand. In regard to this, Paul Eluard has published an article containing the following lines, which touch upon the very essence of cinematic art:

> Wrong or right, I hold that the essential thing about art is its eternal nature. . . . Artistic creation does not lay claim to absolute eternity. Naturally, it does not exist outside the world as a separate entity. It is not rigid, outside the passing world. But its essential aim is to transmit, to endure, to maintain itself as long as possible. How could artistic creation be related to the cinema, which constantly devours itself, nothing of which can remain outside of a fragile existence as a novelty?

We hope that cinematic creation will transmit, endure and maintain itself as long as possible. To those for whom the cinema is not merely a business and industrial item, belongs the

---

[1]The French equivalent of American copyright practices requiring publishers to give copies of each copyrighted publication to the Library of Congress.—ED.

task of preparing its future. Theirs too is the duty to save its past.

1970. Is the essential thing about art its eternal nature? Eluard's remark is arguable, but what he says about the film work's "fragile existence as a novelty" is all too true.

Even if the film work remained physically intact, what in it would continue to live? The outward appearance of men—not only their fashions in dress but also their gestures or their tone —probably evolves more quickly than we thought before the film allowed us to ascertain it for the first time. An old film is said to have aged. But the truth is that it has stayed the same —if not in form, at least in spirit—and it is we who have changed. The cinema remains and will doubtless long remain an art dedicated to the present. We belong to the time that goes by. Its works belong to the time that does not go by.

A Motionless Cinema

Long ago, on the Boulevard of Crime,[1] the actor who had played
the villain was awaited in the street by spectators who wanted
to make him expiate his misdeeds. If you think our contemporaries are less naïve, look at the excited ringside spectators booing
the honest wrestler who is doing his best to fake a performance
in which he plays an expert at illegal holds. But do not take
credulity to task; without it the entertainment world could not
exist. If you are inclined to believe that the blood flowing from
Oedipus' eyes is only make-up, you would do better not to go
to the theater.

At the time when *The Two Little Urchins* was being shown at
the Gaumont-Palace, a suitor wrote the young star of this film
novel asking her for a date *after the performance at the stage door.*
This love-smitten fellow, choosing to ignore the invention of
the cinema, refused to believe that the object charming his eyes
was not real. That occurred around 1920, but—let us be glad
of it—the cinema has not lost its powers of fascination, to judge
by a news item that appeared recently on the crime and disaster
pages:

SPECTATOR STABS FILM ACTOR ON SCREEN

The showing of the film *Commando-Suicide* at the Cornouaille
Theater in Quimper was disrupted last night by a spectator who
was overexcited by a scene of violence. Christian L., age thirty-
one, decided to influence the course of the story. He leaped from
his seat, knife in hand, and struck one of the actors. The screen
was the only victim of the brawler's enterprise. Christian L. was
taken away by the police.*

Do you know that comic strips are capable of arousing the
same passions as the cinema? The cinema shows us shadows,
the comics show us figures constructed by a few strokes of the
pen, and no more is needed to furnish a springboard to our
passions or our dreams. Comic strips recall the images that
freeze on the screen when the projection of a film is suddenly

---

[1] In the nineteenth century, a part of the Paris boulevards was called the
Boulevard of Crime because the theaters situated there concentrated on melodramas and romantic dramas, all rich in illicit deeds.—ED.

Paris-Presse, December 1969.

halted. Their relationship to the cinema is obvious. A motionless cinema, like the Bayeux Tapestry, which seemed to be waiting since the century of Queen Matilda for the wand of a magical director.

The things called *bandes dessinées* in French are called *fumetti* in Italian.* But the French term does not take into account the stories that are illustrated with photographs, and is thus too limited, while the Italian term refers only to the balloons surrounding dialogue, thus excluding wordless images. The German word *Bildstreifen* is not much more satisfying, and the American name "comic strips," applied arbitrarily to works of a dramatic or sentimental nature, is the most imperfect of all. It is the last-mentioned, however, which is used in the international argot of the specialists, though it is quite ill suited to the works of the great ancestors like Busch, Töpffer and Christophe.[1]

This inadequacy of terminology reveals the lack of esteem accorded to an object which no one has found worthy of a proper definition. *Bande dessinée, fumetti* and "comics" are all pejorative, in a goodhumored way. Thus, in the seventeenth century the name of "bagatelle" was given to entertainments not worthy to figure among the arts. Whenever a new medium of expression appears, people say at first that it has nothing to do with art. That was the case for a long time with the cinema and with jazz, which, according to some people, was not music. Even to-

---

*Preface to *I primi eroi* [The first heroes], an anthology of comic strips edited by F. R. Caradec (Garzanti, Milan, 1962) .

[1]*Bandes dessinées* literally are "drawn strips"; *Bildstreifen* means "strips of pictures," and *fumetti* are "little puffs of smoke."

Rodolphe Töpffer (1799–1846) , native of Geneva, is the father of the comic strip in that he was the first to integrate sequential drawings with narrative text in an extended form. His delightful inventions include *The True Story of M. Crépin*, dealing mainly with nineteenth-century pedagogy, and *The True Story of M. Jabot*, the adventures of an ineptly foppish *arriviste*.

Wilhelm Busch (1832–1908) , native of Hanover, continued the tradition, working in verse rather than prose for his text, and creating such memorable characters as *Max and Moritz*, who later became familiar to American readers as Hans and Fritz of *The Katzenjammer Kids* and *The Captain and the Kids*, both of which were originally drawn by R. Dirks under the strong influence of Busch.

Christophe (Georges Colomb) was their French correspondent. Clair will describe him more fully in a few pages. His pseudonym derives from the French name (Christophe Colomb) for the man we call Christopher Columbus.—ED.

day, the comic strip, in the eyes of many observers, is nothing but fodder for illiterates. Certainly, most contemporary comics are depressingly bad, but is all of literature condemned because of the mediocre books published every season? People are unaware that in Finland, for example, the national poet, Mika Waltari, has been writing the verse legends for the series of drawings for children *Kieku and Kaiku* for thirty years. In the United States, John Steinbeck is not afraid to assert that the author of the strip *Li'l Abner*, Al Capp, is the greatest satirist since Laurence Sterne.

It is by reading *Li'l Abner* in American papers every day that I came to understand what the comic strip could be: an original medium of expression that lends itself as well as any other to the possible revelation of talent or genius, a medium that would make it possible to create for the benefit of the greatest number of readers new works like *Pantagruel, Gulliver* and *Ubu*, if people like Rabelais, Swift and Jarry could be found to use it.[1] *Li'l Abner*, which is unfortunately too American to be enjoyed outside the United States, has actually given rise to popular customs in its own country. Every year students celebrate Sadie Hawkins Day, imitating the imaginary inhabitants of the village invented by Al Capp, where once a year the girls chase the boys of their choice and force the ones they manage to catch to marry them.

But Al Capp's fictions are not the only ones that have become grafted onto reality. In *Terry and the Pirates*, a series which enjoyed great success during the last war, a young Oriental girl lent her charms to the service of a spy ring that was highly dangerous to American interests. One day the author patriotically executed her. The papers that printed *Terry and the Pirates* received hundreds of letters of protest and scores of telegrams expressing regrets and condolences. In fact, the story goes that three people sent flowers for the funeral of this charming figment of the pen.

Please do not tell me that this is symptomatic of an unsettling

---

[1]Clair spent the war years in Hollywood, and was able to follow the comics for an extended period of time. It might be noted, incidentally, that comic strips appear only sparsely in European newspapers. American strips are generally regarded in France by those who have seen them as a strange aberration not unlike popcorn, for which Americans have developed a peculiar and inexplicable fancy. On the other hand, the French are very fond of comics in book form.—ED.

of the mind that is cause for alarm. There is nothing less new than these phenomena. At all times and in all lands men have needed heroes. The heroes of the *Iliad* and of the epics of chivalry are the ancestors of Superman and the science-fiction adventurers, and Superman is only dangerous when embodied by a real man whose gigantic portraits tower above the heads of the masses. Let us add in passing that lending human qualities to creatures composed of a few lines is not more unreasonable than attributing ideal virtues to a politician barely known except from photographs.

Comic strips have been studied in very few publications, and these have been relatively incomplete. That should not be surprising. If it is difficult to estimate the number of their readers (sixty million, we are told, but how can we be sure?), it is still more difficult to locate and assemble the considerable number of works that this mode of expression has produced in the four corners of the world. Copies of newspapers, like the comic books put into children's hands, are blown away by all the winds of the past, and the survival of comic strips is entrusted only to these two types of printed matter, which are the most perishable.

Therefore the author of this book has ventured onto practically virgin territory. In the absence of general studies of popular art and comparative works on children's literature, he had to blaze his own trail and then, to avoid getting lost, had to set up a rule and abide by it. This rule was: be less concerned with art criticism than with sociology. A comic strip is not included here because of its visual merits alone, but primarily because of the popularity it enjoyed at a given time and place. This was the guideline followed by the contributors from different countries, who may have had to overlook their personal preferences and be content to express those of their compatriots. Thanks to these correspondents, whom it is a pleasure to thank, thousands of pages were assembled, from which a choice had to be made.

It was most regretfully that the author had to omit a number of works which he would have liked to present at least in excerpts. But it was not his intention to offer a sampling of all comic strips from their beginnings up to our day. What he wanted was to offer an entertaining book that would include selections long enough to permit the reader to get acquainted with the nature of the main character and get interested in his adventures. Fault will surely be found with this necessarily limited selection: perhaps the author will be blamed for overlooking a certain hero, for preferring one episode to another, for interrupting some incident at its most interesting point, for strongly favoring humorous subjects. . . . But what anthology is not subject to similar complaints? It would be too good to be true if this one, the first of its type, were to meet with general approval while no anthology of poetry has ever completely satisfied all its readers.

The author also wanted this anthology to be international, seeking not so much to gratify the taste of its country of publication as to give an honest accounting of the tastes prevailing in every country. His most ardent wish is that readers of all age groups will not only rediscover in this book the heroes dear to them in their childhood, but will also become acquainted with those who delighted other children in other countries. The little Americans who used to read Outcault[1] and the little Frenchmen who used to read Christophe later found themselves side by side fighting the Germans who had read Busch when they were little. Having themselves become the sad heroes of the most incoherent of adventures, they were then able to perceive, if they remembered their childhood reading, that common sense is not always on the side it appears to be on, and that madness exerts a stronger hold on reality than on fiction.

As an epigraph to his *Leçons de choses en 650 gravures* (Lessons on things in 650 engravings) , Georges Colomb (Christophe) wrote: "The child is all eyes. The things he sees strike him more than the things he hears." Why hasn't the cinema benefited by that statement?! It is no accident that comic genius has practically disappeared from the screen since the film began to speak. Characters who were heroes, action, inventiveness, a style allowing the transition from the burlesque to the miraculous—that was the secret of the great films of the past, and that is what characterizes the best comic strips. The pedants, an eternal breed, profess that the cinema is making progress because films

---

[1]Outcault created *The Yellow Kid*, the turn-of-the-century American comic panel that began the whole tradition of American newspaper comic strips.—ED.

are taking on vaguely literary airs and are aiming at Art with a capital A. Whereas in reality its decline begins the moment it breaks away from its popular origins. It is fortunate that the comic strip is saved from this contagion by its need to reach a public composed of children of all ages.

In commuter trains and in the New York subway, most riders open their paper to the funny pages before casting the slightest glance at national news. Let other people object to this! I find this sight reassuring, and I would like it to be repeated in every country in the world. It is amusing to think that after people have completed their morning ablutions, they want to take a bath in the Fountain of Youth, and that at the moment of getting back to the place assigned to them in the modern anthill, they are in a rush to find out the latest news from the world of surreality.

1970. Comic strips have the same right to be considered as a medium of mass communication as the cinema, radio and television. This list is not restrictive. New inventions will probably give our descendants other means for expressing themselves. And just as the flints and bones chipped and carved by our ancestors gave rise to the hazy beginnings of art, it is permissible to imagine that these modes of expression, unknown and undefinable today, will become media of artistic creation.

Similarly, people have wondered whether machines, which are open to unlimited improvement, could not do creative work in the different branches of art. It seems that it is already possible to answer this question in the negative.

If the machine, thanks to its unusual productive powers, were to assemble tens of thousands of words or lines until the moment that the combination of some of these words or lines formed a poem or a drawing, the result would be the product of chance and not of genius. The machine will never have inspiration, unexpected intuitions or one of "those sudden flashes of intellectual light which remain the privilege of human thought."*

Nevertheless, if the machine is incapable of creative work, it can have a decisive influence on the development of art and thought. The invention of printing signaled the start of a new

---

*Louis de Broglie.

era, but, according to Mr. McLuhan, the civilization that began at the time the use of printing spread is a civilization of a temporary nature. An indefinite amount of time had passed before man felt the need for that mode of communication, which is of course artificial, and in the future it is possible that visual and audial means, which are already competing with the written word, will gradually take its place, and that printing will become a thing of the past that was prevalent only for a limited number of centuries.

¶ We mentioned above the name of Professor Colomb, who, under the pseudonym of Christophe, created the most famous French comic strips of the past *(Le Savant Cosinus, La Famille Fenouillard, Le Sapeur Camember)*,[1] and we ask for a moment of silence to attest our respect.

While the nations are rocking the world with explosions that express better than anything else the peaceful intentions of their heads of state, it is proper to salute the men who prophesied the times in which we have the privilege to live: Colomb (alias Christophe), Alphonse Allais and Alfred Jarry.[2]

If Jarry's *King Ubu* is to the leaders of the world today what Machiavelli's *Prince* was to the statesmen of his time, *The Scientist Cosine,* fathered by Christophe, is the inspiration for contemporary science. The majestic atomic mushrooms erected to the glory of Cosine from one continent to another remind our contemporaries that they are urgently invited, in Christophe's

---

[1] Translated, The scientist Cosine, The Fennily family, and Camembert the army engineer.—ED.

[2] Alfred Jarry, founder-in-spirit-emeritus of pataphysics, is best known for his outrageous play *King Ubu*, in which the protagonist bulls his way to power, listening to no one, levying taxes as he pleases, spending the revenue as fancy strikes him, and generally displaying complete boorishness and egocentricism.

Alphonse Allais specialized in wild leaps of the imagination coupled with an inveterate delectation for elaborate awful puns. Here is a typical Allais poem, consisting of two lines that are pronounced alike, although their meanings, of course, differ.

> *Alphonse Allais de l'âme erre et se f*** à l'eau*
> *Ah! l'fond salé de la mer! Hé! Ce fou! Hallo!*

(Alphonse Allais with his soul wanders and tosses himself
  into the water
Ah! The salty bottom of the sea! Hey! The nut! Hello!)   —ED.

words, "to tread the flower beds of pure science and to extract therefrom a mass of practical . . . consequences—that is, if it is possible to extract a consequence from a flower bed!"

Of all the inventions of Alphonse Allais there is perhaps not one which does not have its counterpart in the news items published in our dailies. You will recall that the author of *Amours, délices et orgues* (Love, pleasure and pipe organs) proposed covering warships with mirrors instead of steel plating. Thus, the enemy fleet, seeing in front of it the reflection of an adversary of equal strength, would quickly sail away without engaging in battle.

But what did we read in the papers a short while ago? "The technical services of the American army have perfected a vest made of a new material which no projectile can pierce. The technical services of the army are now beginning to work on the manufacture of a new projectile capable of piercing this material."

Jarry, Christophe, Allais. Any homage paid to these thinkers seems laughable in comparison with that we pay to them unconsciously every day, now that the most gratuitous proposals they made in their teachings are only apparently different from the most absurd realities.

Index of Films

Films are listed under English titles only, except for a few normally identified by their foreign titles. In each case, the original foreign-language title (where applicable), the name of the director and the year of release are given within parentheses. Unnumbered illustration pages are given as 12A (page following 12), 12B (the page after that) and so on.

Index of Persons

Unnumbered illustration pages are given as 12A (page following 12), 12B (the page after that) and so on.

A CATALOGUE OF SELECTED DOVER BOOKS
IN ALL FIELDS OF INTEREST

A CATALOGUE OF SELECTED DOVER BOOKS
IN ALL FIELDS OF INTEREST

AMERICA'S OLD MASTERS, James T. Flexner. Four men emerged unexpectedly from provincial 18th century America to leadership in European art: Benjamin West, J. S. Copley, C. R. Peale, Gilbert Stuart. Brilliant coverage of lives and contributions. Revised, 1967 edition. 69 plates. 365pp. of text.

21806-6 Paperbound $3.00

FIRST FLOWERS OF OUR WILDERNESS: AMERICAN PAINTING, THE COLONIAL PERIOD, James T. Flexner. Painters, and regional painting traditions from earliest Colonial times up to the emergence of Copley, West and Peale Sr., Foster, Gustavus Hesselius, Feke, John Smibert and many anonymous painters in the primitive manner. Engaging presentation, with 162 illustrations. xxii + 368pp.

22180-6 Paperbound $3.50

THE LIGHT OF DISTANT SKIES: AMERICAN PAINTING, 1760-1835, James T. Flexner. The great generation of early American painters goes to Europe to learn and to teach: West, Copley, Gilbert Stuart and others. Allston, Trumbull, Morse; also contemporary American painters—primitives, derivatives, academics—who remained in America. 102 illustrations. xiii + 306pp.

22179-2 Paperbound $3.00

A HISTORY OF THE RISE AND PROGRESS OF THE ARTS OF DESIGN IN THE UNITED STATES, William Dunlap. Much the richest mine of information on early American painters, sculptors, architects, engravers, miniaturists, etc. The only source of information for scores of artists, the major primary source for many others. Unabridged reprint of rare original 1834 edition, with new introduction by James T. Flexner, and 394 new illustrations. Edited by Rita Weiss. 6⅝ x 9⅝.

21695-0, 21696-9, 21697-7 Three volumes, Paperbound $13.50

EPOCHS OF CHINESE AND JAPANESE ART, Ernest F. Fenollosa. From primitive Chinese art to the 20th century, thorough history, explanation of every important art period and form, including Japanese woodcuts; main stress on China and Japan, but Tibet, Korea also included. Still unexcelled for its detailed, rich coverage of cultural background, aesthetic elements, diffusion studies, particularly of the historical period. 2nd, 1913 edition. 242 illustrations. lii + 439pp. of text.

20364-6, 20365-4 Two volumes, Paperbound $6.00

THE GENTLE ART OF MAKING ENEMIES, James A. M. Whistler. Greatest wit of his day deflates Oscar Wilde, Ruskin, Swinburne; strikes back at inane critics, exhibitions, art journalism; aesthetics of impressionist revolution in most striking form. Highly readable classic by great painter. Reproduction of edition designed by Whistler. Introduction by Alfred Werner. xxxvi + 334pp.

21875-9 Paperbound $2.50

DESIGN BY ACCIDENT; A BOOK OF "ACCIDENTAL EFFECTS" FOR ARTISTS AND DESIGNERS, James F. O'Brien. Create your own unique, striking, imaginative effects by "controlled accident" interaction of materials: paints and lacquers, oil and water based paints, splatter, crackling materials, shatter, similar items. Everything you do will be different; first book on this limitless art, so useful to both fine artist and commercial artist. Full instructions. 192 plates showing "accidents," 8 in color. viii + 215pp. 8⅜ x 11¼.   21942-9 Paperbound $3.50

THE BOOK OF SIGNS, Rudolf Koch. Famed German type designer draws 493 beautiful symbols: religious, mystical, alchemical, imperial, property marks, runes, etc. Remarkable fusion of traditional and modern. Good for suggestions of timelessness, smartness, modernity. Text. vi + 104pp. 6⅛ x 9¼.
20162-7 Paperbound $1.25

HISTORY OF INDIAN AND INDONESIAN ART, Ananda K. Coomaraswamy. An unabridged republication of one of the finest books by a great scholar in Eastern art. Rich in descriptive material, history, social backgrounds; Sunga reliefs, Rajput paintings, Gupta temples, Burmese frescoes, textiles, jewelry, sculpture, etc. 400 photos. viii + 423pp. 6⅜ x 9¾.   21436-2 Paperbound $4.00

PRIMITIVE ART, Franz Boas. America's foremost anthropologist surveys textiles, ceramics, woodcarving, basketry, metalwork, etc.; patterns, technology, creation of symbols, style origins. All areas of world, but very full on Northwest Coast Indians. More than 350 illustrations of baskets, boxes, totem poles, weapons, etc. 378 pp.
20025-6 Paperbound $3.00

THE GENTLEMAN AND CABINET MAKER'S DIRECTOR, Thomas Chippendale. Full reprint (third edition, 1762) of most influential furniture book of all time, by master cabinetmaker. 200 plates, illustrating chairs, sofas, mirrors, tables, cabinets, plus 24 photographs of surviving pieces. Biographical introduction by N. Bienenstock. vi + 249pp. 9⅞ x 12¾.   21601-2 Paperbound $4.00

AMERICAN ANTIQUE FURNITURE, Edgar G. Miller, Jr. The basic coverage of all American furniture before 1840. Individual chapters cover type of furniture— clocks, tables, sideboards, etc.—chronologically, with inexhaustible wealth of data. More than 2100 photographs, all identified, commented on. Essential to all early American collectors. Introduction by H. E. Keyes. vi + 1106pp. 7⅞ x 10¾.
21599-7, 21600-4 Two volumes, Paperbound $11.00

PENNSYLVANIA DUTCH AMERICAN FOLK ART, Henry J. Kauffman. 279 photos, 28 drawings of tulipware, Fraktur script, painted tinware, toys, flowered furniture, quilts, samplers, hex signs, house interiors, etc. Full descriptive text. Excellent for tourist, rewarding for designer, collector. Map. 146pp. 7⅞ x 10¾.
21205-X Paperbound $2.50

EARLY NEW ENGLAND GRAVESTONE RUBBINGS, Edmund V. Gillon, Jr. 43 photographs, 226 carefully reproduced rubbings show heavily symbolic, sometimes macabre early gravestones, up to early 19th century. Remarkable early American primitive art, occasionally strikingly beautiful; always powerful. Text. xxvi + 207pp. 8⅜ x 11¼.   21380-3 Paperbound $3.50

VISUAL ILLUSIONS: THEIR CAUSES, CHARACTERISTICS, AND APPLICATIONS, Matthew Luckiesh. Thorough description and discussion of optical illusion, geometric and perspective, particularly; size and shape distortions, illusions of color, of motion; natural illusions; use of illusion in art and magic, industry, etc. Most useful today with op art, also for classical art. Scores of effects illustrated. Introduction by William H. Ittleson. 100 illustrations. xxi + 252pp.

21530-X Paperbound $2.00

A HANDBOOK OF ANATOMY FOR ART STUDENTS, Arthur Thomson. Thorough, virtually exhaustive coverage of skeletal structure, musculature, etc. Full text, supplemented by anatomical diagrams and drawings and by photographs of undraped figures. Unique in its comparison of male and female forms, pointing out differences of contour, texture, form. 211 figures, 40 drawings, 86 photographs. xx + 459pp. 5⅜ x 8⅜.

21163-0 Paperbound $3.50

150 MASTERPIECES OF DRAWING, Selected by Anthony Toney. Full page reproductions of drawings from the early 16th to the end of the 18th century, all beautifully reproduced: Rembrandt, Michelangelo, Dürer, Fragonard, Urs, Graf, Wouwerman, many others. First-rate browsing book, model book for artists. xviii + 150pp. 8⅜ x 11¼.

21032-4 Paperbound $2.50

THE LATER WORK OF AUBREY BEARDSLEY, Aubrey Beardsley. Exotic, erotic, ironic masterpieces in full maturity: Comedy Ballet, Venus and Tannhauser, Pierrot, Lysistrata, Rape of the Lock, Savoy material, Ali Baba, Volpone, etc. This material revolutionized the art world, and is still powerful, fresh, brilliant. With *The Early Work,* all Beardsley's finest work. 174 plates, 2 in color. xiv + 176pp. 8⅛ x 11.

21817-1 Paperbound $3.00

DRAWINGS OF REMBRANDT, Rembrandt van Rijn. Complete reproduction of fabulously rare edition by Lippmann and Hofstede de Groot, completely reedited, updated, improved by Prof. Seymour Slive, Fogg Museum. Portraits, Biblical sketches, landscapes, Oriental types, nudes, episodes from classical mythology—All Rembrandt's fertile genius. Also selection of drawings by his pupils and followers. "Stunning volumes," *Saturday Review.* 550 illustrations. lxxviii + 552pp. 9⅛ x 12¼.

21485-0, 21486-9 Two volumes, Paperbound $7.00

THE DISASTERS OF WAR, Francisco Goya. One of the masterpieces of Western civilization—83 etchings that record Goya's shattering, bitter reaction to the Napoleonic war that swept through Spain after the insurrection of 1808 and to war in general. Reprint of the first edition, with three additional plates from Boston's Museum of Fine Arts. All plates facsimile size. Introduction by Philip Hofer, Fogg Museum. v + 97pp. 9⅜ x 8¼.

21872-4 Paperbound $2.00

GRAPHIC WORKS OF ODILON REDON. Largest collection of Redon's graphic works ever assembled: 172 lithographs, 28 etchings and engravings, 9 drawings. These include some of his most famous works. All the plates from *Odilon Redon: oeuvre graphique complet,* plus additional plates. New introduction and caption translations by Alfred Werner. 209 illustrations. xxvii + 209pp. 9⅛ x 12¼.

21966-8 Paperbound $4.00

ALPHABETS AND ORNAMENTS, Ernst Lehner. Well-known pictorial source for decorative alphabets, script examples, cartouches, frames, decorative title pages, calligraphic initials, borders, similar material. 14th to 19th century, mostly European. Useful in almost any graphic arts designing, varied styles. 750 illustrations. 256pp. 7 x 10.   21905-4 Paperbound $4.00

PAINTING: A CREATIVE APPROACH, Norman Colquhoun. For the beginner simple guide provides an instructive approach to painting: major stumbling blocks for beginner; overcoming them, technical points; paints and pigments; oil painting; watercolor and other media and color. New section on "plastic" paints. Glossary. Formerly *Paint Your Own Pictures*. 221pp.   22000-1 Paperbound $1.75

THE ENJOYMENT AND USE OF COLOR, Walter Sargent. Explanation of the relations between colors themselves and between colors in nature and art, including hundreds of little-known facts about color values, intensities, effects of high and low illumination, complementary colors. Many practical hints for painters, references to great masters. 7 color plates, 29 illustrations. x + 274pp.
20944-X Paperbound $2.75

THE NOTEBOOKS OF LEONARDO DA VINCI, compiled and edited by Jean Paul Richter. 1566 extracts from original manuscripts reveal the full range of Leonardo's versatile genius: all his writings on painting, sculpture, architecture, anatomy, astronomy, geography, topography, physiology, mining, music, etc., in both Italian and English, with 186 plates of manuscript pages and more than 500 additional drawings. Includes studies for the Last Supper, the lost Sforza monument, and other works. Total of xlvii + 866pp. 7⅞ x 10¾.
22572-0, 22573-9 Two volumes, Paperbound $10.00

MONTGOMERY WARD CATALOGUE OF 1895. Tea gowns, yards of flannel and pillow-case lace, stereoscopes, books of gospel hymns, the New Improved Singer Sewing Machine, side saddles, milk skimmers, straight-edged razors, high-button shoes, spittoons, and on and on . . . listing some 25,000 items, practically all illustrated. Essential to the shoppers of the 1890's, it is our truest record of the spirit of the period. Unaltered reprint of Issue No. 57, Spring and Summer 1895. Introduction by Boris Emmet. Innumerable illustrations. xiii + 624pp. 8½ x 11⅝.
22377-9 Paperbound $6.95

THE CRYSTAL PALACE EXHIBITION ILLUSTRATED CATALOGUE (LONDON, 1851). One of the wonders of the modern world—the Crystal Palace Exhibition in which all the nations of the civilized world exhibited their achievements in the arts and sciences—presented in an equally important illustrated catalogue. More than 1700 items pictured with accompanying text—ceramics, textiles, cast-iron work, carpets, pianos, sleds, razors, wall-papers, billiard tables, beehives, silverware and hundreds of other artifacts—represent the focal point of Victorian culture in the Western World. Probably the largest collection of Victorian decorative art ever assembled— indispensable for antiquarians and designers. Unabridged republication of the Art-Journal Catalogue of the Great Exhibition of 1851, with all terminal essays. New introduction by John Gloag, F.S.A. xxxiv + 426pp. 9 x 12.
22503-8 Paperbound $4.50

A History of Costume, Carl Köhler. Definitive history, based on surviving pieces of clothing primarily, and paintings, statues, etc. secondarily. Highly readable text, supplemented by 594 illustrations of costumes of the ancient Mediterranean peoples, Greece and Rome, the Teutonic prehistoric period; costumes of the Middle Ages, Renaissance, Baroque, 18th and 19th centuries. Clear, measured patterns are provided for many clothing articles. Approach is practical throughout. Enlarged by Emma von Sichart. 464pp.   21030-8 Paperbound $3.50

Oriental Rugs, Antique and Modern, Walter A. Hawley. A complete and authoritative treatise on the Oriental rug—where they are made, by whom and how, designs and symbols, characteristics in detail of the six major groups, how to distinguish them and how to buy them. Detailed technical data is provided on periods, weaves, warps, wefts, textures, sides, ends and knots, although no technical background is required for an understanding. 11 color plates, 80 halftones, 4 maps. vi + 320pp. 6⅛ x 9⅛.   22366-3 Paperbound $5.00

Ten Books on Architecture, Vitruvius. By any standards the most important book on architecture ever written. Early Roman discussion of aesthetics of building, construction methods, orders, sites, and every other aspect of architecture has inspired, instructed architecture for about 2,000 years. Stands behind Palladio, Michelangelo, Bramante, Wren, countless others. Definitive Morris H. Morgan translation. 68 illustrations. xii + 331pp.   20645-9 Paperbound $2.50

The Four Books of Architecture, Andrea Palladio. Translated into every major Western European language in the two centuries following its publication in 1570, this has been one of the most influential books in the history of architecture. Complete reprint of the 1738 Isaac Ware edition. New introduction by Adolf Placzek, Columbia Univ. 216 plates. xxii + 110pp. of text. 9½ x 12¾.
21308-0 Clothbound $10.00

Sticks and Stones: A Study of American Architecture and Civilization, Lewis Mumford.One of the great classics of American cultural history. American architecture from the medieval-inspired earliest forms to the early 20th century; evolution of structure and style, and reciprocal influences on environment. 21 photographic illustrations. 238pp.   20202-X Paperbound $2.00

The American Builder's Companion, Asher Benjamin. The most widely used early 19th century architectural style and source book, for colonial up into Greek Revival periods. Extensive development of geometry of carpentering, construction of sashes, frames, doors, stairs; plans and elevations of domestic and other buildings. Hundreds of thousands of houses were built according to this book, now invaluable to historians, architects, restorers, etc. 1827 edition. 59 plates. 114pp. 7⅞ x 10¾.
22236-5 Paperbound $3.00

Dutch Houses in the Hudson Valley Before 1776, Helen Wilkinson Reynolds. The standard survey of the Dutch colonial house and outbuildings, with constructional features, decoration, and local history associated with individual homesteads. Introduction by Franklin D. Roosevelt. Map. 150 illustrations. 469pp. 6⅝ x 9¼.   21469-9 Paperbound $4.00

THE ARCHITECTURE OF COUNTRY HOUSES, Andrew J. Downing. Together with Vaux's *Villas and Cottages* this is the basic book for Hudson River Gothic architecture of the middle Victorian period. Full, sound discussions of general aspects of housing, architecture, style, decoration, furnishing, together with scores of detailed house plans, illustrations of specific buildings, accompanied by full text. Perhaps the most influential single American architectural book. 1850 edition. Introduction by J. Stewart Johnson. 321 figures, 34 architectural designs. xvi + 560pp.

22003-6 Paperbound $4.00

LOST EXAMPLES OF COLONIAL ARCHITECTURE, John Mead Howells. Full-page photographs of buildings that have disappeared or been so altered as to be denatured, including many designed by major early American architects. 245 plates. xvii + 248pp. 7⅞ x 10¾. 21143-6 Paperbound $3.50

DOMESTIC ARCHITECTURE OF THE AMERICAN COLONIES AND OF THE EARLY REPUBLIC, Fiske Kimball. Foremost architect and restorer of Williamsburg and Monticello covers nearly 200 homes between 1620-1825. Architectural details, construction, style features, special fixtures, floor plans, etc. Generally considered finest work in its area. 219 illustrations of houses, doorways, windows, capital mantels. xx + 314pp. 7⅞ x 10¾. 21743-4 Paperbound $4.00

EARLY AMERICAN ROOMS: 1650-1858, edited by Russell Hawes Kettell. Tour of 12 rooms, each representative of a different era in American history and each furnished, decorated, designed and occupied in the style of the era. 72 plans and elevations, 8-page color section, etc., show fabrics, wall papers, arrangements, etc. Full descriptive text. xvii + 200pp. of text. 8⅜ x 11¼.

21633-0 Paperbound $5.00

THE FITZWILLIAM VIRGINAL BOOK, edited by J. Fuller Maitland and W. B. Squire. Full modern printing of famous early 17th-century ms. volume of 300 works by Morley, Byrd, Bull, Gibbons, etc. For piano or other modern keyboard instrument; easy to read format. xxxvi + 938pp. 8⅜ x 11.

21068-5, 21069-3 Two volumes, Paperbound $10.00

KEYBOARD MUSIC, Johann Sebastian Bach. Bach Gesellschaft edition. A rich selection of Bach's masterpieces for the harpsichord: the six English Suites, six French Suites, the six Partitas (Clavierübung part I), the Goldberg Variations (Clavierübung part IV), the fifteen Two-Part Inventions and the fifteen Three-Part Sinfonias. Clearly reproduced on large sheets with ample margins; eminently playable. vi + 312pp. 8⅛ x 11. 22360-4 Paperbound $5.00

THE MUSIC OF BACH: AN INTRODUCTION, Charles Sanford Terry. A fine, nontechnical introduction to Bach's music, both instrumental and vocal. Covers organ music, chamber music, passion music, other types. Analyzes themes, developments, innovations. x + 114pp. 21075-8 Paperbound $1.25

BEETHOVEN AND HIS NINE SYMPHONIES, Sir George Grove. Noted British musicologist provides best history, analysis, commentary on symphonies. Very thorough, rigorously accurate; necessary to both advanced student and amateur music lover. 436 musical passages. vii + 407 pp. 20334-4 Paperbound $2.75

JOHANN SEBASTIAN BACH, Philipp Spitta. One of the great classics of musicology, this definitive analysis of Bach's music (and life) has never been surpassed. Lucid, nontechnical analyses of hundreds of pieces (30 pages devoted to St. Matthew Passion, 26 to B Minor Mass). Also includes major analysis of 18th-century music. 450 musical examples. 40-page musical supplement. Total of xx + 1799pp.

(EUK) 22278-0, 22279-9 Two volumes, Clothbound $17.50

MOZART AND HIS PIANO CONCERTOS, Cuthbert Girdlestone. The only full-length study of an important area of Mozart's creativity. Provides detailed analyses of all 23 concertos, traces inspirational sources. 417 musical examples. Second edition. 509pp.

(USO) 21271-8 Paperbound $3.50

THE PERFECT WAGNERITE: A COMMENTARY ON THE NIBLUNG'S RING, George Bernard Shaw. Brilliant and still relevant criticism in remarkable essays on Wagner's Ring cycle, Shaw's ideas on political and social ideology behind the plots, role of Leitmotifs, vocal requisites, etc. Prefaces. xxi + 136pp.

21707-8 Paperbound $1.50

DON GIOVANNI, W. A. Mozart. Complete libretto, modern English translation; biographies of composer and librettist; accounts of early performances and critical reaction. Lavishly illustrated. All the material you need to understand and appreciate this great work. Dover Opera Guide and Libretto Series; translated and introduced by Ellen Bleiler. 92 illustrations. 209pp.

21134-7 Paperbound $1.50

HIGH FIDELITY SYSTEMS: A LAYMAN'S GUIDE, Roy F. Allison. All the basic information you need for setting up your own audio system: high fidelity and stereo record players, tape records, F.M. Connections, adjusting tone arm, cartridge, checking needle alignment, positioning speakers, phasing speakers, adjusting hums, trouble-shooting, maintenance, and similar topics. Enlarged 1965 edition. More than 50 charts, diagrams, photos. iv + 91pp. 21514-8 Paperbound $1.25

REPRODUCTION OF SOUND, Edgar Villchur. Thorough coverage for laymen of high fidelity systems, reproducing systems in general, needles, amplifiers, preamps, loudspeakers, feedback, explaining physical background. "A rare talent for making technicalities vividly comprehensible," R. Darrell, *High Fidelity.* 69 figures. iv + 92pp. 21515-6 Paperbound $1.25

HEAR ME TALKIN' TO YA: THE STORY OF JAZZ AS TOLD BY THE MEN WHO MADE IT, Nat Shapiro and Nat Hentoff. Louis Armstrong, Fats Waller, Jo Jones, Clarence Williams, Billy Holiday, Duke Ellington, Jelly Roll Morton and dozens of other jazz greats tell how it was in Chicago's South Side, New Orleans, depression Harlem and the modern West Coast as jazz was born and grew. xvi + 429pp.

21726-4 Paperbound $2.50

FABLES OF AESOP, translated by Sir Roger L'Estrange. A reproduction of the very rare 1931 Paris edition; a selection of the most interesting fables, together with 50 imaginative drawings by Alexander Calder. v + 128pp. 6½x9¼.

21780-9 Paperbound $1.50

AGAINST THE GRAIN (A REBOURS), Joris K. Huysmans. Filled with weird images, evidences of a bizarre imagination, exotic experiments with hallucinatory drugs, rich tastes and smells and the diversions of its sybarite hero Duc Jean des Esseintes, this classic novel pushed 19th-century literary decadence to its limits. Full unabridged edition. Do not confuse this with abridged editions generally sold. Introduction by Havelock Ellis. xlix + 206pp. 22190-3 Paperbound $2.00

VARIORUM SHAKESPEARE: HAMLET. Edited by Horace H. Furness; a landmark of American scholarship. Exhaustive footnotes and appendices treat all doubtful words and phrases, as well as suggested critical emendations throughout the play's history. First volume contains editor's own text, collated with all Quartos and Folios. Second volume contains full first Quarto, translations of Shakespeare's sources (Belleforest, and Saxo Grammaticus), Der Bestrafte Brudermord, and many essays on critical and historical points of interest by major authorities of past and present. Includes details of staging and costuming over the years. By far the best edition available for serious students of Shakespeare. Total of xx + 905pp. 21004-9, 21005-7, 2 volumes, Paperbound $7.00

A LIFE OF WILLIAM SHAKESPEARE, Sir Sidney Lee. This is the standard life of Shakespeare, summarizing everything known about Shakespeare and his plays. Incredibly rich in material, broad in coverage, clear and judicious, it has served thousands as the best introduction to Shakespeare. 1931 edition. 9 plates. xxix + 792pp. (USO) 21967-4 Paperbound $3.75

MASTERS OF THE DRAMA, John Gassner. Most comprehensive history of the drama in print, covering every tradition from Greeks to modern Europe and America, including India, Far East, etc. Covers more than 800 dramatists, 2000 plays, with biographical material, plot summaries, theatre history, criticism, etc. "Best of its kind in English," New Republic. 77 illustrations. xxii + 890pp. 20100-7 Clothbound $8.50

THE EVOLUTION OF THE ENGLISH LANGUAGE, George McKnight. The growth of English, from the 14th century to the present. Unusual, non-technical account presents basic information in very interesting form: sound shifts, change in grammar and syntax, vocabulary growth, similar topics. Abundantly illustrated with quotations. Formerly Modern English in the Making. xii + 590pp. 21932-1 Paperbound $3.50

AN ETYMOLOGICAL DICTIONARY OF MODERN ENGLISH, Ernest Weekley. Fullest, richest work of its sort, by foremost British lexicographer. Detailed word histories, including many colloquial and archaic words; extensive quotations. Do not confuse this with the Concise Etymological Dictionary, which is much abridged. Total of xxvii + 830pp. 6½ x 9¼. 21873-2, 21874-0 Two volumes, Paperbound $6.00

FLATLAND: A ROMANCE OF MANY DIMENSIONS, E. A. Abbott. Classic of science-fiction explores ramifications of life in a two-dimensional world, and what happens when a three-dimensional being intrudes. Amusing reading, but also useful as introduction to thought about hyperspace. Introduction by Banesh Hoffmann. 16 illustrations. xx + 103pp. 20001-9 Paperbound $1.00

POEMS OF ANNE BRADSTREET, edited with an introduction by Robert Hutchinson. A new selection of poems by America's first poet and perhaps the first significant woman poet in the English language. 48 poems display her development in works of considerable variety—love poems, domestic poems, religious meditations, formal elegies, "quaternions," etc. Notes, bibliography. viii + 222pp.

22160-1 Paperbound $2.00

THREE GOTHIC NOVELS: THE CASTLE OF OTRANTO BY HORACE WALPOLE; VATHEK BY WILLIAM BECKFORD; THE VAMPYRE BY JOHN POLIDORI, WITH FRAGMENT OF A NOVEL BY LORD BYRON, edited by E. F. Bleiler. The first Gothic novel, by Walpole; the finest Oriental tale in English, by Beckford; powerful Romantic supernatural story in versions by Polidori and Byron. All extremely important in history of literature; all still exciting, packed with supernatural thrills, ghosts, haunted castles, magic, etc. xl + 291pp.

21232-7 Paperbound $2.00

THE BEST TALES OF HOFFMANN, E. T. A. Hoffmann. 10 of Hoffmann's most important stories, in modern re-editions of standard translations: Nutcracker and the King of Mice, Signor Formica, Automata, The Sandman, Rath Krespel, The Golden Flowerpot, Master Martin the Cooper, The Mines of Falun, The King's Betrothed, A New Year's Eve Adventure. 7 illustrations by Hoffmann. Edited by E. F. Bleiler. xxxix + 419pp.

21793-0 Paperbound $2.50

GHOST AND HORROR STORIES OF AMBROSE BIERCE, Ambrose Bierce. 23 strikingly modern stories of the horrors latent in the human mind: The Eyes of the Panther, The Damned Thing, An Occurrence at Owl Creek Bridge, An Inhabitant of Carcosa, etc., plus the dream-essay, Visions of the Night. Edited by E. F. Bleiler. xxii + 199pp.

20767-6 Paperbound $1.50

BEST GHOST STORIES OF J. S. LEFANU, J. Sheridan LeFanu. Finest stories by Victorian master often considered greatest supernatural writer of all. Carmilla, Green Tea, The Haunted Baronet, The Familiar, and 12 others. Most never before available in the U. S. A. Edited by E. F. Bleiler. 8 illustrations from Victorian publications. xvii + 467pp.

20415-4 Paperbound $3.00

THE TIME STREAM, THE GREATEST ADVENTURE, AND THE PURPLE SAPPHIRE—THREE SCIENCE FICTION NOVELS, John Taine (Eric Temple Bell). Great American mathematician was also foremost science fiction novelist of the 1920's. *The Time Stream,* one of all-time classics, uses concepts of circular time; *The Greatest Adventure,* incredibly ancient biological experiments from Antarctica threaten to escape; The *Purple Sapphire,* superscience, lost races in Central Tibet, survivors of the Great Race. 4 illustrations by Frank R. Paul. v + 532pp.

21180-0 Paperbound $3.00

SEVEN SCIENCE FICTION NOVELS, H. G. Wells. The standard collection of the great novels. Complete, unabridged. *First Men in the Moon, Island of Dr. Moreau, War of the Worlds, Food of the Gods, Invisible Man, Time Machine, In the Days of the Comet.* Not only science fiction fans, but every educated person owes it to himself to read these novels. 1015pp.

20264-X Clothbound $5.00

LAST AND FIRST MEN AND STAR MAKER, TWO SCIENCE FICTION NOVELS, Olaf Stapledon. Greatest future histories in science fiction. In the first, human intelligence is the "hero," through strange paths of evolution, interplanetary invasions, incredible technologies, near extinctions and reemergences. Star Maker describes the quest of a band of star rovers for intelligence itself, through time and space: weird inhuman civilizations, crustacean minds, symbiotic worlds, etc. Complete, unabridged. v + 438pp. 21962-3 Paperbound $2.50

THREE PROPHETIC NOVELS, H. G. WELLS. Stages of a consistently planned future for mankind. *When the Sleeper Wakes*, and *A Story of the Days to Come*, anticipate *Brave New World* and *1984*, in the 21st Century; *The Time Machine*, only complete version in print, shows farther future and the end of mankind. All show Wells's greatest gifts as storyteller and novelist. Edited by E. F. Bleiler. x + 335pp. (USO) 20605-X Paperbound $2.25

THE DEVIL'S DICTIONARY, Ambrose Bierce. America's own Oscar Wilde— Ambrose Bierce—offers his barbed iconoclastic wisdom in over 1,000 definitions hailed by H. L. Mencken as "some of the most gorgeous witticisms in the English language." 145pp. 20487-1 Paperbound $1.25

MAX AND MORITZ, Wilhelm Busch. Great children's classic, father of comic strip, of two bad boys, Max and Moritz. Also Ker and Plunk (Plisch und Plumm), Cat and Mouse, Deceitful Henry, Ice-Peter, The Boy and the Pipe, and five other pieces. Original German, with English translation. Edited by H. Arthur Klein; translations by various hands and H. Arthur Klein. vi + 216pp. 20181-3 Paperbound $2.00

PIGS IS PIGS AND OTHER FAVORITES, Ellis Parker Butler. The title story is one of the best humor short stories, as Mike Flannery obfuscates biology and English. Also included, That Pup of Murchison's, The Great American Pie Company, and Perkins of Portland. 14 illustrations. v + 109pp. 21532-6 Paperbound $1.00

THE PETERKIN PAPERS, Lucretia P. Hale. It takes genius to be as stupidly mad as the Peterkins, as they decide to become wise, celebrate the "Fourth," keep a cow, and otherwise strain the resources of the Lady from Philadelphia. Basic book of American humor. 153 illustrations. 219pp. 20794-3 Paperbound $1.50

PERRAULT'S FAIRY TALES, translated by A. E. Johnson and S. R. Littlewood, with 34 full-page illustrations by Gustave Doré. All the original Perrault stories— Cinderella, Sleeping Beauty, Bluebeard, Little Red Riding Hood, Puss in Boots, Tom Thumb, etc.—with their witty verse morals and the magnificent illustrations of Doré. One of the five or six great books of European fairy tales. viii + 117pp. 8⅛ x 11. 22311-6 Paperbound $2.00

OLD HUNGARIAN FAIRY TALES, Baroness Orczy. Favorites translated and adapted by author of the *Scarlet Pimpernel*. Eight fairy tales include "The Suitors of Princess Fire-Fly," "The Twin Hunchbacks," "Mr. Cuttlefish's Love Story," and "The Enchanted Cat." This little volume of magic and adventure will captivate children as it has for generations. 90 drawings by Montagu Barstow. 96pp. (USO) 22293-4 Paperbound $1.95

THE RED FAIRY BOOK, Andrew Lang. Lang's color fairy books have long been children's favorites. This volume includes Rapunzel, Jack and the Bean-stalk and 35 other stories, familiar and unfamiliar. 4 plates, 93 illustrations x + 367pp.
21673-X Paperbound $2.50

THE BLUE FAIRY BOOK, Andrew Lang. Lang's tales come from all countries and all times. Here are 37 tales from Grimm, the Arabian Nights, Greek Mythology, and other fascinating sources. 8 plates, 130 illustrations. xi + 390pp.
21437-0 Paperbound $2.50

HOUSEHOLD STORIES BY THE BROTHERS GRIMM. Classic English-language edition of the well-known tales — Rumpelstiltskin, Snow White, Hansel and Gretel, The Twelve Brothers, Faithful John, Rapunzel, Tom Thumb (52 stories in all). Translated into simple, straightforward English by Lucy Crane. Ornamented with headpieces, vignettes, elaborate decorative initials and a dozen full-page illustrations by Walter Crane. x + 269pp.
21080-4 Paperbound $2.50

THE MERRY ADVENTURES OF ROBIN HOOD, Howard Pyle. The finest modern versions of the traditional ballads and tales about the great English outlaw. Howard Pyle's complete prose version, with every word, every illustration of the first edition. Do not confuse this facsimile of the original (1883) with modern editions that change text or illustrations. 23 plates plus many page decorations. xxii + 296pp.
22043-5 Paperbound $2.50

THE STORY OF KING ARTHUR AND HIS KNIGHTS, Howard Pyle. The finest children's version of the life of King Arthur; brilliantly retold by Pyle, with 48 of his most imaginative illustrations. xviii + 313pp. 6⅛ x 9¼.
21445-1 Paperbound $2.50

THE WONDERFUL WIZARD OF OZ, L. Frank Baum. America's finest children's book in facsimile of first edition with all Denslow illustrations in full color. The edition a child should have. Introduction by Martin Gardner. 23 color plates, scores of drawings. iv + 267pp.
20691-2 Paperbound $2.25

THE MARVELOUS LAND OF OZ, L. Frank Baum. The second Oz book, every bit as imaginative as the Wizard. The hero is a boy named Tip, but the Scarecrow and the Tin Woodman are back, as is the Oz magic. 16 color plates, 120 drawings by John R. Neill. 287pp.
20692-0 Paperbound $2.50

THE MAGICAL MONARCH OF MO, L. Frank Baum. Remarkable adventures in a land even stranger than Oz. The best of Baum's books not in the Oz series. 15 color plates and dozens of drawings by Frank Verbeck. xviii + 237pp.
21892-9 Paperbound $2.00

THE BAD CHILD'S BOOK OF BEASTS, MORE BEASTS FOR WORSE CHILDREN, A MORAL ALPHABET, Hilaire Belloc. Three complete humor classics in one volume. Be kind to the frog, and do not call him names . . . and 28 other whimsical animals. Familiar favorites and some not so well known. Illustrated by Basil Blackwell. 156pp.
(USO) 20749-8 Paperbound $1.25

EAST O' THE SUN AND WEST O' THE MOON, George W. Dasent. Considered the best of all translations of these Norwegian folk tales, this collection has been enjoyed by generations of children (and folklorists too). Includes True and Untrue, Why the Sea is Salt, East O' the Sun and West O' the Moon, Why the Bear is Stumpy-Tailed, Boots and the Troll, The Cock and the Hen, Rich Peter the Pedlar, and 52 more. The only edition with all 59 tales. 77 illustrations by Erik Werenskiold and Theodor Kittelsen. xv + 418pp. 22521-6 Paperbound $3.00

GOOPS AND HOW TO BE THEM, Gelett Burgess. Classic of tongue-in-cheek humor, masquerading as etiquette book. 87 verses, twice as many cartoons, show mischievous Goops as they demonstrate to children virtues of table manners, neatness, courtesy, etc. Favorite for generations. viii + 88pp. 6½ x 9¼.
22233-0 Paperbound $1.25

ALICE'S ADVENTURES UNDER GROUND, Lewis Carroll. The first version, quite different from the final *Alice in Wonderland,* printed out by Carroll himself with his own illustrations. Complete facsimile of the "million dollar" manuscript Carroll gave to Alice Liddell in 1864. Introduction by Martin Gardner. viii + 96pp. Title and dedication pages in color. 21482-6 Paperbound $1.25

THE BROWNIES, THEIR BOOK, Palmer Cox. Small as mice, cunning as foxes, exuberant and full of mischief, the Brownies go to the zoo, toy shop, seashore, circus, etc., in 24 verse adventures and 266 illustrations. Long a favorite, since their first appearance in St. Nicholas Magazine. xi + 144pp. 6⅝ x 9¼.
21265-3 Paperbound $1.75

SONGS OF CHILDHOOD, Walter De La Mare. Published (under the pseudonym Walter Ramal) when De La Mare was only 29, this charming collection has long been a favorite children's book. A facsimile of the first edition in paper, the 47 poems capture the simplicity of the nursery rhyme and the ballad, including such lyrics as I Met Eve, Tartary, The Silver Penny. vii + 106pp. 21972-0 Paperbound $1.25

THE COMPLETE NONSENSE OF EDWARD LEAR, Edward Lear. The finest 19th-century humorist-cartoonist in full: all nonsense limericks, zany alphabets, Owl and Pussycat, songs, nonsense botany, and more than 500 illustrations by Lear himself. Edited by Holbrook Jackson. xxix + 287pp. (USO) 20167-8 Paperbound $2.00

BILLY WHISKERS: THE AUTOBIOGRAPHY OF A GOAT, Frances Trego Montgomery. A favorite of children since the early 20th century, here are the escapades of that rambunctious, irresistible and mischievous goat—Billy Whiskers. Much in the spirit of *Peck's Bad Boy,* this is a book that children never tire of reading or hearing. All the original familiar illustrations by W. H. Fry are included: 6 color plates, 18 black and white drawings. 159pp. 22345-0 Paperbound $2.00

MOTHER GOOSE MELODIES. Faithful republication of the fabulously rare Munroe and Francis "copyright 1833" Boston edition—the most important Mother Goose collection, usually referred to as the "original." Familiar rhymes plus many rare ones, with wonderful old woodcut illustrations. Edited by E. F. Bleiler. 128pp. 4½ x 6⅜. 22577-1 Paperbound $1.25

TWO LITTLE SAVAGES; BEING THE ADVENTURES OF TWO BOYS WHO LIVED AS INDIANS AND WHAT THEY LEARNED, Ernest Thompson Seton. Great classic of nature and boyhood provides a vast range of woodlore in most palatable form, a genuinely entertaining story. Two farm boys build a teepee in woods and live in it for a month, working out Indian solutions to living problems, star lore, birds and animals, plants, etc. 293 illustrations. vii + 286pp.

20985-7 Paperbound $2.50

PETER PIPER'S PRACTICAL PRINCIPLES OF PLAIN & PERFECT PRONUNCIATION. Alliterative jingles and tongue-twisters of surprising charm, that made their first appearance in America about 1830. Republished in full with the spirited woodcut illustrations from this earliest American edition. 32pp. 4½ x 6⅜.

22560-7 Paperbound $1.00

SCIENCE EXPERIMENTS AND AMUSEMENTS FOR CHILDREN, Charles Vivian. 73 easy experiments, requiring only materials found at home or easily available, such as candles, coins, steel wool, etc.; illustrate basic phenomena like vacuum, simple chemical reaction, etc. All safe. Modern, well-planned. Formerly *Science Games for Children*. 102 photos, numerous drawings. 96pp. 6⅛ x 9¼.

21856-2 Paperbound $1.25

AN INTRODUCTION TO CHESS MOVES AND TACTICS SIMPLY EXPLAINED, Leonard Barden. Informal intermediate introduction, quite strong in explaining reasons for moves. Covers basic material, tactics, important openings, traps, positional play in middle game, end game. Attempts to isolate patterns and recurrent configurations. Formerly *Chess*. 58 figures. 102pp.   (USO) 21210-6 Paperbound $1.25

LASKER'S MANUAL OF CHESS, Dr. Emanuel Lasker. Lasker was not only one of the five great World Champions, he was also one of the ablest expositors, theorists, and analysts. In many ways, his Manual, permeated with his philosophy of battle, filled with keen insights, is one of the greatest works ever written on chess. Filled with analyzed games by the great players. A single-volume library that will profit almost any chess player, beginner or master. 308 diagrams. xli X 349pp.

20640-8 Paperbound $2.75

THE MASTER BOOK OF MATHEMATICAL RECREATIONS, Fred Schuh. In opinion of many the finest work ever prepared on mathematical puzzles, stunts, recreations; exhaustively thorough explanations of mathematics involved, analysis of effects, citation of puzzles and games. Mathematics involved is elementary. Translated by F. Göbel. 194 figures. xxiv + 430pp.   22134-2 Paperbound $3.00

MATHEMATICS, MAGIC AND MYSTERY, Martin Gardner. Puzzle editor for Scientific American explains mathematics behind various mystifying tricks: card tricks, stage "mind reading," coin and match tricks, counting out games, geometric dissections, etc. Probability sets, theory of numbers clearly explained. Also provides more than 400 tricks, guaranteed to work, that you can do. 135 illustrations. xii + 176pp.

20338-2 Paperbound $1.50

MATHEMATICAL PUZZLES FOR BEGINNERS AND ENTHUSIASTS, Geoffrey Mott-Smith. 189 puzzles from easy to difficult—involving arithmetic, logic, algebra, properties of digits, probability, etc.—for enjoyment and mental stimulus. Explanation of mathematical principles behind the puzzles. 135 illustrations. viii + 248pp.
20198-8 Paperbound $1.75

PAPER FOLDING FOR BEGINNERS, William D. Murray and Francis J. Rigney. Easiest book on the market, clearest instructions on making interesting, beautiful origami. Sail boats, cups, roosters, frogs that move legs, bonbon boxes, standing birds, etc. 40 projects; more than 275 diagrams and photographs. 94pp.
20713-7 Paperbound $1.00

TRICKS AND GAMES ON THE POOL TABLE, Fred Herrmann. 79 tricks and games— some solitaires, some for two or more players, some competitive games—to entertain you between formal games. Mystifying shots and throws, unusual caroms, tricks involving such props as cork, coins, a hat, etc. Formerly *Fun on the Pool Table*. 77 figures. 95pp.
21814-7 Paperbound $1.00

HAND SHADOWS TO BE THROWN UPON THE WALL: A SERIES OF NOVEL AND AMUSING FIGURES FORMED BY THE HAND, Henry Bursill. Delightful picturebook from great-grandfather's day shows how to make 18 different hand shadows: a bird that flies, duck that quacks, dog that wags his tail, camel, goose, deer, boy, turtle, etc. Only book of its sort. vi + 33pp. 6½ x 9¼. 21779-5 Paperbound $1.00

WHITTLING AND WOODCARVING, E. J. Tangerman. 18th printing of best book on market. "If you can cut a potato you can carve" toys and puzzles, chains, chessmen, caricatures, masks, frames, woodcut blocks, surface patterns, much more. Information on tools, woods, techniques. Also goes into serious wood sculpture from Middle Ages to present, East and West. 464 photos, figures. x + 293pp.
20965-2 Paperbound $2.00

HISTORY OF PHILOSOPHY, Julián Marías. Possibly the clearest, most easily followed, best planned, most useful one-volume history of philosophy on the market; neither skimpy nor overfull. Full details on system of every major philosopher and dozens of less important thinkers from pre-Socratics up to Existentialism and later. Strong on many European figures usually omitted. Has gone through dozens of editions in Europe. 1966 edition, translated by Stanley Appelbaum and Clarence Strowbridge. xviii + 505pp. 21739-6 Paperbound $3.00

YOGA: A SCIENTIFIC EVALUATION, Kovoor T. Behanan. Scientific but non-technical study of physiological results of yoga exercises; done under auspices of Yale U. Relations to Indian thought, to psychoanalysis, etc. 16 photos. xxiii + 270pp.
20505-3 Paperbound $2.50

Prices subject to change without notice.
Available at your book dealer or write for free catalogue to Dept. GI, Dover Publications, Inc., 180 Varick St., N. Y., N. Y. 10014. Dover publishes more than 150 books each year on science, elementary and advanced mathematics, biology, music, art, literary history, social sciences and other areas.

9651